THE IMMIGRANT

PART ONE

THE IMMIGRANT

PART ONE

SANDY SIMON

The Cedars Group
Delray Beach, Florida
2013

Copyright © 2013 by Sandy Simon

ISBN 0-9669625-8-3
Printed in the United States of America

This book is a work of fiction. Names, characters, places, and incidents either are products of the author's imagination or are used fictitiously. Any resemblance to actual events or locale or persons, living or dead, is entirely coincidental.

Published by
The Cedars Group
220 MacFarlane Drive, Suite PH-6
Delray Beach, Florida 33483

www.sandysimon.com

This book is dedicated…

to my father, Alexander Eassa Simon Chalhoub and my mother, Linda Helen Zaine Thomé Simon whose lives inspired this book.

to all those tenacious, resilient, and dedicated immigrants from Lebanon and Syria who, since 1850, have sought freedom and opportunity in America, and have contributed their heritage, culture, and wealth to the fabric of their adopted country.

and, finally, to St. Jude Children's Research Hospital in Memphis, Tennessee, which will receive a portion of the proceeds from sales of this book.

Acknowledgements

I am most grateful…

To my mother and father whose life stories inspired this book.

To my family in Douma, Lebanon for their hospitality and insights.

To Papatya Bucak, Professor of Creative Writing at Florida Atlantic University, for her guidance and support.

To Consul General du Liban, Abdel Sattar Issa in Marseille, who graciously enlightened me to the historical presence of the Lebanese-Syrian community of Marseille, the *Panier*, and Marseille's role over the centuries.

To the late Richard Shadyac, my brother and mentor, for his incisive counsel.

To Sally Benson for her advice.

To my cousins, Hanna, Nicola, Ibrahim Chalhoub, Douma, Lebanon.

To my brilliant cousin, Cezar Thome, Sao Paulo, Brazil.

To my graduate school roommate, W. H. "Bill" Stuart of Bartow, Florida, and to the Kissimmee Historical Society.

To my dear friend, Bill Finley, WWII B-17 pilot, Eighth Air Force, U.S. Army Air Corps for his detailed, first hand recollections, counsel and encouragement.

And to Sheryl Ameen Feigel, Washington, DC for her insight into the historical and cultural mores of Lebanon.

Especially, I wish to acknowledge that this book could not have been written without the support, patience, and nurturing of Christiane Collins and to Mary Strobel, for her professional, expert and patient editing of my manuscript.

TABLE OF CONTENTS

Chapter 1 Late Autumn, 1913 1
Chapter 2 Beirut, 1920 12
Chapter 3 Beirut, 1917 18
Chapter 4 Goodbye to Douma 22
Chapter 5 Marseille 30
Chapter 6 Place du Liban 36
Chapter 7 Magic Moments 48
Chapter 8 Love at First Sight 51
Chapter 9 Les Callanques, 1920 60
Chapter 10 Onboard 67
Chapter 11 New York 75
Chapter 12 Boston 80
Chapter 13 Kissimmee, Florida 86
Chapter 14 Abraham, the Rail Peddler 93
Chapter 15 Wilbur McCray, Cowman 102
Chapter 16 Kissimmee - Abigail 111
Chapter 17 Abigail: Alexander's Tutor 115
Chapter 18 The Cottonmouth Encounter 119
Chapter 19 Christmas at the Sommerlands 127
Chapter 20 The Florida Land Boom 135
Chapter 21 Kissimmee - Secrets Shared 142
Chapter 22 Abigail's Dilemma 147
Chapter 23 Hardships: 1926-1941 156
Chapter 24 The Great Labor Day Hurricane of 1935 161
Chapter 25 Years of the Great Depression 174
Chapter 26 December 7, 1941 179
Chapter 27 Marseille, 1920 183

And let your board stand on an altar on which the pure and innocent of forest and plain are sacrificed...
Kahlil Gibran

CHAPTER 1

Late Autumn, 1913
The Bekaa Valley, Lebanon

They spoke in whispers, using arm signals to encourage each other and remaining constantly on the lookout for the feared Turkish soldiers.

The small group of mountain men in their ragged clothing, joined by young Iskandar, clustered on their knees in the forbidden wheat field gleaning the deep red soil of the rich farmland with their bare, calloused hands, seeking the meager uncollected cut wheat. The 400-year occupation of Lebanon by the Ottoman Empire had been especially harsh for decades, but this year proved the most severe. The people turned desperate; their village became impoverished; their clothing worn through; finding enough wheat to survive through the coming winter months an imperative risk; survival the best the villagers could hope for.

Iskandar, a small boy of ten, crouched on all fours deep in the wheat fields of the Bekaa Valley, searching the soil for as many uncollected wheat kernels as he could find. His mother made these morsels into precious bread and every other staple of the Lebanese diet. If his mission was not successful, his family faced certain starvation.

The boy struggled to walk with eight grown men up and down two rugged mountains to come to this rich valley. It was backbreaking, tedious, and dangerous work for the frightened group, and even more so for the young boy. They carefully stayed out of sight from the army patrols by staying low to the ground, and stopped at the slightest sound, their eyes darting side to side.

The Bekaa Valley was warmer than his village, so Iskandar took off his tattered sweater. The late morning sun high in the clear sky beat down making him feel hot. He grew tired; his legs ached from crouching down for several hours within the remaining wheat stalks. Until now, his powerful feelings of determination kept him going. He looked at his small hands realizing that grown men collected much more grain with their large cupped hands. A slight cooling breeze brushed across his face as he looked up. For hours, mixed emotions of concern and pride invaded his thoughts of helping his mother. Fear of being caught, and an adventure so far from home, added to the excitement and knowledge of how critical was the mission to bring home the precious wheat.

The adventure slowly turned into a frightening experience for the boy.

Iskandar's pride and sense of duty were responsible for getting into this dangerous situation…beyond what he could handle…and it would take all his determination, physical strength, and faith to overcome it. He remembered how difficult it was to get to the valley. And now he realized he had to climb back with his load of wheat.

In the village, his mother and brother often admonished him to "get down from that cedar tree," or "get off that roof, don't take such chances, son." But those escapades were his strengths, a vital part of Iskandar's life. Testing fate and his own capabilities taught him how to find solutions.

Iskandar, being the smaller of two sons, felt it necessary to prove himself. He excelled in school, told jokes, took chances, and sought adventure. His mother taught him those lessons that would prepare him for life: Love, be loved, accept love, work hard, be resilient, tenacious and determined. Have faith in the Lord. He will watch over you.

The dichotomy in his young life significantly influenced his thinking. In the village was support, love and a sense of community. From the oppressive Turkish occupation evoked abuse, hatred and terror in the people. At home in Douma, everyone knew everyone else. Cousins, aunts and uncles served as surrogate parents. And, while love flourished in that small, intimate, somewhat isolated village, the outside forces of the harsh Turkish occupation terrorized the villagers, and the barren hills left few options in life. Locusts and other unforeseen catastrophes invaded the region beyond the norm. So, even in his early, formative years, the boy had to find different ways to enjoy each day. Watching his father struggle and his mother make do with little taught him that his life became his own responsibility and that even though life was hard, one should never give up. His family endured many hardships in this harsh region barren with the loss over the centuries of most of its lush, majestic cedar trees. Only small scattered forests nearby remained.

During the four-year famine from 1912 to 1916, the Turks tried to starve out the mountain people of northern Lebanon. Only the roughness of the region prevented the army from penetrating or occupying. A few fruit trees and grapes grew on the centuries-old stonewall-terraced slopes and gnarled olive trees, which took hundreds of years to produce their bounty in the valley below the village. Most of the land, too steep and the soil too filled with rocks to grow wheat to make bread, pilaf, and *bulgur*, deprived them of the staples of their Middle Eastern diet. That combined with the occupation forced the villagers to find another source of wheat.

Their favorite food, *tabouleh*, a rich, traditional salad made of chopped parsley, *bulgur*, diced tomatoes, onions, olive oil, and lemon juice, didn't have quite the same taste or feel without the *bulgur*, which grew mostly in the Bekaa Valley. No roads led to the Bekaa, and the Turks stationed army patrols near the mountain trails. They arrested anyone they captured, especially young Christian men, who they conscripted into their army; in 1902 the Turkish government changed the law, now requiring Christians to serve.

As a result, the men of the village had to climb over two rocky, steep, very high treeless mountains, with heights up to 7,000 feet to collect the precious wheat down in the fertile valley. The entire time they traveled, they hid from the Turkish army patrols behind rock outcroppings. It was harrowing and physically exhausting for everyone. After climbing the first ridge, then descending into the valley to cross the full-flowing river at *Farhilda*, they climbed the worn, tortuously narrow, curving path up the second range of mountains. From there they looked down with parochial pride on the warm, fertile Bekaa Lebanon's "bread basket."

The farmers and migrant workers departed when the wheat harvest season in the Bekaa Valley ended. The Turkish army, except for a few patrols, relocated to the port cities of Tyre and Sidon on the southern coast for the winter. Several deeply concerned men of Douma decided to walk over the mountains forty miles east to the Bekaa Valley to glean adequate wheat to survive that coming winter. Overhearing their plans, ten-year-old Iskandar jumped at the chance to go. A chance for an adventure. As he listened to the men talk, crouched behind a large stone in the *souk*, he made his plans. He took a burlap sack made of goat's hair and filled it with wheat for his mother. Even though too young to make the trip, he desperately wanted to help his mother. His father, in search of a better life for his family, migrated to America with his sister, hoping to send for all of them soon. Because his older brother, Milhelm, traveled down the mountain to the port city of Tripoli seeking fish, Iskandar decided to do his share. His age didn't matter.

Early the next cold, dark morning, the men gathered together as Iskandar sneaked out of his house to join them.

"I'm going too," exclaimed Iskandar to the group. "I have my sack."

"You are too small, my cousin. It is very difficult and dangerous," said one of the men.

"Stay here with your mother," said another as he brushed Iskandar aside.

That last remark convinced him he *had* to go. Iskandar, determined and stubborn, knew that the men were going to gather wheat for their own families. He too must provide for his family despite his youth.

The men reluctantly allowed him to join them in this dangerous journey realizing his mother needed help and he had to learn sooner or later. His persistence finally convinced them.

The small group began their struggle up the mountain path before daybreak. Despite the very cold air, the steep climb kept them warm in their worn sweaters.

The massive rock outcroppings of the barren, stone-filled slopes made the climb all the more difficult. Late that night they reached the 7,000-foot crest of the second mountain range. As they reached the top, the much colder air made them shiver, making them wonder if they had waited too long to undertake their mission. They slept uncomfortably, sat and rested until dawn. A couple of the men, more tired than the others, lay down on the stony patch of soil. Not wanting to convey his exhaustion, Iskandar crouched against a stone outcropping. But in time he slept curled up in a fetal position.

Before the first warm rays of the morning sun appeared across the eastern horizon, Anthony, their determined leader, shook the men, one at a time.

"Get up quickly," he said. "We must get down to the Bekaa Valley immediately. I don't like the weather signs up here. It may get colder, but I hope that there will be no snow."

They spent four more hours walking down the difficult winding mountain path to the valley floor. Once there, one by one, they selected their areas and, on their knees, quickly began sweeping the ground with their bare, cupped hands, collecting the remnants of the harvest, and filling their sacks and bags, a slow, frustrating, but necessary process.

Anthony, hearing voices in the distance, alerted the others once again. "Watch out for the Turkish soldiers!" he said in a loud whisper.

In order to collect the remnant grains, they spread out and searched the ground for loose wheat cut and left by the farmers. In this way, they wouldn't follow one another and inadvertently seek the same morsels. The stiff, brittle, and thick wheat stalks made it hard to move around, making their efforts even more difficult. It took several hours to collect enough scattered unharvested wheat to fill their bags, sometimes with as much soil as wheat kernels. One of the villagers, wiping his brow with a kerchief, complained how the crouching and gathering harvest made his back and legs burn with pain.

"I am so tired," he groaned, accurately reflecting the feelings of the entire group, including young Iskandar.

When they were finished, they needed to rest. They laid down in a small circle on the soft soil and slept in the fields for an hour, using their filled sacks as pillows. Soreness and painful cramps crept into their backs and legs from bending over, kneeling, and crawling along the ground.

"My God," complained one, stretching his pained back, "how much we must go through for so little wheat."

After nearly an hour, Anthony spoke to his tired group, "Our sacks are full, thank God. We must begin our return to the village. The clouds are building on the mountains. It will be dark soon. *Yallah.*"

Knowing the return walk home would be difficult and treacherous, they gathered their belongings, heaved the heavy sacks over their shoulders, and began their trek back to the village. The pain made it difficult for most of them, but especially for the young boy, even though their strong legs, developed over a lifetime of climbing up and down the rugged mountains to visit neighbors, and tend to their goats, fruit trees and terraced vineyards, endured the trek.

Anthony glanced back at Iskandar and watched him struggle. "Are you able to continue, boy?"

Iskandar stifled a breathless grunt, and replied, "Yes, sir. I am fine," while praying the leader would tell them to stop and rest. He shook with fear because his body ached all over, yet he forced himself onward.

One spoke to his neighbor, "Sometimes these mountains can be your friends, but other times, like now, they can be your enemy."

He replied, frustrated, "I'm beginning to hate this damned bag of wheat."

Breathing hard, and feeling the weight of their heavy sacks, the group finally reached the crest of the first mountain.

The leader raised his arm to stop the stretched caravan of men. "We will rest here."

Without any hesitation, they gratefully dropped their heavy sacks on the ground at their feet, using them for back rests. They sat in a circle and drank water from their sheepskin pouches, breathed easier, and stretched their sore legs.

One man, feeling sorry for Iskandar, offered water to him from his pouch. The boy drank readily. He welcomed the wonderful flow of cool water down his parched throat, refreshing his small body. He tried to straighten his legs. His whole body ached. Even though colder in the mountains, he felt his body dripping with perspiration. Yet, he dared not let the men see his tired face as he turned and winced with great effort, wiping a tear from his cheek.

One villager said, "My God, that was difficult. I am so tired. And yet, we have so far to go."

"Yes, *khali*, but look down to the valley and see how far we have come. And we have wheat for the winter."

Another spoke, "Yes, we must be grateful to God we have full sacks for our children. I feel good that we are safe up here and we have once again cheated those damned Turks."

"Did you hear any birds while we were in the valley?"

"No, I didn't. I'll bet the soldiers shot them all. It is so bad that the whole world is in such a state of war. And we are but a small part of the craziness. But this winter we will not see our children starve to death at the hands of the Turks!"

To Iskandar, after what seemed to be only a few minutes, the leader led them down the mountain as they resumed their arduous trek on the steep trail down the mountain to the river where they could refresh themselves in the cool mountain waters. Each stride painful. Their thighs ached with every step as they constantly shifted their sacks of wheat from one side then the other.

"One more mountain and we'll be home, men," said Anthony, venturing a smile of impending success, and seeking to encourage his weary group. "Stay close, Iskandar. I don't like the weather signs. The clouds from the sea are getting darker."

As they slowly climbed up the last mountain, the sacks of wheat grew heavier and heavier, more cumbersome, and more unwieldy.

One yelled back, "Iskandar, keep up with us."

Another complained, "I knew he shouldn't have come along. He is too young... too small. I told him so."

"But his family needs wheat too," interjected another villager. "And he said he would keep up with us."

Iskandar was in great pain and began to lag farther behind the group. His legs like logs. His thighs cramping. His muscles cried out for rest. His body dripped with perspiration, but he didn't falter in his determination. No complaints. No requests for the men to go slower. Every step tested his will, but his resolve and strength prevented him from collapsing. This was his nature. The thought of his family starving this winter without his bag of wheat pushed him forward.

"Die here on this mountain if you quit, or join your family in your home if you continue," the leader encouraged the weary group.

I cannot shame my father. I must not stop. I must keep up, Iskandar repeated to himself. He willed his body to move. *I can make this body do anything. My mind is stronger than my body.*

They pressed on. Finally, they reached the 6,500-foot second crest. Their village, about 3,000 feet below appeared below them.

Anthony, the leader, exclaimed, "Oh, my God, I see snow ahead."

A second man pointed down and shouted, "There must have been a surprise snowfall up here during the night. It looks at least a foot deep on the crest."

Another looked up and yelled, "Oh, my God, look, here comes more snow from the sea!"

The approaching, freak snowstorm frightened them even more. In minutes, the wet, heavy snow quickly deepened on the ground as the moisture-laden dark-gray clouds blowing east from the sea unleashed a potential disaster. Snow sometimes accumulated more than twenty feet on this mountain. The wind-driven snow stung their bare faces and hands as they quickened their pace. The men did not own adequate warm caps, boots, stockings or heavy coats and gloves they needed. During these times of desperation and starvation, everyone in the impoverished village existed with only the barest necessities.

Iskandar, poorly prepared, only wanted to surprise his mother with a supply of precious wheat, and now he shivered from the cold, his hands and feet freezing.

They trudged through the deepening snowdrifts along the crest, leaning into the wind and blowing snow, covering their faces as best they could as they shifted their sacks. Their feet grew even colder.

Iskandar now walked with only stockings on his feet. His feet, so numb he did not know that he had stepped out of his shoes, leaving them behind on the snowy trail.

After nearly an hour of walking through nearly knee-deep snow, Iskandar, stumbling with great difficulty, and more stubborn than wise, straggled behind the men. Each step a major effort. With frozen tears around his eyes and nose, in great pain and totally exhausted, he finally collapsed and fell face down in the snow.

A man nearest him saw him fall and, alarmed, yelled ahead to the others, "Give me a hand, the boy has fallen down."

Iskandar's feet felt like ice to the village man, hard as stone.

"We must take shelter and build a fire. Some of us, Iskandar for sure, cannot go on in this deep snow. There!" Anthony pointed to a large overhanging stone, "We can find refuge for the boy under that."

Iskandar, shivering from the cold, did not say a word as they carried his limp body. In great pain, embarrassed, frightened and exhausted, he closed his eyes and silently prayed, *Dear Lord, please save me.*

The small group worked their way under the large rock protruding from the mountain and quickly stacked their wheat-filled sacks, making a low makeshift barrier to protect them from the wind and blowing snow. They quickly gathered sticks and built a small fire. In the bitter cold, as they huddled together for warmth, the men placed their bodies next to the boy to warm him.

"Put the boy's feet near the fire to try to get them warm and cover his shoulders," yelled Anthony, taking charge. "He is freezing. I will go down to the village and get Milhelm. He is young and strong, and will come here to take his brother home. He isn't called *Markab el Bar* for nothing."

Milhelm's strength, size and endurance, well known in the province, earned him the nickname "Ship of the Land."

Milhelm, visiting in the *souk* in the middle of the village, saw the man running toward him. He stumbled, dropping his bag of wheat on the ground, and breathing hard as he bent over, hands on his knees.

"Come, Milhelm, come now." Waving his arm frantically, and gasping for air, he pointed to the mountain. "Your brother is in trouble. His feet are frozen and he cannot walk. He is weak and cannot carry his wheat down the mountain. He has been brave, but he is just a boy."

"Damn! We have been looking for that boy for two days, Where is he? Take me to him now. I'll get a blanket at the house and tell Mother that I'll return soon, but we can't tell her about Iskandar yet."

Milhelm and the neighbor ran down the village dirt road toward the mountain slope. Their hurried climb took nearly two hours instead of the normal three. They finally reached the group by the small fire.

"Iskandar, what has happened?" Milhelm asked his frightened brother.

"My feet are frozen, Milhelm," he cried out. "They are turning black. What is going to happen to me, *khai-yi*, my brother? Am I going to die?" Tears were flowing down his young cheeks.

Alarmed, Milhelm spoke. "I will take you home now, Iskandar. Here," he called to the others, "put him on my back. Someone wrap his feet and cover him. We have to go immediately."

With both his brother and the sack of wheat on his back, fifteen-year-old Milhelm carried a double load through the deepening snow on the crest, then down the steep 3,500-feet of mountain path to rescue his brother. It took nearly another two hours. He called on all of his strength to save his brother's life.

Milhelm prayed for God's help during the entire difficult trek back to the village. He nearly ran down the mountain with his brother on his back, slipping and falling several times, shifting his brother and his sack of wheat.

Finally, nearly exhausted, Milhelm slammed his muscular body against the heavy, wooden door to enter his family's crude, dirt-floored hovel, *Biet* Chalhoub, home of Chalhoub. His mother kept a small fire in the house during the cold winter, keeping it warm and dry inside. He carried his brother and the sack of wheat inside and gently placed Iskandar on the small carpet by the fire. Iskandar, now more like a whipped puppy, gratefully lay near the fire getting warm, looked at his mother with sheepish eyes. "Mama, I…"

"Aieee," shrieked Katrina. "What is wrong?" She placed her hands over her mouth, frightened at the sight. Her eyes widened as she surveyed the scene, her children obviously in great trouble.

"His feet are frozen," exclaimed Milhelm to his mother, nearly out of breath. "Iskandar went to the Bekaa with the village men to gather wheat for the winter. The men were surprised by a sudden snowfall on the mountain, and Iskandar lost his shoes in the deep snow. I think he was embarrassed and scared. He knew he should not have gone." Milhelm caught his breath and paused, "He thought the men would be angry with him, so he never complained. He just stubbornly kept walking in the snow still carrying the sack of wheat without saying anything to anyone. You know how determined he is, *Imei*."

"Milhelm, run for the *khoury*, the priest," Katrina cried out. "I'm sure he is at the church. And find the doctor…even if you have to go to Tripoli!" she commanded her son, pointing to the door.

She put more water in a kettle over the fire and began to heat a pot of olive oil, the miracle from God. She began soaking rags in the warm water and carefully wrapping the boy's feet as he lay on the carpet near the fire.

Finally, after what seemed like hours, she heard voices outside the door. "Milhelm! Come in here, *ta ha la hawn*. Is the doctor with you? The priest, *khoury*?"

The doctor knelt by the boy, one knee on the rug, and quickly did those things rural doctors did in those austere, difficult times of 1913. He felt the boy's temperature at his forehead, and then his chest. He checked his pulse and looked into the boy's eyes. Then he turned to his legs and feet. Iskandar's toes were already hard and turning black. The doctor silently frowned. They were frostbitten.

With a serious look on his face, he turned to Katrina and said, "We must watch the boy's feet for a few days. I will send to Beirut for another doctor. Keep him warm, and wrap his feet with warm, not hot, blessed olive oil. Be very careful. Hot wrappings will make the pain he will experience even worse, almost unbearable. This will not be a pleasant experience for the boy." He thought for a moment, and looking into her eyes, added, "It will be very difficult for you both."

Collecting his thoughts, Milhelm spoke, "*Imei*, I couldn't find the priest. But I will." Milhelm knew his mother would want the *khoury* to come and comfort her and the boy.

The doctor returned in two days. He and his colleague silently studied Iskandar's feet. With a sharp pin, they carefully poked his calves, ankles, feet, and toes. There had been no positive change. After a careful examination, the doctors stepped to the side inside the bare one-room house, away from the boy near the fire, and began conferring in whispers, gesturing as they spoke.

"What is it? Tell me!" exclaimed Katrina in a whisper as she stepped toward them, away from her son. "What shall I do?" She bowed her head and wrung her hands.

The doctor softy put his hands on her shoulders, looked into her eyes with great sadness, then whispered, "Katrina, I am so sorry to tell you, but your boy's feet are frostbitten. They are dead. They must be cut off immediately to save his life."

"No!" she hissed in a loud whisper as she stiffly squared her shoulders and turned her body, rejecting that statement. Outraged, tears already flowing in desperation, her narrowed eyes pierced the doctor's. "Never! You will not cut off his feet! You may as well cut his throat! How can this boy live without feet?" She pointed to her young son. "Should he be a beggar in the *souk*? Impossible. Never! With God's love and guidance, I will save his feet and his life. Tell me what to do!"

Iskandar, frightened, huddled by the fire and could only hear whispers, wondering what was being said. He felt sadness as his eyes filled with tears and he stifled a need to cry, knowing it wasn't good news.

"*Imei*..." Iskandar cried out, reaching for his mother with both arms. She was so beautiful to Iskandar, so gentle and loving. She was perfect.

What Katrina endured was a monumental task of a loving and totally dedicated mother. That very day, she began a two-year regimen that taxed her, while bringing her and her son even closer together. Twice a day, day after day, by the fire, Katrina lovingly massaged Iskandar's feet with warm olive oil. She completely devoted herself to saving her son's feet. When Iskandar jerked away from the terrible pain with tears in his eyes yelping, "Oowww...," his mother comforted him with a kiss as she touched his face gently. Only after many months, into the summer, did the pain began to lessen.

"You are a brave young man," Katrina whispered to him as she rubbed his feet. "I know it is difficult. If I could take the pain instead of you, my son, I would gladly bear it for you."

"Oh, *Imei*, I'm so sorry I worried you. Please forgive..."

"Shhh, my little one, be still. It is alright," she interrupted him.

Meanwhile, Milhelm called on their neighbors' homes and borrowed olive oil when they ran out. In the late summer, he made more oil from their olive trees by harvesting, then carrying the *zeytoon* to the village's olive presses. The whole village came to their assistance, aiding this family throughout the crisis. Cousins and friends brought whatever food they could spare. After all, Ibrahim, their father, a former leader of the village, stonemason, builder, and cultural pillar of his church and the village, now lived across the sea in America, working to bring his family to join him there. Meanwhile, his wife barely survived without her husband and his sons without their father.

After two years, Katrina restored Iskandar's feet and his life. Everyone in the village celebrated at mass in the churches of Douma as he gingerly took his first steps. His healing testified to their faith in God and belief in Katrina's love and devotion. His feet recovered, but they remained very dark, nearly black, for the rest of his life.

During his recovery, his mother gently rubbed his feet in her lap with the warm oil, speaking to him with loving tenderness, almost in a whisper, all those many days. She spoke to Iskandar of his father's courage, the difficulties he overcame, his mastery at building homes for his neighbors, his strength and his principles.

"He built this very house with his bare hands. He gathered each stone from the mountain and placed it with loving care. Then he cut the limbs of the olive trees for the door lintels and the ceiling. He placed the stones and soil on the limbs to make our roof, and brought the heavy, ancient Roman marble column section and rolled the roof each day to keep us dry. He never gave up, *habibi*, never. And we must not ever give up. We must stay strong," she would tell him. "Remember these things I tell you, Iskandar."

"Yes, *Imei*, I will. I will always remember."

She told him the stories of his ancient heritage, of how their family forebearers, six brothers Chalhoub, Hanna, Eassa, Maloof, Bashir, Simaan, and Ayoub had settled in this very place before the Greeks, long before Christ, and how there were on these mountains, in those times, thousands of cedar trees that harbored bear and deer. Some even said lions lived in the mountains when they were blanketed with cedar trees. She taught him about his Phoenician heritage and how he must be brave like them and follow God. "You must have faith, Iskandar," she whispered to him, "because your faith is your destiny." She told him all these things from her heart.

She told him of all the difficulties his family and all the Lebanese had endured over the centuries. "From the Greeks, Romans, the Europeans, and the Turks, it has been Lebanon's destiny to be where everyone wants to be, to provide the great cedar wood, plentiful water, food, labor, ingenuity for the world. Our people have always been resilient and come back from adversity." He listened intently. There had always been a deep, loving bond between mother and her youngest child. And these two years brought them even closer. All his life, Iskandar remembered his conversations with his mother during these two years of recuperation. He deeply felt and appreciated his heritage and all that it meant as he witnessed his mother's total dedication and commitment to her family.

Yet, the impoverished people of the village, powerless in the face of the Turkish occupation, lived without freedom under siege. Because of the locust infestation which lasted four years, the villagers had little or no food. It caused him great pain to know his father sacrificed so much by leaving his family to go far away to America to provide a better life for them all. Thirteen-year-old Leila had gone to America with her father to care for him, as was the custom.

Three years after his frostbite, during the severe famine and Turkish blockade, his mother died of malnutrition in his arms. Now, after years of her gentle touch and endearing affection, she was gone. Her death left an enormous void in his emotional being. He grew more determined to go to America where he would have the opportunity to free himself of being so poor. He couldn't fill the void of his lost mother's love. But, he believed God would provide him with someone to love, someone who would love him as deeply as he wanted to love her. Iskandar never forgot those terrible and painful days of his youth. He never, ever forgot his mother's love.

Your joy is your sorrow unmasked...
Kahlil Gibran

CHAPTER 2

Beirut, 1920

Iskandar stood alone at the rail of a rusting World War I Turkish freighter, now a passenger ship, still tied up at the Beirut pier. His eyes impatiently searched the milling crowd on the docks below looking for his older brother Milhelm, who was staying in Lebanon, and his Uncle Elias.

He could see the faces of most of the people waving to their departing loved ones, his fellow passengers. The older men and women dressed in *kiffeyehs* and *afeyehs*, loose, flowing cotton gowns, the traditional clothing of the Arab Middle East. Like Milhelm, some of the men still wore the Turkish pants with the loose-fitting waist, balloon-like upper legs and tight-fitting calves, and the Turkish fez. Others wore flat, wound turbans on their heads. A few businessmen wore fedoras, European-styled brimmed hats, worn by the more sophisticated and well-traveled.

Like many younger men, Iskandar chose to wear the more Western European style of clothing, a close-fitting blouse that emphasized his physique, and long double-pleated, cuffed pants in the French tradition that concealed his athletic, strong legs. A cousin in Beirut introduced him to the more contemporary look and bought him clothes imported from France. Iskandar proudly sported a mustache, also a part of the Lebanese culture. The stark contrast of tradition and the introduction of European influence changed the mores of Beirut.

Iskandar's father, Ibrahim, left for America early in 1912 leaving behind the war, the locusts, and the four-year famine of Lebanon. He settled in a place called Florida. The family waited anxiously for him to save enough money to pay for his trip back to Lebanon to bring his wife and two sons to America. Even though he saved every penny, his meager earnings took much longer than he hoped. World War I further complicated his intentions of coming back to Lebanon and bringing his entire family back to America.

Now, eight years later, Ibrahim, currently owner and operator of a small dry goods store near Orlando, saddened by the loss of his beloved wife who recently died, sent money by telegraph to Elias for the purchase of two tickets for his sons, but only Iskandar was on the ship.

Milhelm planned to go to America with Iskandar mainly to take care of him, but at the last minute, he changed his mind and decided to remain in Lebanon now that World War I, "The War to End All Wars," ended. The hated Turks, forced to leave Syria and its western province of Lebanon three years earlier, and the French government became its "protector" under the League of Nations settlement.

Life in Lebanon improved under the new occupier and Milhelm, the gentle mountain man, decided to stay.

More than 150 other Lebanese, mostly young men like himself, boarded the ship. Leaning on the railings, waving to the crowds on the pier, each filled with the conflicting emotions of leaving their villages, their families, cousins, all things familiar and treasured, and the contrasting mystery and wonder of what their new lives would be. Nervous, eager, some frightened. Some wondering if they made the right choice leaving their beloved homeland; Lebanon, "jewel" of the Middle East; leaving their heritage; and for some, their very souls. The ship stirred as the crew removed the boarding ramp. It acted as a reminder to Iskandar that time ran out for him. But he felt good about his decision, albeit with mixed emotions.

As Iskandar stood at the railing, a young man came and stood beside him. "*Mahrharba*. You look sad. Are you? Or are you excited? My name is Georges. I am from Ehden, in the North...the *Shimal. Shooismi*? What is your name?"

"Oh, *Mahrharba*, *ismi* Iskandar. I am from Douma, near Ehden. Are you going to America too?"

"Oh, yes," replied Georges, "and I have older cousins on this ship who are going to America. They are more anxious than me. They just told me how they really aren't sure they are doing the right thing. They have no money and have left everything behind. It is frightening, isn't it?"

"It is scary, Georges, but what choice do we have? Even though the Turks have gone, we now live under the French."

"But they are better, aren't they?"

"Yes, Georges, they are much better, but are we yet free Lebanese? Or will there always be others who come to rule us? I choose to be free," Iskandar asserted, "and I think America is the only land where that is possible. And besides, my father is there with my sister."

"So, you are not afraid like many on board?"

"No, Georges, I'm not. I've spoken with a few who, with their children, are very unsure and frightened, but deep down I believe they know they must do this for the future of their children."

"It's easy to understand my cousins' concerns. They are like a lot of people. They would rather live with what they know, even if it is terrible, instead of venturing in to the unknown, even if it promises to be better."

"It's always been like that with people, I suppose, Georges. My older brother,

Milhelm, has chosen to stay in Lebanon. He is familiar with the mountains and loves living there even though his future is not bright."

"Is he Milhelm Chalhoub Thomé, known as *Markab el Bar*, the Ship of the Land? Oh, my God!" he exclaimed. "All of us in Ehden know of him and what a good and strong man he is. He has crossed the mountains carrying many kilos of olive oil where no other men dare to go. He saved my father's life last winter. And he is your brother?"

"Yes, Milhelm is my brother, and I am very sad he is not going to America with me. I don't know if I'll ever see him again. I wonder if I should have tried harder to make him leave Douma. It breaks my heart."

"I understand, Iskandar, these days so many families are being separated. Loved ones are being left behind all over Lebanon."

"Will our country ever be the same?"

"I don't know, but as for me, I hate being poor. I want to be free in America."

"I agree with that, Iskandar." Then, nodding his head, Georges stepped away, saying, "I'll catch up with you later."

"There! There is Uncle Elias and Milhelm. Wonderful!" Iskandar exclaimed as he stuck his hand into the air over his head, waved vigorously, and happily yelled, "Milhelm! Here! Here I am, look here!"

Milhelm, an imposing man at six feet three inches tall with a large muscular frame and thick dark hair like Iskandar's, stood out in the crowd. There! Eye contact. He could see Milhelm waving to him, yelling to Iskandar, "*Allah ma'ak! Allah ma'ak! Khai-yi!* Go with God. Be with God. Good-bye my brother. Until we meet again."

Tears welled up in his eyes as he vigorously waved to his brother and uncle.

Suddenly, the steel floor under his feet shuddered as the ship's engines groaned, gained power and the ship's rudders turned, directing the ship from the dock. His hands gripped the iron railings even tighter, not from fear of falling, but from his strong emotions as his homeland of Lebanon moved farther away.

The ship's abrupt movement prompted Iskandar to focus again on his brother's face. He longed to embrace Milhelm one last time. With a sense of longing, his mind raced back to those days of closeness with his mother and brother in their home by the warm fire when his mother massaged his darkened, frozen feet.

"*Imei*, tell me again about how the Lebanese survive when foreign people take over our land," Iskandar asked his mother as she applied the warm olive oil to his feet.

"Our history, my sons, is filled with difficult times because, it seems, so many want what we have. Let that be a good lesson for you both. Before Moses brought the Israelites out of Egypt to Canaan, defeating the people there, the Egyptians conquered this entire region. Those were the days, four thousand years before Christ, during which your forefathers, the Phoenicians, sailed all over the world. They were fishermen and traders, trading as far north as England, long before they knew there were lands beyond our sea. They established trading partners across Africa, Spain, Italy and beyond, always exploring, always profiting in trade, not in conquest. We have always thrived in peace, not war."

Then, Iskandar remembered Milhelm asking, "Why is my school teacher a Russian missionary, *Imei?*"

Katrina responded, "The Russian Czar and Russian Orthodox Church sent missionaries to Syria and Lebanon to teach and protect the interests of the Syrian and Antiochan Orthodox communities, just as the French sent Roman Catholic missionaries to teach and protect the Catholic Church communities."

"And that is why Milhelm and I can speak fluent Russian," I remember saying.

"Yes, and both of you learned very well the mathematics, language, and writing skills from the missionary, the only school teacher we had in Douma."

"Are we to learn Syriac, Christian Aramaic, at home and in church?" Milhelm asked.

"The teacher also speaks Syriac, my child."

"And the Maronites? How did they become such an important part of Lebanon?"

"Ah," their mother, smiled as she thought for a moment, "the Maronites, who never yielded to the pagans or the Moslems, are the reason Christians are still predominant in Mount Lebanon. After the people of Palestine became followers of Jesus, Lebanon was second only to the Palestinians in becoming Christians. After Paul, then Peter and Barnabas went to Antioch, the followers became known as Christians for the first time. Antioch is not far from Lebanon's northern border with Syria."

"Now, about the Maronites," Milhelm asked, listening carefully as he stoked the fire, "where did they come from? And how did they become so strong in Lebanon?"

"If it weren't for the strength and beliefs of the Maronites, Lebanon would be completely Muslim today. For more than fourteen hundred years, the followers of St. Maron stuck to their beliefs and never compromised with the pagans or Moslems. They suffered for years because of their strong Christian beliefs. They are why we Christians are still strong in Lebanon and northwest Syria. There was a monk way back, my son," she replied, remembering her lessons, "who lived very near to Douma, in the Batroun Province of Mount Lebanon. He strongly believed that Jesus was both a divine nature and a human nature perfectly united. There was a major dispute on this very point. The Monophysites adamantly argued Jesus was of but one nature, primarily divine, but had human attributes. St. Maron strongly disagreed.

Iskandar, in his innocent way, suggested, "They sound the same to me, *Imei.*"

"I know, my son, but there is a fine but important difference, and to the Monophysites these two beliefs were different enough to persecute the Maronites and cause them to flee Antioch and seek refuge in these mountains near us. Today, near Douma, there are many villages of Maronites. Douma is principally Antiochan Orthodox. There was a major dispute on this point though. Maronite followers increased in numbers and refused to yield to invaders here in these rugged mountains. They resisted the Islamic movement in the seventh and eighth centuries and were insistent that Mt. Lebanon be Christian. They never gave up. Many years later, they allied with the French who sent forces and missionaries to teach their children and protect them. They have looked to France for their protection since the sixteen hundreds. That is why even today France and the Maronites are closely bonded, and that is why we are safe here in Mt. Lebanon. And that is why the Maronites are able to compete politically with the Muslims."

Milhelm interjected, telling Iskandar and his mother what he had learned in school, "After the Greeks, the Romans controlled Lebanon and Syria. They built Baalbek, their largest eastern city in the Bekaa Valley, named after the god Baal who the local people worshipped before *Allah*, the greatest of all gods. The Bekaa became Rome's eastern 'Bread Basket,' feeding all their armies and citizens in this region for many years."

"Are all Lebanese now Christians, *Imei?*" Iskandar asked.

"Not completely, my brother," Milhelm answered.

"The balance of Syria compromised and became Sunni Muslim because they joined the Islamic movement," said Katrina. "I want you boys to know your inheritance and know it well. We belong to the Antiochan Orthodox Church, the oldest of all Christian churches. It began in Antioch, which was a major city, like Alexandria and Constantinople. Antioch became Christian through the efforts of St. Paul, Barnabas and the growing Christian community there. It was strengthened by St. Peter who founded our church there."

"St. Peter!" Milhelm exclaimed. "Jesus' first apostle founded our church there?"

"Yes, he did. This is the first church of Christianity."

Iskandar remembered feeling so close to his mother as she massaged his feet, and astounded by her knowledge. "Do you mean our church was founded by St. Peter who later went to Rome?"

"Yes, my child."

"So that means our church was before Rome!" he boasted.

"That is true, Iskandar, but the Roman church is just as important, just as much a part of the beginning as are we. But yes, our church was established before Rome. The Greeks became Christian through the travels and preachings of Paul early on too."

"I would like to know more about our Lebanon, *Imei*," Iskandar asked again and again, always wanting to know more. And his mother and Milhelm were always obliging.

"Lebanon, although small, my son, stands for good things. We do not choose war, we seek peace and freedom."

"Where did our families come from, *Imei?*"

"Milhelm, I believe I've told you this story before, but it's important. The elders tell us there were six Chalhoub families led by six brothers who settled in Douma together three hundred and fifty years before Christ, even before Alexander the Great came out of Macedonia and conquered this entire region, including the battles of Sidon, Tyre, and Alexandria, Egypt. That was said to be twenty-five years after the Chalhoubs left the fertile farming of the Golan Heights and came here. At that time, these lands were completely covered in forests, mostly cedars, and wild game was abundant. The men hunted bears, tigers, deer, and almost any animal known to man."

"There were six brothers Chalhoub, right, *Imei?*" Iskandar asked.

"Yes, my darling, they were named Hanna, Eassa, Maloof, Bashir, Simaan, and Ayoub. And members of most of the six families still live here in Douma. Imagine! They have never left their inheritance after so many years."

"That's amazing, Milhelm. I believe we should never leave here after so many years."

Then, Milhelm exclaimed, "I hear the men speak of the rivers in the Bekaa Valley where everything grows!"

"Yes, *Imei*," she replied as she, by custom, affectionately called him with her own title. "The Bekaa has fed the Greeks, the Romans, the Moslems…everyone who comes to conquer us covet our wonderful valley where we grow our wheat, grapes and vegetables."

"Oh, *Imei*," Iskandar sighed, "there is so much to learn, isn't there?"

"Yes, Iskandar, there is. That is why you must always do your lessons at school and at church. We in the *Shimal*, the North, are known for emphasizing education for our children. Learn, son, learn, and you will be free."

The ship hit a wave and jarred Iskandar back to reality from his reverie. Remembering his beloved mother, he reached inside his blouse and gripped the precious gold crucifix which hung against his chest. He made the Orthodox sign of the cross; forehead, heart, right shoulder, left shoulder, heart. "Lord, be with me, protect me." He looked at his right hand. The tips of his thumb, forefinger and second fingers touched each other in the Trinity fashion of the Orthodox Christians. After a moment, he reached into his pocket to assure himself he still had his new friend, the stone he picked on the road above his village at the lookout by the large stone.

Iskandar strained to look back. By now, the shoreline was no longer visible.

"Goodbye, my Lebanon," he whispered.

How can a tyrant rule the free and the proud, but for a tyranny in their own freedom and a shame in their own pride?
Kahlil Gibran

CHAPTER 3

Beirut, 1917
Uncle Salim

Iskandar, now standing near the ship's stern, couldn't tear himself away from the ship's rail, his eyes fixed on the fading mountains above Beirut as the ship sailed east. His new friend, Butrus, and his younger cousin, Kahlil, also from Zahle, shortly joined him.

"Iskandar, are you related to Salim Doumani Chalhoub? We've heard stories about him."

"Yes, Salim is my uncle," he quickly replied "even though he is only two years older than me. He picked up the name Doumani in Beirut because he is from Douma. Salim lived next door to my family there."

"Then you must know the story about his run-in with the Turkish army."

"Oh, yes, Salim told us his story many, many times. All the villagers in Douma know it by heart."

"We in Zahle heard all manner of stories about him. What really happened?"

"Well," Iskandar started, recalling Salim's frightening experience, "Salim, whose reputation as the best singer and *oud* player, charmed Beiruti society with the haunting love songs that we wrote. As his popularity spread, he attracted the attention of the Turks. After entertaining in a Beirut nightclub one night, he left at about four a.m. through a rear alley door to go home to his apartment."

"If he's only a couple of years older than you, he must have been pretty young to be in Beirut by himself. How old was he?"

"Sixteen. His family didn't like his living in Beirut then because of the Turks' strictly enforced martial law prohibiting single men being outside on the streets late at night. He knew the danger, but the thought his family's poverty made it worth taking the risk. Up to that point, the Ottoman Turks weren't too strict about detaining many of the young Christian men."

Butrus interrupted, "Kahlil, the Ottomans, faced with the possibility of war with the West, passed a law a few years earlier, in 1902, that Christian men were to be forcefully conscripted into the Moslem-Turkish army. He was captured in 1917 during the final year of World War I when the Ottoman Turks were being defeated by the Western powers."

"Well, anyway," Iskandar continued, "Uncle Salim told us that just as he left the nightclub and stepped into the dark alley, the neighborhood Army patrol, which he was always very careful to avoid, came out of the early morning fog at an unexpected moment and stopped him in the narrow shadowy alley. They were looking for any young Christian men of Beirut they could arrest. Salim said he was really scared that night, but had no choice but to try to get safely to his home. He said he was shocked when he heard the deep, threatening voice of the mustachioed patrol leader yell, 'Halt! Stay where you are!' while pointing a pistol at him.

"Salim was a singer and poet, not a fighter, a son of the mountains, not a city boy, so he stayed frozen in place, hoping he would not be arrested. He asked, 'What do you want of me? I'm just a singer.'

The Turk told Salim, as he pressed a gun into his chest, 'It doesn't matter what you do for a living. You are the enemy and would kill any one of us if you had the chance. Come with us. Now!'

"One of the soldiers shoved him hard in the back with the butt of his rifle. *'Y'hara deen bladuk!* May your country burn in hell.' He said he muttered under his breath so he couldn't be heard.

"The soldiers forced him to march down the dark alley onto the cobblestone street within the cluster of Turkish soldiers to a waiting flat bed wagon pulled by two horses, where he joined a half dozen other young Lebanese men. Jostling in the back of the wagon as it made its way south to the army encampment outside the city, Salim figured they would either die that night or be taken to Turkey and put into the army."

"Wow!" exclaimed Kahlil, "He must have been really scared, Iskandar!"

Butrus replied, "My dear cousin, Lebanese and others in the Arab world have been abused by the Ottomans for years. They stripped us of our self-esteem, our culture, and our leaders. Can you imagine what it means to be conquered and ruled harshly for five hundred years, always having to bow to arrogant Turkish tribal leaders because they have the armies?"

"Yes," added Iskandar, "Salim's story is just one of thousands. He told us the following anxious days in the outdoor barbed wire stockade passed very slowly for him and the other prisoners, some barely in their teens. He knew of the Allies closing in and the Turks preparing for their final rear guard battles.

"A month later, one of the guards told him that the commander said he had too many prisoners and had to get rid of them. Acting on orders from his superiors, the commander immediately began a systematic process of random executions. Each day they were forced to watch several young prisoners lined up and shot by the firing squad, without a trial, without recourse, and without any hope of rescue. Many were as young as twelve years old."

For more than five hundred years, the Turks ruled Lebanon as a province of Syria; before them, the Western Crusaders, the conquering Europeans; before them, the Muslim hordes; and before them the Romans, the Greeks and the Egyptians.

"Every evening," Iskandar continued, "Salim entertained his fellow prisoners by playing his magical *oud*, and singing the beautiful folk songs of Lebanon and his own poetry. The young men would clap their hands in unison to the happy, vibrant songs, and find their eyes filling with tears as he sang poignant, romantic songs of love. Singing was Salim's passion. It was his escape from the reality of the Occupation.

"He used his feather from the eagle to strum the strings, the fingers of his left hand would slide up and down the tapered bent neck of the *oud*, pressing the strings firmly, resting the rounded bowl-shaped guitar on his thigh. It was a welcome respite as his fellow prisoners awaited their turn to be executed.

"One day, after several weeks of killings and nervous waiting, Salim said his turn arrived. For nearly three horrible months in the stockade, he worried every day, 'Is this the day I am to die?' Two soldiers came into the fenced area, marched to him and grabbed both arms, one of which continued to grip his *oud*, practically dragging him off. He would die with his precious *oud*.

"But," Salim smiled as he told this next part. "They took me to the commander's office instead and he asked me, 'Aren't you the young man whose voice I hear singing to the prisoners at night?'

"'*Na'am*, yes, I am,' Salim told him nervously. 'That is what I do for God, I sing.'

"'You have a gift of *Allah*,' the Muslim Turk responded, nodding kindly. "You have a magnificent voice, young man. And, although I am ordered to shoot every prisoner, I cannot kill your voice.'

"Salim said he could not believe what he heard. The Commander looked at Salim's sad eyes, and, in a firm, angry tone, said, 'I will not do that.' Then the commander slammed his hand on the desk, and calmed his voice almost to a whisper. 'I will propose an exchange for you. Tonight I will have you brought to my office where you will sing for me. If you sing to me the way you sing to your fellow prisoners, I promise I will set you free. Go now. I will send for you later,' the Turk admonished as he waved his hand toward the door.

"Salim memorized the commander's every word, he was so grateful to God that his life was spared. He did sing for the commander that night. He sang his heart out knowing it was for his very life. He sang and sang, watching the commander's face, sensing what he enjoyed the most. The Turkish officer, with his eyes closed, listened intently, sometimes swaying his head to the music.

"Salim told us he was amazed when that night he was dressed in a Turkish uniform and taken to the railroad station where he caught a train north to the seaport of Tripoli, about twenty miles north of Beirut. Once in Tripoli the next morning, he said he felt like he was almost home. In his hated used army uniform, with his *oud* in his hand, he nearly ran the remaining thirty miles up the winding gravel and dirt mountain road to his family's village. The entire village came out and embraced him. We were so happy to have Salim home. Safe in the haven of the mountains, he stayed for the remainder of the war. He really didn't know what happened to the other prisoners, probably dead, he said to us, always with tears in his eyes."

"Those bastards," Butrus exclaimed. "Imagine, killing young boys like that. It's no wonder the Lebanese feel such anger for the Moslems and the Turks. It will take generations for that feeling to go away!"

"I agree," said Kahlil. What an amazing story, Iskandar! Thank you for sharing it with us."

"After Salim settled in at home, we spent many days and evenings together gratefully playing *towleh* (backgammon), laughing, shouting, sometimes cursing under our breath as the other got a *shaish-baish* (six-five), roll. We grew up like twin brothers.

"After his ordeal, Salim realized he would never be safe in Lebanon and, in 1918, as soon as he could get passage after the war ended, he found his way across the Atlantic, Americanized his name to Sam and settled in someplace called Boston. There can't be many *oud* players in Boston. It shouldn't be too hard to find him."

Your friend is your needs answered.
He is your field which you sow with love...
Kahlil Gibran

CHAPTER 4

Goodbye to Douma

The ship continued its voyage to Marseille, leaving Beirut far behind, no longer in view. Almost everyone had left the deck and went below to their quarters when the shoreline disappeared from sight. But Iskandar remained at the rail, watching the sunset and thinking of Uncle Salim in America. Then, he heard a familiar voice that broke his solitude.

"We've left Lebanon, Iskandar," Butrus announced. "The future is ours to make, isn't it? Now come join us below! We are having a *hafli*. We're going to dance and celebrate our new beginnings!"

In steerage, the least expensive deck at the bottom of the ship and just inches of steel plate from the sea, the party was already in full swing when Iskandar and Butrus arrived in the large, high-ceilinged space where the Lebanese voyagers slept, ate their food, congregated and partied. One could easily become depressed if left alone in the barren hold. Banks of bare, incandescent light bulbs along the cold, gray steel walls at the ceiling were fully bright eighteen hours a day. "It's for security" the crew responded officiously when asked later in the voyage if they could be darkened during the day so some could makeup for their sleepless nights. Canvas-stretched hammocks stacked four layers high hung on the walls along the side bulkheads with just two feet of vertical space between each bunk, better conditions than when his father traveled to America. In 1912, the steerage passengers slept in small groups on the floor using each other's bodies for pillows and for warmth.

Iskandar knew most of the Lebanese emigrants, like himself, to be hearty, young men from poor backgrounds, hardly anyone past the age of thirty. Below, he found a group of ten men, arms interlocked in a semi-circle dancing the *debkeh*. Standing along the steel wall, two men played the *defs*, hand-held drums; a third shook and hit with his other hand a *darbuka*, the tambourine, and a fourth played the clarinet, emphasizing the sharps of their favorite songs. Just like at home, all participated in the favorite Lebanese recreational group pastime of dancing, singing and laughing. A few women on the voyage, mostly young wives, sisters, and several young brides, sat together in clusters along the cold, steel bulkheads.

"Here Iskandar, have some *arak*. I secretly packed it in my carry bag" shouted Butrus, so he could be heard above the rhythmic hand clapping, the drums and the occasionally loud outbursts from the dancers. Iskandar smiled and eagerly reached for the cup, quickly sharing the clear anisette liquor. The Lebanese enjoyed *arak* best when sharing it with others.

"Ahhh!" he exclaimed. "The Greeks knew what they were doing when they created their ouzo, Butrus, but I like our *arak* even better. We always have *arak* on special occasions at home."

Iskandar took another sip from a small cup and smiled at Butrus. "*Shookrun, sahbi*, thank you, my friend!"

Happiness consumed them in spite of the meager provisions and lack of any furnishings in the cold and barren steerage class area.

Just as the Irish started migrating to America around 1850 because of their potato famine, so too did the Syrian and Lebanese people. The massive emigration from Syria actually began in 1902 with the newly enacted laws by the Turks requiring Christians conscripted into their army.

Lebanese communities arose across the Americas from New York to California, from Montreal, Canada south to Buenos Aires, Argentina. With the encouragement of fathers, brothers, a cousin, or friends, a new generation of young people fled their homeland and the encroachment of the Turks for a new start in a new country.

Iskandar's father chose Boston joining his already established cousins. Even his *Khali* Salim, whom Iskandar loved so dearly, lived there now.

Cuba and other islands of the Caribbean, Brazil, and Chile attracted large populations of Lebanese and Syrian immigrants instead of the United States, because of America's 2% immigration limitations, a national policy to keep the population proportionately the same as it already was; mostly Western and Northern European. Those like Iskandar and Butrus, approved to enter the United States, considered themselves extremely fortunate. For the first time in their lives, they would be a minority in a society to which they would have to adjust. They were justifiably excited and optimistic about seeking new lives in America, the "Land of Milk and Honey."

Iskandar recalled that those were the same words used by God to Moses in the books of Exodus and Deuteronomy as he described the "Land of Milk and Honey" to the Israelites as they came out of Egypt to settle in the land of Canaan.

After sipping more of his *arak*, Iskandar became a little light-headed, left his nostalgia of remembering his family, and joined his fellow travelers in dancing. He was an energetic *debkeh* dancer, stomping his left foot as he crossed his shin with his right foot while he hopped into the air a few inches, keeping in rhythm, double stepping so expertly with his happy compatriots. It was a joyful time. Those not dancing were laughing and watching as they happily clapped their hands in unison to the infectious rhythms.

Butrus joined the end of the line, while Iskandar boldly stepped over and took the lead place in the dancing line. It was the place where, while his left arm was interlocked with the person's arm next in line, his right hand twirled a rolled, twisted kerchief above his head. As leader, he could be creative in his dance steps. He was really happy now, shouting out exclamations like *yeh*! or *yih*!, jumping, slapping his elevated foot, some steps and movements like Greek dancers, spinning under his now-unlocked right arm while holding his neighbor's right hand with his out-stretched left hand. He was now showing off for the crowd, smiling and laughing. They loved his display and began clapping louder and louder in rhythm. The drumbeats got louder and more pulsating, the musicians responding to the *arak* most had shared and relished. Suddenly, captured by emotion and joy, the *darbuka* player stepped off the box he had been sitting on, stood tall, and shouted, "Dance, Iskandar, dance like you are a reborn man! We are going to America, Iskandar!" Now, he was shaking the tambourine over his head, making as much noise as he could, staying in rhythm with the drums. The laughter, chanting, singing and clapping of the musicians and more than one hundred young people with their joyous excitement vibrated loudly off the steel walls of the large, cavernous room, intoxicating and infectious. The *arak* was having an effect on Iskandar now, making him more daring in his steps. The drumbeats grew louder as more and more people began to feel the affects of the *arak* and the rhythm of the drumbeats. They were feeling so happy! So free! Finally, in time, as the song ended, the dancers laughingly stumbled to the edge of the dance area and hugged their fellow travelers. Some sat down. Some bent over, perspiring and spent from exhaustion. And some fell down and lay on the floor, laughing out loud. Iskandar found Butrus and wrapped his arm around his young friend's shorter and heavier shoulders.

"We are going to America, Butrus! We are going to America!" Iskandar repeated excitedly, exuberant from dancing, with a hint of slurring in his speech. "How lucky we are, *sahbi*!"

"We are fortunate, Iskandar. We will be in America. Imagine! If we work hard, we can be anything we want. Not like in Lebanon under the Turks."

They walked to the side of the room and, together, slumped to the floor and leaned against the ship's steel wall. Each eagerly finished their cup of *arak*. With a flourish, Butrus, who always somehow was able to find just what was needed, reached to his left into his bag beside him, and pulled out a sack of natural *fistok*, pistachios, offering the open sack top to Iskandar.

"Aah, heaven," he smiled to Butrus. "*Arak* and *fistok*!...After the *debkeh*. I feel so complete!"

"I think you were showing off for the ladies," laughed Butrus.

Iskandar winked, "I love to dance, Butrus. Back in Douma, I often led the dance, but there, everyone was my cousin. Here, for the first time, I am dancing with people from all over Lebanon. Until now, everyone I knew was a cousin and we all lived in the mountains."

It was the same for all of them in the group. Most were not allowed by the Turkish army to travel far from their towns and villages where they could make new friends. Until the end of the war, all Lebanese had to stay in their regions.

Butrus and Paul were from farming families who likely lived for many generations in the Bekaa Valley, by far Lebanon's largest and richest agricultural region; a valley measuring seventy-five miles north to south, an average of ten miles wide. Located about twenty miles east of Beirut on the coast, the fertile valley is bounded by the Lebanon Mountains to the west and the Anti-Lebanon Mountains to the east, the ridge boundary between Lebanon and Syria. Until 1943, when Lebanon declared its independence, Lebanon was a province of Syria populated mostly by Christians.

The Bekaa, Lebanon's breadbasket today as it was for the Eastern Roman Empire, is rich in soil, fruit orchards, hay and wheat producing pasture lands in the northern portion and, in the southern reaches, because of more rainfall and sunshine, abundant crops of all kinds, including corn, potatoes, vegetables, tomatoes, vineyards of Chardonnay and other types of grapes. For thousands of years, the Bekaa, a major part of the famous "Fertile Crescent," produced food stuffs for the entire eastern Mediterranean region and, with its historical Roman and Omayyad monuments still present, added a high sense of pride to those who lived in the valley. The Bekaa is steeped in history with ruins from as early as the Phoenician presence at least two thousand years before Christ. Two major rivers dominate the Bekaa, the Orontes (Asi) which originates in the Valley and flows north into Syria, and the Litani which flows southward from Zahle.

Butrus loved the Bekaa Valley as Iskandar loved the mountains. "Anything and everything grows in the Bekaa," Butrus would say proudly. Butrus leaving this rich heritage, hoped the area to which he was emigrating would be at least as prolific a region to farm as he had in the Bekaa. Butrus's father was now located in Stockton, California, finding the San Joaquin Valley very much like the Bekaa, with its rich soil, plentiful water, good weather, and vineyards growing in the north. While Butrus would miss Zahle, the ancient Roman and Greek ruins, the Omayyad dynasty arches and the Roman temples, he was happily destined for California.

"I will miss the lakes and ponds too," Butrus reminisced. "What a beautiful place to grow up. But now, like you, Iskandar, I am joining my father in America. You are eighteen years old, but I am just sixteen. So, I will, tag along with you for it is said: 'one who is even one hour older is wiser. Listen to Him.' There is so much I don't understand, Iskandar. Everything is new to me."

"Everything is new to me too, Butrus," he replied, laughing, "but as long as you can find *arak* and *fistok*, you can be close to me, *sahbi*!" They were both rural innocents about to experience for the first time unbelievable new sights and cultures.

As the trip slowly continued at sea, every day was like the day before. During the twelve-day voyage to Marseille, when they weren't seasick, many passengers slept late, and walked the outer deck as often as possible to view the open sea. The days were long and boring, with only the sound of the passing sea beneath them.

Sometimes, as the ship sailed near to the Mediterranean islands, they would get excited and talk among themselves of their heritage. For many, like Iskandar, these were the first islands they had ever seen. First came Cyprus, then Rhodes, both former Phoenician trading settlements, and then, near the tip of Italy's boot, they passed ancient Sicily on the starboard. As they turned north, Sardinia was passed on the left. These were large islands and could easily be mistaken for the mainland of Greece or France.

In the evenings, each would find his own hammock, collect their handbags and place them under their heads for comfort and security.

Iskandar, too, located his handbag and placed his head on his arm as he lay on his right side, his favorite position. As he lay in his hammock on this voyage, the first time in his life away from Douma, he thought of his father in America, and then about his mother and how much he missed her. His thoughts always returned to his small village of Douma, the only life he had ever known. As was his habit, he fondled the gold crucifix resting on his lean chest, hanging by an almost pure gold chain. Holding it in his hand somehow helped him fall asleep easier. How he loved his gold cross. It was so special when his mother draped the chain over his head that Sunday at St. Mary's church just a few yards down the road from their home. He was twelve years old. It was his Confirmation Day at church when he took on the responsibility of leading his life spiritually.

This gift from his mother was even more treasured now that she was gone. He found himself fondling it often, rubbing it between his fingers every day when he thought about his mother, whom he loved so much. He recalled when his mother had had Iskandar's aunt, Ibrahim's sister Sara go to Beirut to have it made especially for him by a cousin who was a gold merchant and goldsmith. It seemed like almost every Lebanese or Syrian family had a gold merchant for a cousin. Discounts and fair negotiating were assumed between seller and buyer, and business volume depended on "word of mouth."

This particular 20-karat gold cross was designed to reflect the characteristics of the Antiochan Orthodox church, St. Paul's first church, his mother told him. It was beautiful and unique. It always reminded him of his mother's love. As Iskandar remembered her, he brought the cross to his lips and kissed it. This night, he gripped the cross, asked God for a safe voyage, then fell asleep on his cot remembering that winter day four years earlier, when his mother was so very sick.

"Quickly, Iskandar, get me some soup from the kettle so I can feed your mother," shouted Aunt Sara.

"Katrina, how could you go so long without telling me, your own husband's sister, that you were ill?" Then, shaking her head, Sara asked, "I am like your sister. Haven't we known each other all our lives? Wasn't I there when you and Ibrahim were married in St. Mary's church? And wasn't it I who helped you bring Milhelm, Leila, and Iskandar into this world? And wasn't I the one you came to when you were lonely after Ibrahim left for America? I was the one who went to Beirut to have the special gold crucifix made for Iskandar's 12th birthday. Now, my dear cousin, you are very sick. And I am here. Thank God Iskandar came to me and asked me to come to you. You are terribly ill. When was the last time you ate decent food? The locusts and those bastard Turks! They are determined to kill us all."

Sara carefully brought the spoonful of soup to Katrina's lips, angry and frightened at what she saw. Katrina tried to eat, but she had not eaten much beyond broth for weeks, saving the bulk of their food for her growing sons. She was actually becoming unable to eat and did not feel the need for food.

"Eat, eat, my sons," she would scold. "You are growing and you are young. Eat."

"But what about you, *Imei*? When will you eat?"

"Don't worry about me, Milhelm," she would reply, smiling softly, hiding her pain. "I eat while you and Iskandar are out during the day. I am fine." But she was not fine, looking tired and worn all the time, getting thinner and thinner, and having less energy each day.

The boys had no idea their mother was so sick and was actually dying. They could see she was sad most of the time, not as hopeful for them as before. It was only when she began coughing...hacking deeply, that they felt something was very wrong. Already, more than two hundred people in Douma had died of malnutrition or pneumonia during the past year. Those were terrible, agonizing days for the people of the mountains.

It had only been a dozen years since the cruel decimation of the Armenian people to the north by the Turks. Nearly all two million Armenians had been systematically killed in the holocaust. Those who could, escaped to Syria, then to Lebanon, exacerbating Lebanon's social problems. But since the Armenians were mostly Orthodox Christians, the Lebanese welcomed them even though it would be difficult. Culturally, they were the same peoples. And now, since the Turks could not move their armies across the steep northern Lebanese Mountains, and especially could not cross the *Wadi Kadeesha*, "Valley of Passion," that deep narrow rift that runs north and south through the north half of central Lebanon which is so steep it cannot be traversed, the Turkish Army chose simply to starve the

Lebanese to death by blockading all routes into and out of the mountains.

And now, lovely Katrina would become another of their casualties.

That day, in their two-room stone home, Katrina was wearily lying in her bed covered in blankets. She waved her hand to her son as she spoke in a soft whisper, "Iskandar, come sit beside me. I want to speak with you. It is very important that you understand what I am going to tell you." She paused as he sat beside her. "You are a strong young man now. You must know how much I love you, my son, more than life itself. You are my very heart."

She reached for his hands, tears welling in her eyes. "From the moment you were born, you were different. You were special. Of course, I love Milhelm and Leila too. I would give my life for any of you, Iskandar. And perhaps I have. But it is right, and it is good." She paused to breathe, her eyes deep with sadness. "I want you to know your father and I are so very proud of you, how bright you are and how you have grown into a fine, handsome, good man. You, your brother and sister are gifts from God and have made us so proud of you."

Iskandar became frightened, listening to her as his eyes became moist too. He interrupted her, "*Imei*, please, you are tired. I...I...don't understand. You make me sad. You have always been the strong one." He reached out to her.

"Even though we know you and Milhelm are different, you both make us happy." She smiled wanly and continued, "He is very strong. He loves you as he loves God. I know you love me and that you know how to love completely. In the lessons of life, you have excelled." She breathed deeply, sighing, "Milhelm will always stay here in Lebanon. He is not like you. He will never leave these mountains." She tightened his hand for emphasis as tears began to overflow on Iskandar's cheeks. She focused deeply on his eyes, summoning all her strength, and, in a higher pitched voice, firmly said, "But you, Iskandar, you *must* go to America."

"But I want him and you to go with me," he cried, pleading, tears now flowing from his eyes.

Katrina paused slightly for a moment, gathering her thoughts, "You belong in America where there is opportunity. As long as the hated Turks stay in Lebanon, there is nothing for you here. It is too difficult simply to live, especially for you, my son. You must be free or you will have no life."

She was pleading now, her hands on his hands as he knelt beside his mother to get closer to her face. "Your father saw that. I know you love these mountains, that you enjoy the ancient cedars, our beautiful but poor village, and our way of life. But, it is not enough for you to thrive. You cannot not stay here and meet your true destiny, Iskandar. Your heart is where you are free, where your talents will thrive. Your future is in America. You must promise me, my beloved Iskandar. You must tell me now, for I am very sick. Promise me that you will go to America and seek fulfillment of your dreams. Find a good woman, be a fine husband, and love her as your father and I love each other. Go join your father."

As she spoke, she caressed Iskandar's hands. He felt the tears steadily slip down his cheeks as he brought his face to hers, touching her moist cheek with his. Impulsively, he hugged her tightly with both arms, both now crying silently but openly.

Iskandar had watched intently as his mother spoke to him. He was choked, unable to speak. He kept shaking his head, and whispered, "No, *Imei*, please. No! You must go with me."

Only now did he realize she was truly very ill. But he still did not know how seriously. He became more frightened by her words, portending something he wasn't prepared to face. He could see tears in her eyes. Yet, he could also see her smile of pride in her son. Katrina had twice given Iskandar his life. She had saved his feet and his life only four years earlier. And now she spoke to him with her final advice and hopes. She knew it would be for the last time.

When she finished speaking to him, they embraced and kissed each other's cheeks. He cupped his hand under her chin, and he kissed her cheek again. They gently looked into each other's eyes and saw their tears overflow. He lovingly stroked her hair, clinging to her, not willing to accept her sense of finality, unable to let her go.

"*Imei*, I love you so much. I cannot bear to leave you. I will stay with you forever. I will protect you."

"No, *Imei*," Katrina replied, addressing her son with his name for her in the customary way, "You must promise me one day soon you will leave this place for a new life of opportunity. Seek your adventures in America, not here. Promise me, *Imei*, this minute. I must hear your words so that I may sleep in peace tonight knowing you will fulfill my dreams for you. Speak the words, my son, so that I may sleep now. Promise me, Iskandar, you will leave these mountains and go…go beyond the cedars."

His tears were now welling again, greater than he could hold back.

"Yes, *Imei*, I promise you, but you must be with me," he sighed sadly.

"Remember, Iskandar, my beloved son, I will always be with you."

Her head turned on the pillow toward him as her eyes closed and she whispered, "You have made me happy, my son. Thank you and God bless you." He pressed his open hand in hers and held it there, not wanting to let go.

That night Katrina peacefully fell asleep for the last time.

With tears welling in his young eyes, Iskandar rolled over in his hammock fastened to the ship's hull, and after a few more minutes recalling his mother's last wishes, he finally fell asleep.

Your joy is your sorrow unmasked-
When you are joyous, look deep into your heart…
Kahlil Gibran

CHAPTER 5

Marseille

Iskandar awakened from his sleep and felt the tears flowing down his cheeks.

"Get up, Iskandar, we are arriving in Marseille! The ship will soon dock at the wharf. Get up. Join us. We are all going on the outside deck. It's so exciting, *sahbi*. Let's go see."

Iskandar shook off his emotional dream and joined Butrus. They stood with the other passengers at the starboard rail as the ship neared Marseille from the southeast, gazing on a coastline of high, steep ridges and scattered rocky islands offshore. They were glad to be outside and eager for the voyage to end.

"How different from Lebanon," exclaimed Butrus, pointing to the shore. "Our mountains sit at least a mile, maybe two, from the sea, but these butt right up to the sea. We grow bananas and tomatoes along our coast. I don't think they can grow anything along this French coast!"

"I wonder what they call this place?" asked Iskandar, sweeping his arm across the view of the French coastline.

As they sailed past Les Calanques, the white-faced steep cliffs climbed as high as 500 feet above the sea. They watched as many coves and secluded beaches nestled in the meandering water's edge passed by revealing people walking along the crests, pleasure boats heading out from the coves, and pockets of people sunning on the stones at the shore.

"Well, it is Saturday, so maybe the people of Marseille come here on weekends," decided Paul, standing nearby.

"Weekends we go to the Litani River near Zahle," replied Butrus proudly.

"Well, I'm from Mount Lebanon, so I'm feeling pretty good about seeing these cliffs and mountains. Pretty special, wouldn't you say?" Iskandar reminded them with a smile.

"Yes, beautiful!" yelled Butrus. "And over there on the other side of the ship, all those islands offshore. Marseille is incredible! I'm going to own one of those islands one day, he blustered."

"Butrus," Iskandar responded to his young friend and the others nearby, waving his arm across the shoreline, "A wonderful life awaits us. Hopefully, good, not bad."

"And I hope you're right, Iskandar," Butrus smiled.

As the ship neared Marseille, the cliffs wore to rounded hills and gave way to scattered buildings along the shore as the city came into view. A large structure near the city, the magnificent mansion called *Jardin du Pharo*, appeared first.

As they slowly approached the port, the two massive fortresses, Fort Saint-Jean and Fort Saint-Nicolas on either side of the entrance to the Old Port, *Vieux Port*, prominently welcomed them.

"Look at those!" yelled Butrus, as he pointed. "I'll bet nobody got passed them. They're just magnificent."

A deckhand interrupted him. "Believe it or not, those were built to keep the Marseille citizens from exiting the city when parochial and wealthy residents of Marseille were battling the royals of Paris during the rule of Louis XIV in the seventeenth century."

Iskandar made a mental note, planning to record it in his diary later.

Instead of entering at the Old Port, the passenger ship docked at the newer, larger docks in the Bassin de la Grande Joliette, where seagoing ships following World War I could be accommodated. Only small fishing boats and those wealthy enough to have a private boat used *Vieux Port* now.

The city was huge, spreading over many hills. But for Lebanese travelers, other immigrants and the poor, the Panier District, "the Basket," provided their temporary lodgings because of its convenient location just across the road from the Joliette docks, very nearby their disembarkation dock, and near the railway station.

The ship pulled slowly and unsteadily to the dock at the western portion of the city, where the crew, under the watchful eyes of the captain, raced to and fro tying the ship's lines to the large mooring piers.

The city's earth-toned brick buildings in many ways resembled Beirut's, with rail yards and hills in the background. Longshoremen busily loaded and unloaded the ships at the piers as dusk approached. The sun bounced off the light ochre buildings and glistened on the clear blue waters. Taking in the whole scene, looking up at a mostly clear sky dotted with a few puffy clouds, and feeling a light breeze drifting across his face, Iskandar pronounced it a good omen.

Iskandar took in the human beehive of activity surrounding the dock, grateful to end the long, uncomfortable, exhausting trip made even worse by frequent bouts of seasickness. Now the adventure of exploring this magnificent city of France for the first time was the number one priority.

From the moment their feet stepped onto the Joliette pier, the passengers, most from poor remote villages, admired the bustling, vibrant shipping activity, and over-whelming French presence in Marseille. France's national and regional flags fluttered in the breeze as groups clustered on the pier seeking directions, looking for waiting relatives, gaping at the busy port.

Iskandar and Butrus were no exception. They took in all the confusion happening around them at the port. Vendors carrying their goods walked among the newcomers shouting out prices of their myriad variety of wares — always with a smile and ready for bargaining, the culture of the Mediterranean merchant.

Dockworkers hauling freight and luggage with their wagons and carts, some pulled by horses, some pushed by hand, rushed in every direction.

"Butrus, let's ask one of the workers where all these goods are arriving from. I'm curious."

"Well, alright, but you can be the one to ask, my friend."

Iskandar spotted a large man standing near them at the dock who was giving orders to a small group of workers. Squaring his shoulders, Iskandar boldly stepped up to him and asked, in French, "Monsieur, my friend and I have just arrived in Marseille from Beirut, and we are interested to know about all these wares."

In a friendly tone, he answered, "We have oranges from Jaffa, Palestine and Sardinia, and bananas from Lebanon. Citrus is my main import. Other items are Egyptian cotton from Alexandria, silk, cloth, olives and cork from Spain, and Eastern spices, olives and wheat shipped from Latakia, Syria's major port. Now, you boys better move on. This is a dangerous unloading dock area."

They watched the large, mechanized cranes and machinery transfer enormous bundles of goods. Only two years after World War I and its devastation of Europe, especially France, companies hired dockworkers either too young or too old to have served in the army. Marseille, clearly one of the most active and entertaining cities, offered a laissez-faire attitude. The mood reflected the postwar relief and carefree behavior that spread across most of Europe, except Germany, which was bankrupted by the Draconian provisions of The Versailles Treaty, "the spoils to the victor" agreement that would come back to haunt Europe and especially France, in less than two decades.

This early "Roaring Twenties" era embraced an euphoric consumption of anything that made one "feel good," including copious consumption of France's more than ample supply of wine and its companions of women and song. The spring weather felt temperately cool, but comfortable, with a late afternoon light breeze off the sea

"I am amazed to see so many shops here," exclaimed Butrus. "My uncle has a shop in the Zahle *souk* where he sells mosaic boxes, backgammon games and tables. Zahle is a big city, but we don't have this many stores."

"Wonderful, isn't it?" responded Iskandar, as they passed by brass and copper pots and trays hanging from hooks above and around the entrance, dangling in their shiny hand-tooled shapes and sizes and making singing sounds as they bounced together gently in the breeze.

As Iskandar and Butrus walked along the promenade, they came to a *zeytoon* shop.

"Iskandar, they must have a dozen kinds of olives in all those barrels!"

"These shopkeepers look Lebanese or Syrian."

"I agree, Iskandar. They all look like my cousins in Zahle!"

A small, narrow shop, reminiscent of one in Beirut's *souk*, crammed barrels of a variety of nuts in front of the shop and on either side of a small passage into the store. A scoop lay atop the mound in each three foot high barrel, with paper bags stacked near by. The mustached shopkeeper, his round belly hanging over his belt, smiled and beckoned with his hands.

"Five francs! Only five francs for a bag of the finest almonds and pistachios! One bag free if you buy two! Come here, *ta ha la hawn*."

"I knew he'd have *fistok*!" Iskandar nudged Butrus toward the shop. "Let's have a look. I'm getting hungry now."

"*Ibn Arab?* Are you of Arabic heritage?" the shopkeeper asked the boys.

Both nodded their heads yes.

"You will love these *fistok*! Take some. You are young and look hungry."

Iskandar and Butrus grinned happily, "*Shookrun*. These are delicious and remind us of home."

Iskandar whispered to Butrus, "We'd better be going now. We'll go crazy here with no money to spend. Let's go find my Uncle Hanna at *Place de Liban*. The French call it *Place de Lenche*. That's where Uncle Elias told me I'd find the *mushthamah Libnani*…in the Panier District. He said that there's been a Lebanese colony in Marseille since the Phoenicians. I should go there now to find my Uncle Hanna. I'm certain he can provide us with a room because he's a wealthy businessman here who owns many buildings."

"*Yallah*! Let's go, Iskandar." Smiling mischievously, he added, "And now I want to see the pretty French girls."

"*Yallah*! I am ready too, Brutus!"

As the two excited teenagers walked along the boulevard, they felt a soft, cool breeze muting the warmth of the bright sunshine that fell on their faces. Carefully spaced tall sycamore trees planted along the cobblestone sidewalks of Rue de l'Evêché added a natural softness to the stark rows of storefronts and brick buildings. Because it was late spring, young, pale green leaves sprouted everywhere in the trees creating a dabbled effect on the marketplace.

"Iskandar, I think we've landed in heaven. Have you ever seen so many pretty girls in one place?"

"They are pretty, aren't they?"

"And none of them are cousins! I like the way they look at us, Iskandar. I'm glad we speak French fluently!"

After twelve days at sea reeling of seasickness Iskandar and Butrus had to find their balance on land, shedding their unfamiliar "sea legs" that they had constantly braced against the ship's rocking movements. Now, seeing this free city for the first time, they soon found themselves in the "Lebanese Quarter."

"Just think, Iskandar," laughed Butrus, "if Marseille is this different to us, imagine what America will be like! But I'm glad we are staying here for a few weeks until our ship to New York arrives. So many others are going to take the train to Paris and to Le Havre to get to New York faster."

He turned to watch a cluster of teenage girls walk nearby. "Now I know I want to stay here for awhile," he added with a wink.

Watching the girls, Iskandar happily nodded in agreement and then continued, "Six weeks, Butrus! We should be able to meet lots of pretty girls in six weeks! I think we're going to like being in Marseille for awhile. I mean, you never know who might come into your life in a city like this…I don't think there's another city like it!"

After WWI, there were ten women for every man in Marseille because so many French men were killed or maimed during the war.

Some of their fellow passengers they knew would leave by train to Le Havre within a week to board a ship there that would take them to America along the North Atlantic route and get them to Canada and the United States faster. Iskandar and Butrus planned to remain in Marseille for several weeks before boarding their passenger ship bound for America via the South Atlantic route. Some of their fellow voyagers would end up in New York, while many would disembark in the Caribbean islands, or in Central America or the South American countries of Brazil, Argentina or Chile.

Iskandar recalled his father's wishes that he not take the train to Le Havre, but wait in Marseille as long as necessary before sailing to America. The southern route was safer he had said. In February 1912, Ibrahim, his father, and Leila, his sister, arrived in Marseille, and like the others had the same choice: stay in Marseille and wait several weeks for a ship that would take them across the Atlantic Ocean via the southern route or board the train for Le Havre. "It is a faster trip to America from Le Havre," they had been told. His father's passage ticket could have included the train, but he decided to stay in Marseille and not go to Le Havre. This was lucky for him and Leila. The ship boarded by those who went to Le Havre en route to New York was the Titanic, then on its ill-fated maiden voyage. Almost all of those Lebanese émigrés were in steerage with the equally poor Irish. Most of them perished at sea, although a few did survive to tell the story of the horror of that night.

But Ibrahim and Leila, with others who chose to wait, were spared, and with grateful thanks for their good fortune, thanked the Lord everyday in America.

So, rather than tempt fate to hurry to America, Iskandar followed his father's wishes and waited in Marseille for the next ship to America where his father would be waiting for him in New York.

That decision would be of enormous importance to him. For during his lengthy stopover in Marseille, he would meet someone who would have an impact on him for the rest of his life.

*A Teacher…gives not of his wisdom
but rather of his faith and his lovingness…*
Kahlil Gibran

CHAPTER 6

Place du Liban

"We need to find your uncle's place. There is a policeman, Iskandar," Butrus exclaimed, pointing. "Let's ask him before we get lost."

"*Pardon, monsieur,*" Iskandar raised his arm and called out in fluent French as he approached the uniformed gendarme who was walking toward him with a smart gait. "Gendarme, s'il vous plaît, can you tell us where 216 *Place de Lenche* is located?"

"*Oui,* I can," responded the friendly policeman, quite accustomed to requests for directions from incoming passengers from other ports. "It is here in the Panier District and very near by." He continued, pointing with his arm, "Follow Rue de l'Evêché straightaway. You will come to a stone stairway on your left. It is wide, and perhaps a climb of only three meters. At the top is *Place de Lenche*. You cannot miss it. It has many trees and is surrounded by handsome apartment buildings, cafes and restaurants."

"Let's go, Butrus. We're nearly there!"

In moments, the two found the steps leading to the plaza.

Place de Lenche was an intimate courtyard less than fifty meters square. From the plaza, they could see a huge church with the figure of St. Mary on the top coated in pure gold on a hill in the distance. Tables set for a meal stood ready for customers under the mature sycamore shade trees, some occupied with *towleh* sets and men already occupied playing the game. The smell of food cooking permeated the air.

"Oh, smell that. They're baking lamb. I'd know that aroma anywhere. I'll bet they're baking *kibbee, tabouleh, koosa,* and *imjadara ma' roz*...I love beans and rice! We have found the right place!" exclaimed Butrus.

As he turned to look around at the shops that lined three sides of the park, he caught his foot on a cobblestone edge and tumbled to the ground. Laughing at his clumsiness, he added, "And pastries, and desserts! I can't wait for some fresh baklava! It's been a longer ride on that ship than I thought!" He laughed at himself. "I can hardly walk."

"You have to slow down, Butrus."

Iskandar and Butrus found the four-story row building along the south side of the square-shaped plaza as the *gendarme* had instructed. They looked at the number over the entry door carefully, verified his uncle's offices on the directory, entered the doorway into the small alcove, climbed the fourteen well-worn unpainted wooden steps to the second floor and walked into the hallway.

"Ah, 216. Here it is, Butrus. Why don't you go down to the plaza and look for something to do while I speak with my uncle and get us a room? Meet me at the restaurant downstairs in about an hour. Alright?"

"Sure. I won't get lost. It'll be fun!"

After Butrus left, Iskandar turned to the paneled door and anxiously knocked.

"*Entrée, s'il vous plaît,*" spoke the man's accented deep voice behind the door.

Iskandar pushed the door open and confidently stepped into the small, sparsely furnished office. People spent money on the home, not the office. A well-manicured and meticulously groomed, stocky man in his mid-forties rose from behind the unpolished desk and greeted Iskandar with a friendly smile.

"Monsieur Hanna Chalhoub?" Iskandar asked tentatively.

"*Oui*, I am Hanna. And you must be Iskandar! *Ahlen wa sahlen*! Welcome, cousin! Welcome! Look at you!" Hanna exclaimed as he stepped around the desk and, with out-stretched arms, fully embraced Iskandar with a bear hug followed by the customary kiss on both cheeks.

"Ah, *habibi*," he said endearingly, "Elias telegraphed you would arrive today. Coffee, juice, tea? You will love the juice from the fabulous Jaffa orange. We'll have wine later," he smiled.

"*Shookrun*, thank you, Uncle Hanna. It is so wonderful to be here. I have been looking forward to this meeting for a long time. Marseille is so friendly even the *gendarme* who directed me to your office."

He was excited now, and eager to converse with Hanna, who was not really his uncle but was his father's cousin, part of his extended family. He leaned forward. "May I be direct? I need your assistance. My friend Butrus and I need a place to stay." Iskandar spoke very fast, nervously.

"I was told you are an impetuous young man." Hanna smiled as he gestured to one of the two oak chairs opposite his desk. "Of course, but first, calm down, sit and be comfortable, my son. It is better to visit first." As he looked carefully at Iskandar's face, he spoke, "You look just like your father. I cannot believe it. But you have your mother's smile. So, tell me Iskandar, how is your brother Milhelm? Is he well? Why is he not here with you? He was supposed to arrive at the same time…Elias wrote me with the details weeks ago."

"*La'a*, no, *Khali* Hanna," Iskandar shrugged and turned his body away, showing a bit of disappointment. "Milhelm decided at the last moment to remain in Lebanon. He simply could not leave. His heart was too heavy at the thought he might not ever see Lebanon again." Iskandar paused as he watched Hanna's eyes. "So, I am here alone with my friend Butrus." Now his eyes widened and a smile came over his young face as he continued, "And I am to stay in Marseille for the next six weeks until my ship arrives to take me to America."

"And Uncle Elias. How is his health?"

"*Na'am*, yes, he is in very good health and his businesses are going well in Beirut."

He looked around the office taking in everything. A picture of the cedars of Lebanon covered in snow hung on the side wall which was painted off-white. The wood floor was serviceable and plain, like the hallway. The ceiling was made of wooden planks painted white. To one side, a large mosaic backgammon table with two chairs was set to play. A large journal at least two inches thick occupied a small stand behind Hanna's chair. The tall shade trees outside and the hinged outdoor shutters made window dressings unnecessary.

"And the family? Is everyone in Douma in good health? How's the town doing?"

"Yes, *Khali* Hanna, everyone in Douma is doing better now that the war is over and the Turks finally gone. There are a few more jobs now, and the *zeytoon* (olives) are flourishing; the *areeshi* are full and lush now in the vineyards of the productive Bekaa Valley, and Beirut's businesses are getting stronger. It took several years for the vineyards, olives, and the farms to come back in Douma after the locusts. That was a terrible time. No food, no jobs, no medicines, no money those evil Turkish army patrols. I love Lebanon, but I hated life there. It is so difficult. All our freedoms were taken from us. Everyone was so poor."

Hanna, nodding somberly and murmuring as Iskandar spoke, understood. He had heard of the difficulties and glad he was safely living in Marseille.

"Tell me some more about what happened," Hanna encouraged.

Iskandar caught his breath, boldly stood and took a few steps around the office as he thought. Then turning back to Hanna said, "The men slowly lost their confidence and dignity. Some could hardly face their children. They helplessly watched their families grow sick, and many died. Life was mostly filled with fear and a loss of hope. You cannot imagine how meaningless life became. And, you know, those very things took our mother from us."

"Ahhh, beautiful Katrina. *Ya'haram*, poor thing. How it broke my heart to learn that she had died. She was so kind, so sweet, so beautiful. How I always wished she had seen me first! Your father was a very lucky man. I might have been your father, Iskandar," he laughed aloud, extending both arms out in front of him, gesturing. "And that would have been good for me, for I have watched from a distance as you, your sister, and your brother have grown into fine young people. You have always made your mother and father so proud of their children."

Hanna, now standing at the tall, wood-framed window that came within twelve inches of the floor and ceiling, turned, gesturing back to one of the chairs.

"Have a seat Iskandar. Let me tell you about Marseille and the room I have set aside for you and your friend Butrus right here at *Place de Lenche* or *Place de Liban*, the name given in deference to the main plaza of our Lebanese community. Even the French have adopted our name although Monsieur Lenche was quite famous. We Lebanese are quite active here in Marseille. Most of our immigrant community is here in the Panier near the docks and railroad yards. There is so much history here. And our people love being near to each other. Those who have the ability to do so, live in other parts of the city. I myself live on the hill overlooking the harbor. I have lived in Marseille for many years, almost twenty-six now. You know, it is the second largest city in France, Iskandar. Only Paris is larger. But our city is growing fast. It is one of the most active ports on the Mediterranean. It brings good business and has been a stopover for Lebanese and Syrians bound for America since the mid-1800s, more than seventy years." He paused to catch his breath, then resumed, "Although the Greeks claim to have first settled here in 600 BC when they fought the Roman armies for this land, we Lebanese love to say, 'Yes, that is true, but the Phoenicians were here first, way back around 2,000 BC, but they decided to travel to more distant lands including Britain which they called 'The Land of Tin.'" His proud smile showed his prominent gold tooth.

Iskandar laughed with his uncle. "I am told you own many apartments near the docks. Isn't this so?"

"Yes, *habibi*, I do. They have been good investments for me. Lots of trouble sometimes, but like all of our family, I believe in owning land and buildings. I don't trust the bankers, you know. I bought most of my holdings during the Great War when the French were selling their properties…almost giving away everything they had of value. I think, as Lebanese, we have had such a history of being conquered that we do not let mere war deter us from investing." He laughed at his joke. "After all, we have learned that even the conquerors need people in business. We have a sense of history. We have had to learn the hard way, since it seems Lebanon has always been occupied by someone. Of course, we never conquered anybody's lands. And this is a good lesson for you. *Y'eini*, always have cash when others do not. Have faith in the future. If you truly believe, God will watch over you and your faith is what makes all things happen. Then life will be good." He smiled confidently. "But this is most true if you work like hell as you are waiting," he laughed aloud.

"And if you are free, Uncle Hanna." Iskandar interrupted him, remembering his village.

Hanna, focusing on Iskandar's eyes, nodded, "Yes, to be sure."

He stood up, feeling an emotional need to be Iskandar's "Dutch Uncle." He was now exuberant in his advice to his youthful, distant cousin who might have been his own son and admonished him saying, "That is true, my son. Use your brain that God gave you and your faith, and buy when others sell. Sell when everyone else is buying. It is good business. Listen to your own mind. Seek advice, yes, but decide for yourself. You must hide your cash until it is needed. Many people spend their cash on silly things. I do not. But, *y'eini*, you will have a good life in America. Remember, this is your only life. Make the most of it." Waving his finger upward, he continued, "This is a good lesson you must understand. Ah, but now I have rushed to become your teacher. You see, I have no children of my own." He shrugged, "Perhaps I have spoken too much so soon, my son." He smiled as he put his hands on Iskandar's shoulders. "But, I am very happy to see you."

After a moment of thought, Hanna walked back around his desk to his chair. Taking a deep breath, he leaned back comfortably into his soft leather chair.

He continued, "The room I have for you, Iskandar is on the third floor of this very building. *Place de Liban* is where our working people love to visit, congregate, and entertain their friends. As the end of the day approaches, you will see many men at their tables down there playing cards, *towleh*, backgammon, or dominoes. The women visit here also. They often knit in groups under the trees. The favorite pastime for the men is playing *towleh* and smoking *aguilas*, water pipes. If you are anything like your father, you must be very good at the game!"

"I love to play, and sometimes," Iskandar smiled in modesty, "I win my share."

Hanna laughed and slapped his thigh. "I bet you do, my son."

"But my father can beat anyone. He taught me well," responded Iskandar, smiling.

Hanna rose from his chair, walked to the window again and called the young man to his side. They both looked down on the plaza. He affectionately put his arm over Iskandar's shoulder as they both looked out the window. "We are very proud of how beautiful our plaza is. Say, my boy, have you eaten today?"

Iskandar shook his head.

"Then let's go down and have something. Do you want a *shawarma*, a sandwich, or would you like to visit with me over a cluster of assorted appetizers, a mezza of *jibneh*, *hummus*, *kibbee*, and *tabouleh*? The French insist I drink their wine," he chuckled, "but I do enjoy my daily glass of *arak*."

Iskandar took an instant liking to his uncle. It would be a good thing to stay close to this man. The contrasts between his quiet tiny village and this hectic port city might prove bewildering and challenging. He needed his guidance and help.

Hanna moved away from the window and, using both hands, carefully placed his burgundy-colored, flat-topped, tasseled fez on his head, one of the many Turkish customs the Syrians adopted during the years of occupation. As he turned to the side to look at his reflection in the mirror, he smiled with pleasure as he shifted the fez to the correct angle. *Some habits never die*, Hanna thought.

"Follow me, Iskandar," said Hanna as he waved his arm and led him to the plaza below. They strolled among the tables and afternoon pedestrians, across the open, shaded cobblestone park to the opposite side. Hanna pointed as he described everything to Iskandar and they slowly walked nearly two hundred feet across the plaza. Iskandar listened, learned, saw it all and asked questions. They also discussed Lebanon's travails, Beirut, the family, Katrina, and what Iskandar would do with his future.

Hanna smiled proudly. "This city is known as the most exciting city in France, Iskandar. That is especially true these days, *habibi*. We are now just two years after the terrible war throughout Europe, and the French people are euphoric with peace; yet, there is still a struggle. So many young Frenchmen were killed by the Germans that there are many, many young women for every man. Many still look for work. They are poor. Germany too is very poor, as are other lands in Europe. This city, especially near the docks, has bistros, cafes, restaurants and, yes, prostitutes. Everyone wants to enjoy themselves, even though there is difficulty everywhere in Europe. The immigrants and travelers like you attract the 'ladies of the night,' and the risqué 'can-can' is a favorite entertainment for the men. You must be careful with what little money you have, my son. Everyone wants your money because they have so little. They will know you are new to the city and that you are naive. It is good you are fluent in French. At least you will understand what you hear, although your accent signals you are from Lebanon."

Iskandar laughed at Hanna's reference to money, something of which his family had had very little. He noted the old four-story buildings on the three sides of the plaza with their varied fronts. The open fourth side offered a magnificent view of the port. The structures looked somewhat similar to Beirut's: mostly brick, some of old stucco and in need of paint. Wooden shutters hung on either side of the windows, many painted colorfully in turquoise, deep red or yellow.

As if reading Iskandar's observations, Hanna commented, "These buildings have been here a long time. You know, Iskandar, the Panier has been the favored place for all immigrants from the days of the Crusades when tens of thousands came to Marseille to find transportation to the Holy Land. The merchants of Marseille got very rich during those two hundred years, and even became a threat to the crown." He laughed. "Some of these buildings look like they were here even then," he laughed. "But while old, they were mostly built in the past century. They just need some paint, don't they?"

Iskandar laughed and nodded as he continued to observe the waiters scurrying around from table to table, as people began arriving, taking their places at the tables. There must have been a hundred tables grouped throughout the stone plaza. The plaza quickly filled as shadows deepened with the approach of evening. It was an interesting but understandable observation by Iskandar that most people spoke French. Only once in a while did he hear Arabic spoken in conversation by the older people.

Pulling out his pocket watch on a gold chain, Hanna flipped open the cap. Looking up, he smiled, surprised, "My God, it's six o'clock already, Iskandar. The dock and rail workers are finished for the day and getting ready for their evening.

There will be much activity for several hours. Around ten o'clock, prostitutes and single men, mostly travelers, will be on the streets. For now, we will go over there to the *Café Liban* for a glass of *arak*, some *fistok* and *hummus*."

Pointing his arm toward the port, Iskandar asked, "What is that beautiful building in the distance? Over there on the hill. It looks like an old church."

"That, my son," Hanna stated with formality, "is the Notre-Dame-de-la-Garde. It is Marseille's proudest landmark. And on top is the magnificent gold statue of the Madonna. The church is more than one hundred years old, very young for French cathedrals, but very beautiful and very important. They say the sunsets from that hill are the best in Europe. It is magnificent, is it not? All citizens of Marseille revere Notre-Dame-de-la-Garde, Iskandar. It is visible throughout the region and far at sea."

They quickened their pace as they dodged others strolling across the crowded plaza. Hanna was a most friendly man with a broad smile that he shared with the many passersby. He acknowledged his many acquaintances and friends with a cheery nod. But Iskandar knew that when it came to business, he would be like any other successful Lebanese businessman: pleasant but not hesitant while bargaining, friendly yet expecting to be well paid for his services. He would not spend his money freely, nor would he waste his time in fruitless conversation. His hard-earned wealth did not come easily, and he would not let someone else have it without a more than fair "*quid pro quo*." He relied on his experiences and instincts for guidance. However, Hanna, like many successful Lebanese men, knew the benefits of the "good life." He knew how to play, how to enjoy himself, and how to make his woman happy.

"Over there, Iskandar," Hanna pointed with his hand, "several blocks away from the sea and near the east end of *Vieux Port* is the *Canebière*, the main shopping boulevard. You may want to see it. The stores are popular and busy. They are also expensive. I have a dear lady friend whom you will meet later tonight who owns a popular ladies' boutique there. Several parks with fountains are nearby, good for relaxation." Pausing, he motioned to the left, "There is the infamous street named 'The Street Where Women Never Sleep Alone.' That's where the prostitutes gather. It's very near to 'The Street of Forgiveness,' where the prostitutes and their customers go later for confession at the small church that has been there serving the same vital mission with its nuns for more than five hundred years." Hanna laughed at his description. "Ah, no matter when, there is always a need for both. It is famous they are together, eh?" He smiled at his rhetorical question.

As he listened to Hanna, Iskandar's hand went to the gold crucifix at his chest. Needing comfort for his thoughts, he gripped the treasured gift from his mother.

"If you would like to be with a woman some evening, contact me, I have a friend who has many associates and she will provide for you. But you must see me first. There are other kinds of pretty girls and prostitutes on the streets. They are not for you or me, my son."

"Here we are, Iskandar. This is *Café Liban*. Let us sit down. I am hungry and it is time to rest." They found a typical four-legged wooden table covered with a white cloth surrounded by four wooden chairs in front of the café, and took their seats.

Hanna signaled to a waiter in black pants, white shirt and red vest with a white towel apron and called out their order in French, "*Garçon, s'il vous plaît, arak, deux. Et hummus. Nous sommes très faim.*"

They looked around and Hanna recognized a familiar Lebanese face.

"George! *Mon ami*, meet my nephew, Iskandar. He is just in from Beirut. He is eighteen years old and will go to America in a few weeks."

"*Marharbahr*, welcome, Iskandar," smiled George as he offered his hand to Iskandar's and welcomed the fresh-faced newcomer in the typical Arabic way, with an embrace. "And what is the news from Beirut?" he asked, making conversation.

George was sitting at an adjoining smaller table for two, smoking a cigarette and sipping his *arak* as he watched the strollers pass by. "I love to come here each day at this time. Many interesting people to watch, Iskandar," George commented to his new friend. "I am from Zahle in the Bekaa, and Marseille has been very exciting for me. There are so many beautiful French women, and so few French men. It is a good time for us to be here, Iskandar," he grinned.

They both glanced around, watching men and women, some young and pretty, some carrying babies or holding hands with their young children as they crossed the plaza, conversing as the waiters rushed to tend to their tables.

Iskandar laughed at George, "Is there nothing to do in Marseille but look at pretty girls and work at the docks?" As Iskandar looked at George, he noted his stylish tight-fitting clothes; his shoes were French and au courant.

George was in his late twenties, Iskandar reckoned, worldly and more confident than he, and looked like quite the ladies' man. A friendly sort with a ready, almost cocky, smile who should not be underestimated, he thought to himself. Iskandar looked out of the corner of his eye and tacitly asked Hanna if he was correct. Hanna caught his glance, smiled and nodded his head acknowledging that his nephew was judging George exactly right…he would like him, enjoy him, but know he has his own plans that may not be the same as yours. "Another lesson, my son," Hanna quietly told Iskandar. "You are learning; you are a smart young man."

"What more can most men do?" responded George with a knowing smile and a shrug of confidence. "This is the good life, the war is over and the French people have been through hell. They want to have fun now, and they will. So, who am I to try to stop them?" he chuckled, as he shrugged his shoulders and spread his arms, questioning.

"Well, I am not interested in being with just any girl," replied Iskandar as his eyes widened above a warm smile. He was so serious, idealistic, and naively romantic. "I want to be with someone I love. And I will know her when I see her."

"Well," spoke George dubiously, "maybe we can sit here until she comes by, looks at you and says '*Bonjour*, will you come home with me?'" He rolled his fingers as if signaling someone to come to him and laughed out loud at his clever response

"Perhaps that is too much to expect, George," Iskandar shrugged, feeling a bit embarrassed, "but it is a wonderful way for me to think. Remember, all my life I have been surrounded by relatives who loved me, especially my mother. So, how am I to think differently now? I have faith. And when she enters my life, I will know it. Don't you think so, uncle?"

Hanna nodded, while not really following the conversation. He was busy consuming a dip of *hummus* on pita bread. After a moment of chewing and a sip of *arak*, he told Iskandar, "Have your dreams, son, follow your heart. Be patient, and wait for God. He will provide for you, Iskandar." He spoke with an uncle's affection and sincerity. Iskandar smiled and reached for the pistachios in the small bowl.

"How about a game of *towleh*, Iskandar?" asked George, testing his new friend while raising an eyebrow and waving his hand to the table. "Pull up a chair Iskandar and let us challenge each other."

"Yes, let us play *towleh*! But I must keep an eye out for my friend, Butrus. I told him to meet us around this time."

Iskandar stood up and stepped from the larger round table he and his uncle shared to sit opposite George at his table with the backgammon game set to play.

"Roll your die, Iskandar, let us play," extolled George as he threw his die on the board to determine who would be the coveted first to roll the dice. They began their game. George threw a five to Iskandar's four and looked confidently into Iskandar's eyes and said, "My roll."

"Next time I will lead," said Iskandar to George with a confident smile.

"Next time, perhaps, my new friend, but not this time. This time I am first," boasted George. "Be on your guard and do your best, because I am going to win this game."

Iskandar narrowed his eyes as he studied George's first moves and quickly determined his strategy.

And George did win the first game. But Iskandar played well too and impressed George.

"Another," demanded Iskandar with determined confidence, lightly slamming his open hand on the table. "Let us play another," he challenged George as he took a small sip from his glass of *arak* and then confidently swept a dollop of *hummus* on his wedge of bread and brought it to his lips.

After an hour, George led with three games to Iskandar's two.

Hanna exclaimed, waving his arm with a slight sense of importance, "Iskandar, come back to my table, it is time to talk and enjoy our dinner. Join me. I have something to tell you."

Iskandar stood up, stretched and nodded to George who laughingly taunted, "Come back and let's play another time." He stepped over to his uncle's table and sat down. "Yes, *Khali* Hanna?"

"You are a good player, *habibi*," Hanna spoke softly, touching Iskandar's shoulder affectionately, "and you are making a good friend in George. It is good you did not beat him too much too early. You don't want to anger him. *Y'eini*, you will be in Marseille many days before you leave for America. And George is popular. You want him to enjoy being your friend. This is a good lesson in life, *habibi*. Listen to your Uncle Hanna, Iskandar." Somehow, Hanna felt a fatherly need to mentor Iskandar and continued to advise him, surprising himself because he knew he was always focused on his business.

Interrupting Hanna's thought, Iskandar nodded and whispered, "I understand. Thank you for your counsel."

"Iskandar, here is the key to the apartment I have for you and your friend. It is number 3-A. Now, go to the restaurant door, take the stairs on the right, and climb to the third floor with your bag. Then return to me here. I have a friend, lovely Madame DuBois, coming to visit with us. She is my lady, and will be here any minute with a surprise for you. So, go now, wash your face, change your shirt and return here. Do not tarry. I promise you a delicious meal and warm fellowship. *Yallah*, Iskandar!"

He hurried up the stairs, two at a time, and entered the sparse room. There were two small cots with mattresses. It was a much better situation than on the boat, thought Iskandar happily with a smile as he sat on his cot. After a quick face wash and shave, Iskandar looked around the room, saw again the bowl on the wooden commode with a small mirror above hanging from a nail in the wall. He went to the window overlooking the street below and saw the now even busier plaza filling with people. The apartment was perfect, nicer than his own humble home. The bathtub and toilet were located in a communal bathroom at the end of the hall. In the village, his modest stone home had no plumbing and a thick roof composed of a mixture of packed earth and rocks. There, he slept on a leaf-filled wool cloth bag on a hard, stone floor, and washed his face in a bowl near the fire. His toilet was an outhouse, a humble *shishmeh*. His entire two-room home in Douma was not much larger than this room. So, Iskandar was very happy with his good fortune. This is my home for the next six weeks, he thought with pride as he looked around the room, sweeping it with his eyes. And with a smile of excitement, he pulled on his other shirt and his only coat, smoothed the front and checked his buttons. He turned, opened the door and stepped out into the hall. Remembering Hanna's words of caution, he pulled the door closed firmly, carefully turned the key in the lock, and walked to the staircase.

By the time Iskandar returned, primped with his wet hair neatly combed close to his head, the plaza was almost filled with nearly three hundred diners, visitors, and game players. The volume of voices loudly overcoming the rest seemed to have doubled in less than an hour.

"It's perfect, *Khali* Hanna. Thank you so much. It's more than I could have hoped for. You are very kind."

"It is my pleasure, the least I can do for you. Enjoy the room, Iskandar!"

Then, at the same moment they both heard a young man's voice over the growing crowd. Butrus, a young sixteen, excited by the newness of Marseille and eager to explore, was urgent in his movements and always using his hands as he spoke. He approached the table with one arm up and a happy smile as he excitedly yelled out, nearly stumbling, "Iskandar, there you are." He came to the table quickly, and too out of breath to speak softly said, "I am glad I found you. My neck is sore from trying to see all I can see, and all the pretty girls. What a wonderful city," he exclaimed, both arms spread out.

"Ah, Butrus, meet *Khali* Hanna." Iskandar quickly introduced his friend to Hanna. Butrus, calming down, politely extended his hand to Hanna. "He has provided us with an apartment." Reaching out to Butrus, he handed him the key. "Here is the key. It is room 3-A on the third floor. Go see it."

Iskandar gestured to his uncle and then, for Butrus, pointed to the window of their room. "I will be here having dinner with my uncle this evening and will join you later. *Khali* Hanna wants me to meet his lady friend, and I'm not able to invite you to join us."

"No problem, Iskandar. I'm having fun and I'm not really hungry right now."

As Butrus left, Iskandar turned to Hanna and, as he swept his shirt with both hands, said, "Do I look appropriate to meet Madame DuBois? I am wearing my best shirt. I have only two," Iskandar spoke in nearly a whisper because he didn't want to embarrass his uncle.

"You look very nice, *habibi*. Daniella is a very beautiful and kind lady and I think she will be most impressed by you. Her husband François was a good man and my friend. But, sadly, he was killed in the war. It is so unfortunate."

"Oh, killed…that is very sad."

Hanna's voice softened as he spoke endearingly, "I try to help her and her charming daughter as much as I can. I think our friendship is of great comfort to both of us. She is a popular seamstress for the wealthy ladies of Marseille. She owns a boutique where she and her daughter design and custom make fine clothing. She does very well, and although she receives a check from the French government for the loss of her husband, it is very little. Still, she is a magnificent woman. She is well read and makes her own beautiful and, I must say, quite stylish clothes and those of her delightful daughter who is learning the same trade, as an apprentice, from her mother. I am certain you are going to like my friend, Daniella, and, I think you will enjoy her surprise for you," said Hanna with his easy smile. "Her daughter, Madeleine, is such a charming, delightful, young lady. We shall have a lovely evening, *habibi*, the four of us."

They both smiled, enjoying the early evening cool air, the slight breeze off the sea, the birds chirping in the sycamore canopy above. Small wrens were hopping on the ground near the tables picking at particles of food on the plaza stone. Hanna, lifting his glass of *arak*, gestured to Iskandar. "A toast then, Iskandar, to the wonders of what this evening might bring to us."

Your children are not your children.
They are sons and daughters of life's longing for itself...
Kahlil Gibran

CHAPTER 7

Magic Moments

"Ah, Daniella, there you are."

Hanna, stood up as she stepped toward the table, smiled and welcomed her with outstretched arms.

"Come sit with us."

"Hanna, *bonsoir, mon ami*," replied Daniella, emerging from the crowd of strolling pedestrians.

Iskandar turned to his left toward the voice to see a tall, beautiful woman in a bright blue close-fitting sleeveless, chemise dress that flowed to her knees over her sensuous body and emphasized her every movement as she came toward them. A matching Hermes silk scarf draped around her slender neck fluttered in the breeze and brought out her deep blue eyes. Her broad smile revealed perfect teeth that accentuated her clear, unblemished white skin.

Just as his uncle promised, Daniella DuBois proved strikingly attractive with dark hair shaped in a chignon at the nape of her neck, in the fashion of the day. Her 16-year-old daughter, Madeleine, a perfect younger clone of her mother, followed a step behind, her waist-long black hair flowing behind, her full skirt swirling around her calves.

Just as Iskandar followed Hanna's lead to greet Daniella, a young boy came out of nowhere jostling Daniella and knocking her daughter to her knees exposing the upper part of her legs.

Daniella, surprised at her daughter's fall, exclaimed, "*Mon Dieu*! Hanna, please help Madeleine."

Hanna saw what happened and began to rise from his chair, but realized Iskandar was already moving toward Madeleine. Hanna called to Daniella, "My nephew has already reached her." He smiled proudly as he watched Iskandar rescue Madeleine.

The young boy continued darting among the people bumping into some and causing more disruption among the pedestrians. A large man grabbed his arm and scolded him demanding to know where his parents were.

In a blur, Iskandar offered both arms to help her to her feet. Her cheeks burning red, she looked up at Iskandar trying to hide her embarrassment with a slight smile then lowered her eyes as she smoothed her skirt in an attempt to gain back her modesty. Still looking down, she reached up and grabbed his proffered hand. He gripped her hand with his right hand and placed his left hand on her small waist. As she felt his strong but gentle grip on her waist, she moved her left arm up to his shoulder for support and allowed him to pull her up.

As they stood now, face to face, their eyes met for the first time. She was only slightly shorter than he. He tried to hold her gaze as he took in every detail of her face: the deep blue almond-shaped eyes accented by arched eyebrows, her natural rose-colored lips set off by porcelain white skin, but she looked shyly down again releasing a fresh whiff of lavender emanating from the white ribbon tying back her hair. For a second, a slight tightening across his chest caused him to stop breathing in reaction as a warmth moved through his body. A sensation he'd never felt before.

Several people watched as Iskandar assisted the young lady, and together broke into spontaneous applause, cheering his chivalry.

Less bold and still somewhat embarrassed, she finally looked up and locked eyes with him and felt a tingling sensation spreading throughout her young body. She lowered her eyes and blushed again from the unexpected emotions enveloping her. Doing her best to recover, she smiled with the loveliest curl of her full lips and whispered to him, "*Merci, Merci beaucoup.*" Her knees betrayed a weakness, but not from the fall.

His knees buckled too as his libido responded to the softness of her voice. His excitement grew.

Still holding her hand, Iskandar gathered his composure long enough to stammer, a bit embarrassed at his clumsiness. "Are you hurt? Are you alright? Come sit here," he said leading her to a chair. Iskandar gently continued to support Madeleine's arm, not wanting to lose contact with her, as he guided her carefully toward her chair.

"*Oui, Oui, Merci.* I am fine," she replied.

Now aware of still holding her arm, he took her hand and recovered with, "My name is Iskandar. Uncle Hanna is my uncle." He nodded in his direction and quietly withdrew his hand.

"*Bonsoir,*" she whispered. "I am Madeleine, Daniella's daughter. I am so happy to meet you…and so happy you came to my rescue." Now fully recovered, her modesty restored, she beamed at him. She felt safe with Iskandar and regained her confidence. She smiled shyly acknowledging the applause and cheers from the people who had gathered to see what was happening, then turned her attention back to Iskandar.

At that moment, the world stopped for Iskandar. The only sound he heard was her soft voice. He didn't hear the cheering and applause. All the activities and movement of the people in the plaza vanished, he saw only her. No waiters rushing around serving their customers, just the delicate movement of her hands. No chatter of people dining, just the lilt of her giggle. No one playing games at the tables, just her sitting at the table in front of him. The background din, clattering dishes, laughter, loud voices — all faded to the presence of Madeleine.

She, focusing completely on Iskandar, got lost in the moment, unaware of her surroundings, unaware of her mother and Uncle Hanna calling her name almost in unison.

"Madeleine! Madeleine! Are you okay?"

Concerned, Daniella watched her daughter carefully as Iskandar helped her up. She reached out her hand to Madeleine and said, "*Tut'es fait mal, chérie*, did you hurt yourself, my darling?"

The spell broken by her mother's insistence, Madeleine responded, "*Merci, Maman*, I am fine. My knee is a bit scratched, but I am fine." She reached down and rubbed her knee.

Iskandar followed her hand as she lifted her skirt slightly to examine the damage and once again a sensual wave sparked through him.

Afraid everyone could see what was happening to him, he bent over and repeated again, "Please sit down, Madeleine. May I help you? Would you like something to drink?"

A bit flustered and trying to control his behavior, Iskandar let out a sigh as he took a seat next to her. He grabbed a quick peek at his uncle, who gave a smiling nod in return.

A golden moment. Now broken.

A fleeting magic. Now gone.

An awakening of mysterious emotions he'd never felt.

He searched the plaza trying to find answers and explanations for what had just happened to him.

"Iskandar? *Merci*. You are quite the gentleman for helping my daughter," and turning to Hanna, Daniella said, "You have a very fine nephew, Hanna. I see why you are so proud of him. I hope we'll be seeing more of him."

And Iskandar's heart leapt again.

When love beckons to you, follow him, though his ways are hard and steep...
Kahlil Gibran

CHAPTER 8

Love at First Sight

After dinner, Madeleine and her mother left for the night and Iskandar went to his small apartment deep in thought, remembering and recapturing every moment of the evening...Madeleine's enchanting smile, the suddenness of his almost overwhelming feelings, her reciprocation that had given him confidence and daring.

Butrus was already asleep, probably dreaming of America, thought Iskandar. But he could not sleep. His thoughts were only of Madeleine...enchanting Madeleine.

Butrus was snoring lightly so he couldn't share his newfound excitement with his friend. Iskandar was experiencing that exciting, tingling rite of passage, "first love." To anyone, it is a fabulous experience, but at eighteen, every emotion is magnified. Love! What other word could describe what Iskandar was feeling?

After a long time lying on his back in bed, remembering every moment of his encounter with Madeleine, he finally drifted off to sleep, dreaming of her.

Early the next morning, Butrus was awake first. He chided gleefully, "Wake up, Iskandar! Let's go, *Yallah*! We must see the city."

"*Na'am*. Yes, Butrus, let's go see Marseille. But first, I must go and visit Uncle Hanna. Then, I must go to see Madeleine's mother's shop to see her too! I've met my dream. It's amazing! She's so beautiful, Butrus. I believe I'm in love!" Iskandar could not stop thinking or talking of Madeleine.

"Madeleine? Who is she? Is she very pretty? Is she Lebanese? Or is she French? What is she like? In love so soon, Iskandar?" Then, standing with his arms folded across his chest, he laughed, "You are a lucky man! Maybe you are crazy too!" Butrus was excited for Iskandar and couldn't stop his inquiry. They were both young and experiencing a new world.

"Maybe I am crazy, but I don't care! I can't wait for you to meet her, Butrus. She looks Lebanese, although she is French. She has the bluest, loveliest eyes. Like my mother's. Her voice is like a soft breeze, her skin like silk. Her hair is so pretty. She dazzles me!"

"Iskandar, you are speaking so fast. Slow down, *sahbi*."

"You are right. Let's go have some breakfast, Butrus. Then after I will visit with my uncle."

They quickly washed their faces, carefully combed their hair, dressed, and hurried out.

"Good morning, *habibi*. I am glad to see you," welcomed Hanna from his chair behind the desk. "Sit down, have coffee with me and tell me how you find Marseille. Is it to your liking?"

"Oh yes, *khali*. I love Marseille." He was overcome with excitement. "The people seem very friendly. I especially enjoyed meeting your lady friend Daniella last night..." Iskandar felt a bit embarrassed.

"And Madeleine?" inquired Hanna, with a knowing smile. "How did you like meeting Madeleine? It seemed to Madame DuBois and me that you lost your appetite and could do nothing but look on Madeleine all evening."

"She is lovely don't you think, *Khali* Hanna?"

"Indeed she is, just as alluring as her mother." Captured by Iskandar's enthusiasm, he thought for a moment and replied, "Would you like me to arrange another meeting, perhaps dinner another evening, say next week?" Hanna was teasing Iskandar.

"Next week? How could I wait that long? You are playing with me. Why not tonight? Why not this minute?"

"Actually," Hanna responded laughing, "I spoke with Daniella this morning. She told me Madeleine did not sleep at all last night, and she did not eat her breakfast this morning. Daniella had a difficult time getting her to even go to work this morning. I believe she is thinking only of you, *habibi*."

"Oh, *Khali* Hanna. That is how I feel about Madeleine. I'm captured by her. I'm stunned! I can think of no one or anything else."

"Well, that's nice, *habibi*," replied Hanna, trying to calm his nephew by not joining in his exuberance. "I'm glad you are happy. I'll arrange another meeting this very night. Meanwhile, Iskandar, go join your friend Butrus and see some of Marseille. There are many pretty girls here and so few men. There is a very nice park nearby, or the fish market along *Vieux Port* where people go to stroll, shop or meet friends. I suggest you go to the park near the *Aix Marseille*, the University, at midday when it's busy. There is another gathering place where young men play football (soccer) a block or two beyond the *Canebière*." Hanna's mind was exploring all things and places these two teenaged boys might enjoy. "But I think you will have a good day simply seeing the city, the busy docks, and the people. Perhaps you would like to meet me at the same restaurant as last night. You and I can meet earlier, say six o'clock, before we are joined at seven by Daniella and Madeleine, *d'accord*?"

"*Khali*, I will be there, even before the appointed time. I will not be late." He paused, thinking. "Now, I must go join Butrus before he grows too impatient. Until six o'clock, then. *Allah ma'ak*."

Iskandar, filled with energy, bounded from his chair and went to the door, waving as he quickly left the office.

Ah, youth, Hanna said to himself with a smile. *It's a pleasure to watch…sometimes*, he laughed.

After a busy, adventurous day of touring the city, Iskandar and Butrus were able to locate *Place de Liban* again and return to their apartment at four o'clock. They refreshed themselves and lay down on their cots to rest and recapture the day with each other.

"Isn't this wonderful, Iskandar? Here we are in Marseille, France, on our own, in our own apartment. And you, my dear friend, have fallen in love! How lucky you are! Maybe I will find someone too, *mon ami*."

"I am so lucky, Butrus. Imagine meeting the most beautiful girl in my life… here in Marseille. I suppose everyone creates an ideal in his own mind. I have, and she is that person. Her face is perfect. Her smile is perfect. She smells so good. Her eyes drive me mad, especially when she looks at me out of the corner of her eyes. Do girls do that deliberately? It surely works on me! I want to see her everyday. All the time! I hope she wants to see me the same way. If she doesn't, I think I'll die."

"But remember, Iskandar, we leave for America in six weeks."

"Don't remind me, Butrus."

"Why don't you take her for a walk up to the cathedral? There is a beautiful park near there. You could be alone. I can keep myself busy if you like. There is much to see."

Iskandar was daydreaming, lying on his back on his cot, hands under his head, thinking of this dream who had come into his life, and whom he would be with shortly. He was in heaven. Iskandar would surely remember Marseille and his time here for the rest of his life. He was nervous, energized, and bewildered all at the same time. After a while of lying down, he could not be still any longer.

Lifting his head and looking at Butrus, he spoke, "It's time for me to go now, Butrus."

Iskandar stood, sprinkled water on his face, perfunctorily wiped his face with the small towel, dressed quickly, and satisfied with his appearance went to the door, waved good-bye to his roommate, locked the door and walked to the stairs. He hurriedly bounded down the stairs, two steps at a time, to the plaza and walked to the nearby restaurant.

At exactly six o'clock, Iskandar sat at the same table outside the restaurant as the evening before, deliberately sitting in the very chair that was occupied by Madeleine. It felt good.

The waiters were busily setting tables, pouring water into glasses and scurrying around taking orders.

Lots of Lebanese were playing cards at several tables, *towleh* at others, and dominoes at still others. Most of the men were in their forties, fifties, and older. As they played their afternoon games, some smoked elaborate *aguilas* with the mouthpiece attached to the long narrow hose that reached to the top of the bottle of water sitting on the walk beside them. Others were smoking Turkish cigarettes. As time passed, the aguila smoker would stir the charcoals in the top pan and place new tobacco on the glowing red coals to keep the pipe operating. Sometimes, hashish would be placed on the hot coals, sometimes apple slivers.

As he anxiously looked around at the arrivals filling the plaza, searching for Madeleine's arrival, he shuffled the table's cards nervously.

It was difficult for him to think of anything or anyone but Madeleine. What a dilemma he felt. He was already debating with himself as he sat impatiently waiting, reshuffling the cards again and again.

As they approached the table, he looked up, "Oh, Madeleine, there you are. *Bonjour*! And Madame DuBois. How nice to see you." Iskandar smiled as he stood, nearly tipping over his chair as he stood.

"*Allo*, Iskandar. Where is Hanna?" replied Daniella, looking around the plaza. "Is he not here?"

"He'll be with us in a moment. He just stepped into the café. Please sit down."

Iskandar stood and helped first Daniella, then Madeleine to their chairs. "How is your knee, Madeleine? Is it feeling better now?"

Madeleine lowered her face and blushed from a bit of embarrassment, not wanting to draw attention to herself. "It is fine, *merci, mon ami*. I am so embarrassed that I fell down; that was most unusual for me. I am very grateful that you came to my rescue. *Merci*."

"But that boy running through the people bumped you. Don't be embarrassed; it couldn't be helped. It could have happened to anyone!" he shrugged. "I was happy to help you." He caught himself as he almost used the word eager instead of happy!

"*Est-ce que tu aime* Marseille? she asked, looking at him with her blue eyes wide open.

"*Oui*, Marseille is very exciting. I have found the people very friendly, and the city very busy. I want to see more while I am here before I leave for America."

"Oh? When do you leave?" inquired Daniella, surprised at his comment.

"I will be here for six weeks, I believe. My father is to meet me in New York." He smiled, remembering his mother's words. "I must find and fulfill my destiny in America…" The words were hardly out of his mouth when he suddenly felt enormous conflict and wanted to take them back.

"Oh," whispered Madeleine as she lowered her eyes in disappointment. "Just six weeks then?"

"Yes, but I have begun to wonder if I should stay in Marseille. I have felt wonderful since last evening."

"I have enjoyed meeting you also, Iskandar."

Tempting fate, and looking directly at Madeleine, he softly said, "Perhaps I could enjoy Marseille more if I had someone show me the city." Then, remembering Butrus' suggestion, he added, "I would like to see as much as possible. Do you think we could see the Notre-Dame-de-la-Garde together?"

"That would be very nice I think. May I, *Maman*? It is the spiritual symbol of our city," she added with a flourish of pride.

"Perhaps," Daniella responded with a smile.

Iskandar, hoping she would say yes, tried as much as he could not to gaze on Madeleine, but he couldn't take his eyes from her. "May I come by your shop tomorrow?"

"*Oui*. That would be nice." Turning to her mother, she asked "What time, *Maman*?"

Daniella lifted her head as to assert her concern, then discreetly whispered to her daughter so Iskandar could not hear, "Perhaps we should speak about this later, Madeleine."

"*Allo*, Daniella," greeted Hanna with a smile and his arms reaching out to his lady friend as he came to the table, interrupting their thoughts. "I apologize for not being prompt. I was detained and could not arrive sooner. Please forgive me, *mon ami*e."

"We are comfortable," responded Daniella with a smile, acknowledging Iskandar's presence, while remaining seated as she offered her hand to Hanna's. "We have been speaking with Iskandar. He tells us he will be here for only six weeks before he must travel to America."

"Yes," interrupted Madeleine, with widened eyes, "and he has asked me to show him parts of Marseille."

"Ahh!" Hanna whispered aside to Madeleine, "He is happy to meet you Madeleine. Perhaps you both will become good friends. We would like that, wouldn't we, Daniella?"

"Well, I think that would be nice," replied Daniella, a bit reluctantly. "They can become good friends, and yes, they should enjoy themselves. Life is short, as I have learned." Turning to Iskandar, she noted with a smile, "Madeleine is adventurous. I hope you can keep up with her, Iskandar. She loves to see everything and has more energy than most."

Daniella held a reserve inside, concerned for her impetuous daughter, noticing that Iskandar had already turned her head, yet in six short weeks he'd be gone.

Hanna turned to Daniella, "Well then, I will bring Iskandar to your shop on the Canabière tomorrow? At noontime, *n'est pas?*" Now, he spoke as the host of the group. "*t'Fuduloo*, let us dine," easily switching from French to his native Arabic.

Throughout the evening there was laughter, good feelings, and free-flowing, animated conversation in French. Iskandar told of his life in the village, his mother and brother, his voyage from Beirut, and was already clearly anxious about the next day's events. Madeleine was interested in his every description, and showed her carefree spirit. She smiled at Iskandar most of the evening. She also was a bit anxious, yet felt very comfortable with her new handsome friend. He could see she looked up to him.

Iskandar turned his head from side to side as he listened to Hanna speak with Daniella while they suggested places to go, to see.

"Maybe we can go and see Les Calanques with some of my friends who have a boat, or maybe go to the Corniche overlooking the sea, or visiting the seaside les jardins along the way," Madeleine blurted out with excitement.

It was a lovely, cheery evening for everyone. When it drew to a close, more than an hour after dinner, Daniella spoke, "*Pardon, s'il vous plait.* We must return home now. And we shall see you gentlemen tomorrow at twelve o'clock at my shop?" Her tone of voice indicated that the question was actually confirming a definite arrangement.

Hanna turned to Daniella and said, "You and I should meet for dinner tomorrow evening on the *Canebière* and let them make their way. *Ça va bien*, is that acceptable?"

"*Oui*, I believe so," nodded Daniella. "Perhaps tomorrow at noon we can determine where we will dine, so that Madeleine and Iskandar can decide if they wish to come join us." Then, standing and moving her head toward Hanna to receive a kiss on her cheek from him, Daniella nodded to Iskandar and, turning, said with her warm gracious smile, "*Alors, bonsoir, mon ami*s."

Iskandar rose from the table with them. "*Bonsoir*, Madeleine," Iskandar said, wishing the evening would not end so early. He kissed the back of Madeleine's extended hand for the first time, emulating his uncle's gesture.

"*Bonne nuit*, Iskandar. I will see you tomorrow," whispered Madeleine, reluctantly following her mother

As they walked away, Madeleine exclaimed to her mother excitedly, "Isn't he wonderful, *Maman*? He is so gentle, so kind, so handsome. I like him very much."

"*Oui, chérie*. I can tell. He is special to you, isn't he?"

"And I believe he likes me too! Don't you agree? *Maman*, I feel so good. I am happy. It is wonderful to meet Iskandar. I feel so alive. I've never felt like this before. It is good isn't it, mama? Tell me it is good, please."

"*Ma chérie*, I love you so much. The one thing a Mother desires is that her child be happy, carefree and lively."

When they arrived at their home, Daniella sat on the sofa in the parlor and, with Madeleine sitting beside her, they held each other's hands. They spoke into the night; Daniella vicariously enjoying her daughter's excitement and feelings of first love, albeit with caution.

"Madeleine, you must understand that Iskandar will be here only a short time. Be good friends, yes, but be careful with your heart. Please understand that he will be gone in six weeks. I'm a bit worried for you."

She continued, looking lovingly into her daughter's eyes, "You know, don't you, that I was just one year older than you are when I fell in love with your father. We were so happy, and you were born of the love we shared so deeply. And even though your father is no longer with us, I am grateful for the time we had together. But remember, chérie, your father was not leaving Marseille."

"But," Madeleine interrupted, "Papa did leave for the army. And he didn't come back, yet you're happy you fell in love and married him, aren't you?"

"Yes, I believe it is better to feel the excitement and deep caring of true friendship and love even for a short while than it is to let it pass by. So, ma chérie, follow your heart. I have never seen you like this. It is a treasure in my heart to be with you and see you this way. God works in strange ways. Perhaps your meeting was meant to be. I could feel as he spoke that he loved his mother deeply. And that is a good sign. He will treat you well and with respect. And," she reminded her, "He is Hanna's nephew. And I know how you feel about Hanna who is a very good man. Iskandar does seem to like you very much. So, enjoy tomorrow, and sleep well tonight."

With her mother's concerned, yet supportive comments, Madeleine did indeed sleep very well.

Madeleine was just twelve years old when her father had to go off to war to fight the Germans and to protect France, "to protect our Madeleine," her mother had told her so often.

"But why must Papa go away?" Madeleine had cried. "I will miss him terribly. I love Papa. I love to sit in his lap, to have him hug me and tease me. I need Papa, *Maman*."

"I know, *ma chérie*, I know. I will miss him too. But, we must continue. Soon he will return to us," Daniella said to her young daughter that difficult day when he left, trying to comfort her. "We both love papa, and we need him with us. Soon, *chérie*, he will return to us so he can take care of you and love us, like before."

But François did not return. "The War to End All Wars" took François forever. He died protecting them, but he left an enormous pain of loss, especially with the little girl, an emptiness where there had been such joy, laughter and love. She had so much love to give because she was a child of love and affection from her father and her mother. There was a very special bond between father and daughter. Nearly every day during his absence, Madeleine would sit alone by the window, hugging her pillow to her chest, fondling the gold ring her father had given her as he left. She would stare out the window at the street and the short walk to their front door wishing, hoping to see his face, remembering his laughing face as he would pick her up off the ground when she would run from the house to greet him, shouting, "Papa, Papa, you're home!" She was the fulfillment of his dreams. She had so much love to give, and longed to give her love to a man like her father. Her mother tried to be both parents, but could not.

After the ladies had left the *Café Liban*, Iskandar and Hanna stayed at the table speaking with each other for some time as Iskandar gathered in the energy of his mostly fellow Lebanese all around him, making him feel all the more comfortable. He and Hanna played several games of *towleh*, and visited with Hanna's friends who passed by on their evening ritual. Butrus then stopped by their table by ten o'clock and excitedly told Iskandar of his day.

"Six weeks in Marseille! Iskandar. In Beirut, I thought I would die if I had to wait so long before sailing to America. It seemed that too much time would be wasted. But I have met so many nice people here from Lebanon. And the French girls are so pretty. It's a good thing I have so little money. The prostitutes are everywhere, and so enticing. I would gladly have spent all I have," he said with a grin.

Iskandar, thinking about that but not interested in "girls," responded, "I too thought six weeks would be much too long to wait. I even thought that maybe I would go immediately on to Le Havre, but for my father's schedule. But now, after meeting the most wonderful girl in the world, *sahbi*, I wish I was going to stay in Marseille for a long time, years maybe," he laughed. "I'm going to see her again tomorrow, Butrus!" He thought for a moment, looked at Hanna, then back to Butrus. "I want to see her all the time, everyday. Is that crazy, *Khali* Hanna?"

"Yes, Iskandar, it is crazy," responded Hanna with a smile. "But life is short, and one never knows what tomorrow will bring. Enjoy your young life. I think Madeleine likes you very much. She will be a good friend." Looking at Iskandar, he explained, "You know, her father was a good man, a devoted father and husband. But his life was cut short by the war." Hanna remembered all the sadness. "The war changed our ways of thinking. Daniella was only eighteen when Madeleine was born. And Madeleine was just thirteen when her father was killed. I respected him very much, and I waited two years after the sad news before I asked Daniella to share just a dinner with me. And even then, we were with her friends. But now, I can say to you, I consider her my love. She feels the same way. We do many things together. I have watched with pride as Madeleine has grown from a child. Daniella and I have even spoken about marriage one day. I believe, Iskandar, life is a gift from God, and what you do with your precious time is your gift to God. And God is Love, we are told. So what better gift can you give but love? The French people, especially these days, remember how the war took so many young people of France, destroying lives, families, hopes and dreams. Perhaps that is why we treasure each moment, each day, for tomorrow could be painful."

"So, my young nephew, follow your heart. And be grateful for each day. It cannot be retrieved. I know you are smitten with Madeleine. And why not? She is lovely, she is sweet and kind. A fine young woman. But Iskandar, you know you must go to America in six weeks. You must be honest with her...treating her kindly. What will be will be."

A shiver shuddered through Iskandar at the thought of having to leave Madeleine.

And when love's wings enfold you, yield to him...
　　　　　　　Kahlil Gibran

CHAPTER 9

Les Callanques, 1920

For young Iskandar, the following days were filled with the pleasure of Madeleine's company.

"Uncle Hanna, I'd like to take Madeleine to somewhere nice. Is there any place around here where we can spend some time?"

"Why not take her to our lovely jardins overlooking the sea, Iskandar?"

Taking Hanna's suggestion, they visited the seaside parks several times. Madeleine brought a blanket and a picnic basket filled with wine, bread and cheese. They found a tree with shade to enjoy the sea air and watch people pass by. They laughed, touched, and sometimes held each other's hand. Their conversations centered on likes and dislikes, or observations of their surroundings.

On the third day, at the jardin, and half way through the bottle of wine, Iskandar looked over at Madeleine, took her hand, and said, "I know about you and your mother. Would you like to hear about my life in Douma and my family?

She quickly responded, nodding her head anxiously and smiling warmly, encouraging him, "*Oui*, Iskandar. I would like very much to hear about your family." She tightened her grip on his hand affectionately and placed the other one on top of his, scooting around to face him.

"Douma is a tiny, but beautiful little mountain village high in the northern mountains of Lebanon, a blessed country, but the village is so poor. It is uniquely scorpion-shaped as seen from the mountain road above the village. The combination of the four-year locust infestation, the shortage of food, and the Turkish army occupation made it very difficult for the entire region. Many people died of starvation, including my wonderful mother. Yet, my family has survived there for hundreds of years the Greeks came, then the Romans, and on and on. My people, my family endured in poverty. I already miss them very much, Madeleine. My cousins and playmates, and Anthony Bashir...my favorite," he said as their faces flashed in his mind.

His voice trailed off as he remembered his beloved mother's love and dedication to her children. He told Madeleine of the mountains, the goatherds, the village, the orchards, the olive groves, and the incredible vistas. He smiled as he recalled his youth, climbing his treasured cedar trees, and, when looking west from his perch in the trees, seeing the same Mediterranean Sea that Madeleine had seen all her life.

Then, gazing out over the sea, he thought in silence. After a few moments he turned to her. "Let me tell you the story of a small boy just ten years old trying to be a man too soon. But first, let me show you something."

He reached to his feet and began removing his thick, smooth black shoes and white socks. "Look at my feet," he said to Madeleine.

"Why are they so dark? They are almost black," she exclaimed, pointing at his feet.

He frowned every time he looked at his feet, visible, lifelong reminders of the severe poverty of his youth. "They turned black after I suffered terrible frostbite during an unexpected snowstorm. I nearly lost them." He paused, recalling that terrible experience high in the snowy mountains. "We had no food to eat."

"Is this your own story? When you were a little boy?"

"Yes," he responded in a whisper. He felt the sun's warmth as it came from behind the scattered clouds, and heard the reassuring joyous songs of the small birds in the trees fluttering from limb to limb. He was relaxed with her, but became more tense as he began. "This is what happened." Iskandar cleared his throat, closed his eyes, leaned forward and thought in silence for a moment. Then, using his hands as he spoke, "I foolishly sneaked from the house early one late autumn morning to walk to the Bekaa Valley with a group of grown men who were going to climb over the mountains to glean wheat from the soil after the harvest because of the near starvation our village faced. My older brother Milhelm was down at the coast in Tripoli seeking fish."

"Why did the older men allow you to go with them?"

"Because they knew how stubborn and determined I was to help my family. I climbed up the two mountain ranges then down to the valley. Terrified, I hid from the army patrols, and crouched in the wheat field while gathering into my bag what I could with my little hands, just like the men. Afterward we crossed back over the two high mountains to the village."

"Iskandar, how long did that take?" Madeleine asked.

"It took us two full exhausting days," he replied "These are very high mountains, over seven thousand feet. To make matters worse, we were struck by a freak early snowstorm along the second mountain crest. For a long time, we walked in snow that was very deep for me, a little boy. I was so tired and so sore, I could barely keep up. I didn't know it, but I lost my shoes in the snow and my feet froze. The other men protected me under the shelter of an outcropping stone. They built a small fire for me and one man ran down to the village to tell my brother Milhelm that I could not walk any farther. He came up the mountain to save me."

"How was he able to carry you down with your bag of wheat?"

"Milhelm is known in the mountains for his strength and endurance. He is much bigger than me."

Somehow, he felt comfortable telling Madeleine of his life's most harrowing experience. He realized of all people, he could trust Madeleine with his most personal feelings; secrets he would not be able to share easily.

Taking a deep breath, he paused to make certain he had not forgotten any of the traumatic experience before he lay back and said with a strong statement as he looked into her eyes, "Madeleine, my mother saved my feet and my life." He paused, remembering, and after remaining quiet for a few minutes, he looked up to the sky, silently thanked God, sat up again and continued the story. "For two painful and difficult years, my mother lovingly rubbed my feet every day with warm olive oil, while telling me stories about my father and my heritage."

Throughout, Madeleine, fascinated, remained silent. As he completed the story, his fluid brown eyes filled with tears. He wiped his face. "This is the first time I've told anyone this story."

"You loved your mother very much, didn't you, Iskandar?" Madeleine asked in a warm, soft whisper, looking into his eyes.

Iskandar, hearing her voice and loving her presence as he had loved his mother's touch, replied softly, "More than my life itself, Madeleine. I still treasure her deep in my heart. I revere her. I always will. She was everything to me. Can you understand? And now, she is gone." Pausing, reflecting, he lay back on the grass, his eyes moistened as he remembered.

After the fourth week of being together nearly every day and evening, they agreed to meet in the early morning to spend an entire Saturday together.

They started very early in the morning at the fresh fish market along the east side of the *Vieux Port*, opposite the Panier, soon after the last of the small fishing boats returned to port. They walked to the lines of booths along the pier with men selling all kinds of fish from their morning catch.

"This place, near the *Canebière*, Iskandar, is where the fishermen of Marseille return from their excursions in the sea. Sometimes they are gone for several days. They bring their bounty here where it is sold in these booths along the Corniche. Every restaurant owner comes early to select the most succulent fish for their specialties. My mother shops here at least three times a week. You know, Iskandar," she said, smiling while she held his hand as they walked from booth to booth, "bouillabaisse is the trademark of all foods in Marseille. The finest is made here! My mother makes it with four different fish when we have friends over, the same as in the best restaurants."

"Bouillabaisse?" asked Iskandar.

"Yes," she replied. "It is a delicious fish broth. It is best served with several tasty types of fish. They say the best in the world is made in Marseille," she added in a light, playful boast.

He laughed at her as she smiled at him, still holding his hand as they walked, enthusiastically speaking almost non-stop, pointing at each wooden stall, stopping to ask about the specialty of that particular vendor. One booth showed hundreds of snails crawling up the sides of the buckets. Others displayed on their sloped table tops numerous freshly caught fish, some smaller ones he recognized as similar to those in Tripoli. Another stall sold only fresh squid.

"And the escargot, are they all fresh today?" she asked, pointing at the nearly full buckets of squirming, slow-moving snails.

"*Oui*, of course," the fisherman laughed, "my boat is just there." He pointed at the small sailboat nearby.

After spending the morning at the bustling fish market with hundreds of other shoppers, the pair continued along the Quai de Rive to tour Fort Nicholas, built by Louis XIV and located at the port entrance on the way to the *Jardin du Pharo*.

After Madeleine led Iskandar through the old fortress, he announced that he was hungry for lunch.

She laughed. "Let's go back to the market, get a basket of food, some bread and wine, and have a picnic."

"Wonderful," Iskandar replied with a smile, and loving her exuberance, he grabbed her hand as they nearly ran back, not wanting to waste any time.

"I want to see everything you can show me, Madeleine. Marseille is unbelievable, but mostly because I am with you!"

Slightly embarrassed, she gripped his hand and brought her face near his. Kissing his cheek, she whispered, "*Merci beaucoup, mon ami*. I believe you can see that I feel the same way." Then, she pulled him along quickly as they returned to the northern end of the quai, back to a stand where she could purchase the bread, wine, grapes, and cheese for their picnic.

"Grapes?" she asked as they stood at a stall by the boats. "Do you like grapes?"

"*Oui*, of course. I love grapes," he replied as he imagined placing one in her mouth at their picnic.

"I have a wonderful idea, Iskandar!" she exclaimed, pointing to the pier where there were small excursion boats loading passengers. "My girlfriends and I have taken one of those boats to the coves along *Les Calanques*. Let's do that. It will be fun. We can picnic on a beach."

"Yes," he eagerly responded. "That sounds exciting. I've never been on a beach. I'm from the mountains, you know," he laughed.

Holding hands, not wanting to let go of each other, they rushed to the pier where the boats waited.

"There, Iskandar, look up at the hill at the beautiful *Jardin du Pharo* and the huge mansion there on the left," Madeleine said to him as they stepped toward the bow of the boat's deck with a group of perhaps twenty young people.

"This is wonderful, Madeleine! I really like being on this boat with you. My friend, Butrus, and I marveled at these hills. Do you call them Les Calanques?"

"Yes, these Calanques are unique to Marseille, with many coves and beaches. Young people come here all the time to picnic, to swim, to sun, and to climb hills. Some bring their own boats. It's a wonderful place."

As he looked at her, he wondered how it would feel to actually kiss her on the lips. She smelled wonderful each time they kissed on their cheeks. She was so soft, so gentle. While he looked at her as she pointed first to the cliffs on the left, then to the small rocky islands offshore on the right, his urge to hold her grew and grew. Finally, as she turned to him, her face close, he embraced her for the first time. It felt magical.

Emboldened, and willing to express his inner feelings, he said to her, "Oh, Madeleine, it feels so good to hold you. I think I am in love with you. Can we find a place to be alone?"

"*Oui*, Iskandar," she giggled. "I was hoping you wanted to be alone because I feel the same way. We'll find a cove and go to a beach. After our picnic, we can climb to a grassy spot and be alone to look at the sea together."

After they sat on the small secluded beach enjoying their picnic near the water's edge, they could see couples pairing off to be alone. Some found large secluded rocks near the water, and some climbed the hill to the plateaus much higher overlooking the sea. And still others climbed more than three hundred feet to the top of the palisades. There were well-worn paths in every direction. Les Calanques were a very popular place to explore for the young people of Marseille.

"Let's go there, Iskandar. I'll bring the basket and the blanket," Madeleine suggested, pointing to the slope of the hills. "We can be alone for awhile. Is that what you want too?"

"*Oui*, absolutely," he responded quickly. "But let me carry those."

They gathered their possessions and headed for the cliff. After climbing up the path, they soon found a private grassy plateau.

This became their favorite spot overlooking the glistening sea below. The sea breezes brushed their faces gently causing Madeleine's hair to lift and flow with her movements. As she faced the sea's breeze, her hair streamed behind her. She was a goddess to Iskandar who followed her every movement. Madeleine spread their blanket on the lush, soft grass and sat down. He fell to the blanket next to her. For quite a while, they sat together, arms around their knees, quietly looking at the sea, appreciating being by themselves.

She turned and smiled at him. "Isn't this the most beautiful place in the world, Iskandar? This is our special place. It now belongs to us," she giggled happily.

He turned to her and watched her long, beautiful dark hair blow in the wind despite her ribbon and her futile efforts to pull it back. Iskandar playfully reached to help her and, for the first time, felt her silken tresses against her slender back. She shifted her body and, inadvertently, a breeze blew the soft folds of her dress above her knees. He felt a streak of electricity throughout his body as he looked at her long, shapely legs. Spellbound, he grew more excited. He moved his hand to the nape of her neck and caressed her gently. After several electric moments of feeling his fingers resting gently on her neck, his arm against her shoulder, she reached for his hand and slowly moved it across her shoulders and lightly brushed her breasts, inviting him. She turned to him longingly, bringing her face to his. Iskandar pulled her to him, feeling raw sensual emotions rushing through his body.

"Oh, Iskandar, I have wanted you ever since I fell into your arms that first night weeks ago. And it's only gotten better and stronger every time we are together. You have been so good for me," she whispered as she lowered her eyes demurely.

He leaned to her and, with the smell of early summer and the sea in the air, he lightly, tentatively kissed her. Their lips touched softly, with the delicacy of a butterfly, like a soft wisp of a breeze. He felt her eyelashes brush his cheeks. Their first kiss expressed the bond of two young lovers venturing where they had never been before. Neither spoke. Both felt their hearts and emotions yielding their bodies to each other.

She lay back and gently rested her head on the blanket keeping his eyes locked on hers. Drawn to her, he lay close and kissed her full lips that opened… asking. Madeleine melted against him as he pulled her close to him, embracing her completely for the first time and feeling her entire body pressing against his.

To their right, the golden setting sun, a willing participant and observer, spread its last rays of the day, creating millions of diamonds of reflections on the surface of the sea, casting a soft pastel hue across Madeleine's face enhancing her beauty. The sun slowly became a magnificent, exaggerated, red-orange ball silently slipping into the sea. Shadows lengthened and crossed their entwined bodies, exciting Iskandar even more and magnifying their youthful sense of secrecy and adventure. They were in a moment of full, young love and happiness, sharing thoughts and sensations neither had ever felt before.

"This place is so beautiful, Madeleine. Almost as beautiful as you," Iskandar whispered, gazing into her eyes.

She whispered, "I am yours, Iskandar. I love you."

"Oh, Madeleine, let our souls become one. I love you so much too."

They held each other for a long time, never wanting to let go. He embraced her tightly as he raised his head to look at her lovely face and again kissed her inviting lips softly, expressing his total love for her. "*Mon amour.*"

Madeleine whispered, "Oh, Iskandar, you are very romantic. I love that in you. I am so glad we loved each other here today. I give myself to you completely. You are my life."

After a few moments of lingering pleasure, Iskandar looked at her protectively. He loved her so and wanted her to have his most valuable possession. "As a symbol of my love and my lifetime commitment to you, Madeleine, I want you to have my gold cross." He carefully removed it from his neck. "It was given to me by my beloved mother when I was twelve years old. I have never taken it from my neck. It is the most valuable thing I own. I want you to wear it always as a reminder of my love for you. It is my treasure and should be around your beautiful neck." He reached to put the chain over her head. "Please accept this as a remembrance of this day, of our becoming one in deepest love. I promise you, Madeleine, you will never leave my heart. Only you, my love, only you…forever."

Madeleine, her eyes welling with tears from emotion and sincere love, pulled back her long hair as he carefully placed the chain around her neck, carefully placing the cross between her firm breasts.

"And for you, Iskandar," she whispered, "I give you this ring from my finger. My father gave it to me the day he left to go to the war. I have worn it always as a reminder of his love for me and my love for him. Now, I give you my treasure. I commit my heart and my love to you Iskandar, forever and ever, for my whole life. I have found you and I will never stop loving you. Know that…and believe that…forever." She placed the gold ring on the smallest finger of his right hand. It fit perfectly.

"I promise, my love, this ring will never leave my finger. I will be reminded of your beautiful face, your eyes, your love, every day for the rest of my life. You will always be my love, forever, Madeleine. I promise you."

At that moment, almost as a signal blessing their union, the bells of Notre-Dame-de-la-Garde began their evening chime. They looked to the church high on the hill overlooking the city, smiled gratefully and embraced, feeling their union had indeed been blessed.

They lay back together for a little longer, savoring moments of their love, their eyes returning to the other's.

The sun began setting as a full moon emerged from the sea, omens to them of God's blessing.

"This truly is the most wonderful, most beautiful place on earth, Madeleine. And yes, this is our place. It will be ours forever. We will come back here together."

"I will always remember this day, Iskandar. It is our day. This is our place and our secret."

When love beckons to you, follow him,
Though his ways are hard and steep.
And when his wings enfold you yield to him,
Though the sword hidden among his pinions may wound you.
And when he speaks to you believe in him,
Though his voice may shatter your dreams
as the north wind lays waste the garden…
                    Kahlil Gibran

CHAPTER 10

Onboard

Iskandar and Madeleine remained inseparable. They were acutely aware that Iskandar had to go on to America.

The two sat once again on Madeleine's soft blanket in the seaside *jardin* holding hands, Iskandar sometimes stroking Madeleine's hair, the afternoon sun embracing their faces with warmth as the breezes from the sea rustled the leaves above them.

"This is so difficult for me, Madeleine, knowing I must leave Marseille and you. Each day in America will be devoted to saving enough money to return to you. Nothing can get in its way. I know that while I must go to America, I will not be able to fulfill my destiny without you. I love you completely."

"Oh, Iskandar, I didn't know I would hurt so badly, now that I'm convinced you will leave me so soon. But I do not regret one minute of our time together. I do believe our union is blessed and that one day soon you will return to Marseille and me."

"I remember every moment since the evening we first met, *mon amour*. I have even written in my diary every night before I go to sleep. And it's all about you! I fall asleep thinking about you and I think about you every morning as I wake up. I think about you all the time!" he laughed, a bit reluctantly, hoping to turn the conversation to something else. She wanted to do the same and asked him, "What will you do in America, Iskandar? We never spoke about that."

Still holding her hand, not wanting to let go, he looked into her moist eyes that reflected her sadness and wiped the tears from her cheeks as she wiped away his. "My father wrote that he owns a store in a small town near Orlando in Florida. It has a strange name of Kissimmee. He thinks it is derived from the Native American Indians. So my first work will be with my father. He didn't want to work in a textile plant in Boston like my cousins there. He wanted to be free to come and go, so he went to a new frontier where it is warm. The railroad just came there. After a while, I'll see what I must do, even as I honor my father. *Insha Allah*, God willing, one day maybe I will have my own store."

"Your own store? And own property like your Uncle Hanna?" she asked optimistically.

"Yes, Madeleine, I have the same blood as Uncle Hanna and my father. My father already owns his store and some other property too. If he can do it, I can do whatever it takes. I will save every penny so I can return to Marseille and you so that we can be together again. I promise. I'll never love another as we have loved. I'll find you wherever you are."

"And I will wait for you too, Iskandar. I cannot love another as I love you. I'll fondle your…my cross…your mother's gift each day…and I'll want you beside me each day. I am yours forever."

"Wake up, Iskandar!" Butrus exclaimed, standing by Iskandar's bed. "Time to get up, it's eight o'clock, *sahbi*." Butrus shook his friend's shoulder, eager to get out on their final day in Marseille. "*Yallah*! Let's go! We set sail for America tonight!"

"What? Oh, Butrus," Iskandar replied haltingly, wiping his eyes with both fists. "I'm so sleepy, *sahbi*. I…uh…couldn't go to sleep. I am so sad thinking about Madeleine. I didn't fall asleep until nearly dawn. I think I only had two hours of sleep!"

"Well, that's too bad, but it's time to get up. It's our last day and I want to say goodbye to my friends all over the Panier. We've agreed to write each other when we are in America, just as you and I promised."

"Oh, alright, Butrus. I'll get up, but I ache all over and I don't want to leave."

After they both washed their faces, dressed, and finished their packing, with Iskandar almost crying as he packed the last of his belongings, they went down to the restaurant on the plaza in front of Café du Liban where they ordered a typical Mediterranean breakfast of cheeses, hardboiled eggs, bread and fruits. Shortly, Hanna joined them and Butrus, finished with his breakfast and sensitive to Iskandar's misery as he watched him idly push his food around his plate, left the table promising to join Iskandar at the ship shortly before six o'clock that evening.

"I'm not hungry, Uncle Hanna. I'm very sad."

Reluctantly, Iskandar had packed most of his meager belongings the night before after being with Madeleine all that day and into the evening. He had avoided any preparations, hoping against hope it wasn't true that he must leave her. Perhaps something would delay his departure. They had spent several more days together on the promontory above the beach, their favorite place.

As he and Hanna sat at their favorite table, Iskandar printed an image in his mind of the plaza. He wanted to remember the many evenings he waited for Madeleine and the moments they shared together…the familiar store fronts, the scattered tables, the lush sycamores with their colorful trunks spreading their limbs overhead, the neighbors simply sitting and sharing their free time over coffee. His eyes swept across the opening looking north, and there, between the two buildings that formed the east and west boundaries of *Place de Liban*, through the open north end, he focused on the magnificent cathedral, Notre-Dame-de-la-Garde in the distance, and the golden pinnacle of Saint Mary atop the high dome, some four hundred feet above sea level and he prayed for guidance.

"Uncle Hanna," he said softly, "I am going to miss her desperately. Look! Look at Notre-Dame-de-la-Garde, how beautiful she is — the symbol of Marseille. Madeleine took me there many times. How am I going to deal with this, Uncle? How? What should I do? How can I leave Madeleine? I love her so much."

Hanna's eyes looked down as he rubbed his forehead with his hand. "My son, you are a very sensitive, and yes, a very romantic young man. You feel with your heart, like your mother. And certainly, Madeleine is very special."

"But, Uncle Hanna," Iskandar interrupted, not wanting to hear anything but encouragement.

Hanna waved his hand and continued, "I love her as if she were my own daughter. So I am biased. She is in pain too. But neither I nor anyone else can tell you what you should do. You have a full life to live yet, and," he paused, reaching for Iskandar's shoulder, "you alone must decide. America is the hope of so many Lebanese, in fact, the world over. Your father awaits you. You will have opportunities there that do not exist here these days. To be sure, you have a most difficult decision to deal with. If you continue your journey to America and do well, then perhaps you can return to Marseille and Madeleine." Then, looking directly into his eyes, Hanna, sensing this young man's dilemma, asked, "My son, when you consider all things, even at your young and inexperienced age, you will make the correct decision. I do believe completely that Madeleine loves you with all her heart and that no one ever will replace you. These painful conflicts are what make life fascinating and challenging. And none of us knows what the future holds. Trust God."

Smiling sympathetically, he raised his demitasse cup of strong Turkish coffee, inviting Iskandar to do likewise. They touched cups as Hanna, now looking directly into Iskandar's moist eyes, said, "*Bon courage*, Iskandar, *bon courage*."

Iskandar replied, "And to you, Uncle Hanna, *bonne santé*."

After picking at his breakfast, he eagerly went to Daniella's shop to be with Madeleine one last time.

"She is not here, Iskandar, she is in her room. She is very sad today. We both hate that you must leave."

"But I must see her. I must be with her."

Daniella embraced Iskandar and spoke softly to him, "We all knew this day would come, Iskandar. She and I spoke of it many times. C'est la vie is a way we French people have had to learn to think, accepting our fate. She is so sad today; I know this to be true, because she loves you with her whole heart. You are her love, her friend. Your soul has bonded with hers. I bless your beautiful love, Iskandar. Be happy and come back soon. She wants to see you, I am certain. But she needs to be alone for awhile. Why don't you come back at twelve o'clock? Your ship departs at sunset, evening tide, isn't that so?"

"Yes, six o'clock. But I want to be with her this day, Madame DuBois."

"Come back then, Iskandar, at twelve o'clock. I will see that she is here for you."

Frowning, Iskandar left, disappointed and saddened, but accepting.

After spending the next few hours alone walking along the *Vieux Port* quays, recalling their times together in this same place, he returned to Daniella's shop at twelve o'clock.

"Madame DuBois," he asked, "is Madeleine…"

"Hallo, chéri," interrupted Madeleine with a sad smile, reaching out her hands to him. "Please forgive me, Iskandar, this is a difficult day for me."

"It is difficult for me also, chérie. My heart is exploding with sadness. I truly do not know what I must do. I am so torn by this. How can I leave you? But how can I stay? I have nothing; I have no way to earn a living here. My father is in America. I am to go there. But it is an impossible conflict for me. You must be with me today, Madeleine. Come let us go to our favorite place until I have to go to the ship."

That day, their last in Marseille together would once again be filled with passionate emotions. They went to their favorite place on the promontory above the beach, aware this would be the last time they would be together. These two young lovers walked hand in hand to the hill overlooking the sea. With their blanket on the grass, they sat close together. Holding hands, their bodies touching, while looking at the sea together, perhaps for the last time, they embraced longingly, and kissed deeply, several times.

Iskandar held her face close to his as he absorbed her fragrance and whispered, "This is a terribly difficult thing for me to leave you and go to America without you, but I am without any money at all. My father will look for me in New York and I must go. I hope that you understand because we've spoken about it. Yet, I will be empty without you and will think of you every day, wishing you were with me." Then looking into her eyes, he whispered, "I promise…I'll return for you someday."

Madeleine, holding him tightly, whispered back, "I am so grateful that we met as we did and that we love each other so deeply. I will treasure every moment we shared together for as long as I live. These weeks have been heaven on earth. I'll never forget you. I will treasure also the beautiful cross you gave me."

He fondled her ring on his finger, the reminder of her love.

As she finished, he stood up, looked down to her and reached out, helping her up. "Let's go now." They stood together and, looking into each other's eyes, kissed each other deeply, embracing each other as close as they could, lingering.

They arrived just in time at the docks. From a distance, the ship, tied to the dock, was still being loaded with provisions through the side doors as the dock workers wheeled the carts filled with food and supplies, hustling quickly under the steely eyes of the ship's quartermaster yelling, "Let's go!" or "*Yallah*!" depending on the language of the workers, including some Arabic immigrants. "We've got a schedule to meet! Get those boxes in here!" The men pushed and pulled their carts around and over the large ropes used to tie other ships to the dock, some coiled neatly, some stacked loosely.

Nearby, passengers walked up the gangway and onto the ship, most bearing packages and belongings not shipped in the hold. At the top, each in the queue, stopped to wave to their families or friends below standing on the dock waving and yelling farewells.

"There, Madeleine," Iskandar said as they approached the ship, gesturing toward the passenger ramp near them and the officials at the bottom of the ramp. He could see the officials checking the papers of each passenger lined up to board the vessel. That reminded him to gather his own passport, ticket, and identification papers he carried in his leather pouch with the shoulder strap Madeleine had purchased for him as a going away present. As they stepped toward the ship, they reached for each other's outstretched hand until he stepped completely away from her reach.

"I must say goodbye, and I cannot." He felt a tear overflow onto his cheek and watched her face change, reflecting her pain.

She turned her downcast head toward him as he walked to the ramp, tears filling her eyes. He reluctantly walked up the sloped ramp and boarded the ship while she stood on the wooden dock.

In time, she saw him at the railing of the ship. Waving, she called out to him with her beautiful, wide smile, "Iskandar! Remember that I love you. I will wait for you forever."

He could barely see her through his tears as he vigorously waved his arms to her, watching her stand on the pier below. "I love you, Madeleine," he shouted.

"I am so sad," Madeleine whispered to no one. "I am lost without him. How will I live?"

The engines of the ship increased their roar as the ship shuddered and began to slowly pull away from the docks. As Madeleine watched from the pier, the ship moved west away from the port toward the sea, carrying her love far away…to America. She wrapped her arms around her breasts, not moving her eyes from her beloved who was still at the stern's railing.

Iskandar kept waving and noticed her right hand move slowly downward to hold her abdomen followed by her left hand. It puzzled him that she was cradling her stomach and no longer waving at him.

The ship grew smaller and smaller until she could no longer make out his form. Then, finally, the ship disappeared into the sea's last reflections of the golden sunset.

Iskandar stood at the ship's railing he tearfully focused only on Madeleine until she disappeared into the distance. His heart was heavy; the yearning to hold her in his arms overwhelming.

As the ship pulled away, she whispered to herself, trying to be brave, "How fortunate we are to have met each other, even for a short time, and to have found a love so real, so good. Please come back for us."

A woman standing next to her said, "*Excusez-moi?*"

"*Je suis désolé*," Madeleine responded. "I was just talking to myself. I am having difficulty with my love leaving me for America. I pray he will be safe, and finds his father. I miss him already."

The older woman smiled and nodded knowingly. "He will be back. Do not fret too much."

Madeleine turned to watch as the ship sailed away toward the setting sun. She saw Iskandar wave again with both arms as he shouted something she could not hear.

She wiped the tears streaming down her face before she turned from the sea and walked away. She fondled his cross, her hands brushing her breasts and finally resting again on her abdomen.

To her right, on the hill above the beach, the trees stood witness to Iskandar and Madeleine's place of love, preserving their memory. Madeleine smiled broadly and looked up at the sky with scattered pink and lavender clouds reflecting the setting sun. Birds flitted overhead; a sea breeze gently ruffled her hair.

She reached inside her blouse again to feel the gold cross. Rubbing it with her fingers, she lifted her head, straightened her shoulders, stood tall, and confidently walked away from the pier back toward the city and the *Canebière*.

Life goes on, she whispered to herself.

Iskandar could not leave the deck railing at the stern of the ship for hours.

"Come, *sahbi*, come, walk with me," said Butrus as he put his arm around his friend's shoulders, interrupting his preoccupation with Madeleine. "I know you are feeling great sadness, leaving your beloved Madeleine. But you have beautiful memories. I know you will never forget her. And she will always remember you. But now you must focus on your future and how you will soon be able to return for her."

Iskandar again found her ring with his thumb and rubbed it as he had all day. "You are right, Butrus. I ached when I had to leave Milhelm, and, I am torn to pieces having to leave Madeleine. But somehow, I must now turn my thoughts to America. Yet, it is so painful for me. I must find a way somehow to come back to Madeleine. I will work hard, save my money, and come to her." He kept rubbing her, now his, ring on his finger, thinking of that day on the hill.

Later, below on their bunk beds, Iskandar asked, "Butrus, I need paper and a pen. Can you help me find these things? I must write to Madeleine and tell her how I am feeling, if I can."

"*Shookrun, sahbi*. Thank you, my friend," Iskandar said to Butrus when he returned with several sheets of blank paper, envelopes, and a fountain pen with ink. "Where in the world did you get these?"

Butrus smiled, "My Auntie Najla always has writing material with her because she will write many letters to family in Lebanon and in America during the voyage. She is my favorite aunt and I'm her favorite nephew. She loves me and always takes good care of me."

After starting several letters to Madeleine, and not being pleased, Iskandar, determined, finally found a quiet place on the ship where he thought for hours about his six weeks in Marseille with Madeleine. After gathering his thoughts, filled with emotion and romance, he began his first of six letters he planned to post as soon as he arrived in New York. Writing in French, he wrote:

> *My dearest Madeleine,*
>
> *I write to you with my heart filled with sadness and loneliness. I miss you so terribly. But I feel wonderful when I think of you and see your lovely face. And, as we say in Arabic, y'sleme al wish, or may God save your face for me.*
>
> *I have been in love with you from the very moment we met. And it grew everyday in Marseille during our six weeks together.*
>
> *Madeleine, I think of you all day, everyday. I wake up during the night thinking of you. I go to sleep with you on my mind as I fondle your ring, and each morning I wake up thinking of you.*
>
> *It has been five days since we departed. I'm sorry to say that because*

we ran into bad weather, many of us have been seasick. Most of us are not accustomed to being on a ship. I myself have been too sick to write to you for several terrible days. This entire trip has been painful and very unpleasant since we left Lebanon. Many of us had to say goodbye to our homeland, our villages and our families. Those I've talked to miss them so much. And while I look forward to arriving in America, I really don't know what that even means.

As for me, Madeleine, I have had to say goodbye to my father when I was a little boy, then to my mother when she died, then to my brother Milhelm, my cousins, and my village. And now, the hardest of all, I had to say goodbye to you, the only other woman, besides my mother, I have ever loved…you!

But, I promise with all my heart, Madeleine, I will endure this voyage. And I will endure my new life in America, and I will return to you, dearest, just as soon as I can.

I will always love you with all my heart,

Iskandar

The ship sailed west to Malta for refueling and supplies, then stopped in the Azores for replenishments before it turned its course for New York.

Day after day, Iskandar and Butrus stood on the deck at the railing, watching the sea.

"How vast is the sea, Butrus? How great is the distance between my Madeleine and me? It is so enormous. Yet, I must find a way to come back for her after I am able. I must work hard and commit myself to my work. I must succeed, save enough money and return to my Madeleine. I swear I will not rest until I have accomplished that mission."

"Iskandar," Butrus spoke to his friend, "that is a good goal. But we must also live in the present. Let us enjoy the beauty of the sea, the sky, and think of the new life that we will have in America."

When you are joyous,
look deep into your heart and
you will find it is only that which
has given you sorrow is giving you joy…
Kahlil Gibran

CHAPTER 11

New York

"Look, Iskandar, look!" shouted Butrus above the din of the ship's engines. "See the Statue of Liberty? She is holding the torch of freedom, lighting our way to America. Isn't she beautiful! And look at the buildings! I've never seen such tall buildings before! What a city! What a country! I can't believe what I am seeing! We are free!"

Iskandar wept with joy. "God has watched over us. Thank you, Lord. Now we must find our fathers and begin our new lives. Butrus, even though you are going to California and I will be in Florida, we must remain friends."

Their initial excitement of arriving in America soon gave way to the difficult process that lay ahead. They spent most of the day going through the frustrating, bureaucratic, officious immigration process on Ellis Island. They filled out forms, stood in lines, endured humiliating medical examinations, and the other unpleasant procedures required of all immigrants coming to America in the early years of the twentieth century.

Iskandar grew impatient with the delays and turmoil of the process. Hundreds of new immigrants, mostly from his ship, pushed and shoved each other in the overcrowded room. No one understood the English signs or shouts of the immigration officers. They spoke only French or Arabic. The officials used hand signals to lead them to the impersonal and embarrassing physical examinations. The interpreters shouted at them, "Hand me your medical records…let me see your eyes…disrobe and let me examine your body…here, sprinkle this cleansing powder on your body…you cannot enter America unless you are healthy."

"Butrus, I cannot believe how demeaning and crude this process is. This is a terrible experience. I hope the rest of America isn't like this," Iskandar complained.

"We have to go through it, Iskandar. Our fathers did it," Butrus replied.

"I know. The Turks also did it to Salim. If they lived through it, so can we," he resolved.

Finally, after what seemed like hours of humiliation and being treated like animals, the officials directed them to a large room where they stood in line for a long time, papers in hand stamped "Approved for Entry," and their passports.

"What is your name? Where is your passport?" demanded the immigration officer gruffly in English with a thick Irish brogue.

"My name is Iskandar Chalhoub Thomé, *Ibn* Ibrahim." He handed his papers to the official.

"What? Let me see your passport. Uh-huh, mustache, dark hair, five feet, ten inches tall, your number, everything is in order, but you must have an American name. Let's look in the book. Iskandar is Alexander; Ibn is the son of…Abraham Thomé. Hmm, that can be Tomay or Tomei," said the officer, frowning, searching for a phonetic sounding name. "Or, many named Thomé take the name of Thomas. So, will you? How about Alexander Abraham Thomas?"

"*Ma Bakar*, I don't know," responded Iskandar thoughtfully with a quizzical look on his face, not fully understanding the man's question.

"My American name is to be Alexander Abraham Thomas? he asked, then nodded yes in acceptance when the official glared at him.

Iskandar, who endured the Turkish authority for so long, eagerly welcomed the proffered option to agree with, but not required to do. He became refreshed and hopeful.

The officer thrust the official papers back into Alexander's hands and he finally entered America.

"Go through that door to find your family if they are waiting for you," ordered the officer. By this time, Alexander would have agreed to most anything if it meant he could leave the building.

"There! There is my father." He pointed and waved when he recognized Abraham waiting in the crowd of relatives anxiously searching for their loved ones.

"*Biyee*!" he waved and yelled. "Here! Here I am!" He pressed through the crowd, turning his shoulders as he moved between people, his eyes never leaving his father's suntanned face.

"Iskandar, *ta ha la hawn*, come to me," Abraham beckoned and shouted loudly so to be recognized above the din of the noisy, jostling crowd. He opened both arms wide, excited to see his son for the first time in eight years. "Here, my son! Come to me!"

They stood facing each other with outstretched arms, tears of joy pouring out of the eyes of father and son as they embraced, repeatedly kissing each other's cheeks, displaying affection in the custom of their homeland.

"Thank God," he murmured as he felt his father's strong arms wrap around him. He smelled his father's familiar musky scent while absorbing this wonderful moment.

"Eight years! Eight years! So long, my son! How you have grown! You are as tall as me now! I am so happy to see you, Iskandar." Abraham proudly tousled Iskandar's thick hair.

"*Biyee*, you look so good. You are still so strong! What joy to be here with you. Oh, how I wish *Imei* was here with us today."

"And Milhelm too," responded Abraham, sadly. His large hands lovingly swept Alexander's shoulders and the side of his face as he smiled broadly with pride. "Let me look at you. Your shoulders are strong. You look very healthy and handsome, my son! Come, bring your belongings. I will help you. We will go now and be together." Tears began to well up.

"Father, I've missed you so much. You look the same, except I don't remember you with a tan," he smiled broadly.

Slowly they separated, joyous but the sadness of the long separation and the reasons for it hung in the air.

They stood facing each other, "Son, there is so much to tell you. And there is so much for you to tell me. Your sister Leila could not be with us, for she is with child, her third, and the journey would have been too difficult for her. We will see her in due time. She sends her love. Now, are you hungry? Let us eat before we begin our journey."

"Forgive me, Father, my legs are still a bit weak from the journey on the seas. I must walk a bit slowly for a while. I was sick on the ship so much! But yes, *Biyee*, I am hungry. I am hungry for food, for you, for your love, and for my new life in America. I met a wonderful girl in Marseille, *Biyee*. I want to tell you all about her. And *Khali* Hanna sends his love to you as well." Alexander spoke fast and excitedly to his father. He had so much to say.

The moment Alexander and Abraham stepped outside, arms linked together, Iskandar pointed at the tall buildings and exclaimed, "*Biyee*, this city is amazing. Look at all the tall buildings! And crowds of people everywhere!" Abraham guided them quickly through the crowds toward the bus stand. "Come, Iskandar, we must go to the train station. It is on the island over there. It is called Manhattan. Here is the bus. Let us go."

By 1920, New York had more than three million people mostly recent immigrants or first generations. It was the largest city in America, and much larger than Beirut and even Marseille.

He could hardly restrain himself. "Oh, *Biyee*, what a big city! Is it like this where we are going? Is this the way America is everywhere? Everything is so full, so fast, so big, so tall. Everyone is walking fast…so many trolleys with overhead power wires, cars and trucks in the street. It is chaotic! But, everyone seems so free, so happy. It's exciting!" Iskandar watched the cars speed past, drivers honking their horns as they wove in and out of traffic. "The women are dressed stylishly like the wealthy women in Marseille."

He whispered to himself, "Alexander… Alexander Thomas. Everything is strange, even my name!" Then, as he looked up at the clear, blue sky, he felt good about this new world.

"My God, village life was so simple. I never imagined New York would look like this, *Biyee*," he said to his father.

"Iskandar, New York is different from everywhere else in America. There is only one New York," Abraham said to his son, still using his Arabic name. "I would rather live in a village where I know everyone and everyone knows me. I feel safer there than here. Everyone is an immigrant here in New York, speaking his own language until some of them go on to other places. Their young go to school to learn English, but the older people do not. That is why they live in separate places. Brooklyn, in New York, has many Syrians. You can purchase any kind of food from Syria you wish: bulgar, *fistok, jibneh, zeytoon*, herbs and spices. Everything is there. The same is true for the Irish, the Greeks, the Jews, the Italians and others. Most Armenians are with the Lebanese. New York is a big place with many kinds of people. Somehow, in America, they all get along without wars. That is the miracle of America. Now, we must eat something."

They went to a restaurant near the terminal building that was quickly filling with new immigrants and their welcoming families, speaking to each other in their native Arabic. They found an empty table and sat down to wait to place an order.

Abraham spoke enthusiastically in his native language to his son across the table, loud enough to be heard above the cacophony of the other diners, "Rest, my son. You have had a very long journey. And today was difficult. But it will get easier and less confusing in time. You will find it much simpler after you have learned to speak and read English. English is a hard language, Iskandar. I have not yet learned to speak it well. But you are young and must learn as soon as possible. I have arranged a speaking tutor for you in Florida, and you must attend school there to learn the customs as well, and make friends. There is so much to talk about. We will speak more about these things later."

Then, looking into his son's dancing eyes, he said lovingly, "Oh, I am so happy you are finally here with me, my son." Pausing, he decided he must discuss his plans with Iskandar. "We will have a long journey, my son. America is a large country. Our village in Florida is fifteen hundred miles away. That is nearly ten times the length of Lebanon. A new frontier, so they say, far to the south where it is warm all year. There is no snow where we will live. But before we go there, I think we should go see your cousins, my brothers and your Uncle Salim and Uncle Mike. They wait for you. So, after we eat, we will go to the station and take a train to Boston."

They sat on a wooden bench the entire seven-hour train ride with the windows open, wind rushing to their faces. Alexander, seated next to the window, eagerly pointed at the forests and towns the train passed through. His eyes rarely left the sights whizzing by. Iskandar laughed when he heard the bells ringing…ding, ding, ding…at the town crossings when the gates went down to warn automobile drivers and pedestrians to stop at the railroad tracks. The two, father and son, spoke in their native tongue and exchanged banter and recollections. It seemed a bit strange to be with his father for the first time in eight years.

"You were just a boy of ten, my son, when I had to leave you. If I stayed the Turkish army would have taken me. I had no choice. Like so many other Christian Lebanese and Syrian men, there was no hope for us under the Ottomans."

Alexander, remembering the separation, his mother's sense of loss, and his trials following the freak snow storm, recalled to his father, "*Biyee*, it was so awful without you. I missed you so much, but she took good care of Milhelm and me. She never took good care of her own health, but worried about us…too much…and now…" he ended in a sad whisper, tears welling up.

"But now, we must turn to the future, Iskandar. We must remember her and love her. She would want more than anything that you are happy in America."

Your friend is your needs answered.
He is your field which you sow with love
and reap with thanksgiving.
Kahlil Gibran

CHAPTER 12

Boston

"*Ahlen wa sahlen!*" exclaimed Uncle Mike, Abraham's brother, with both arms outstretched, welcoming his nephew with a big smile and a strong embrace.

"Come in, come in. We are so happy to see you. Ah, Iskandar, you are a young man now. Eighteen, eh? You were just a boy when last we saw you in Douma during the winter of 1911. We all came to say goodbye to your mother and you boys. Learning of her passing saddened us. Beautiful Katrina. She was everyone's favorite. And now, Milhelm is the only one still in the village," Uncle Mike exclaimed, gesturing. "Please sit, rest, and have coffee. We have food for you both. How was your voyage?"

Alexander, smiling, simply said, "It was difficult." He didn't feel much like talking yet. He was just excited to see everyone.

Mike turned to Abraham. "And, *khai-yi*, how good to see you. It's been too long. How are you, my brother? Our voyage was very difficult too, eh?" They laughed and embraced, two men in their fifties, affectionately kissing both cheeks. They all sat around their room on cushions scattered on the floor carpets, a custom they brought with them from Lebanon. For a long moment, they gazed at each other, savoring their reunion, loving the sight of each other, and then, all resumed speaking at the same time, then laughing at themselves.

"This is like the end of the Prodigal Son parable that Jesus spoke of in the Bible, isn't it, Abraham? We must dine on the fatted calf, rejoice and be happy for your son who has come to you after so many years."

"I am so happy, Mike," replied Abraham sitting next to Alexander, and with a broad smile, his hand never leaving his son's arm. "I am rejoicing the whole time. Yet, I must confess, I am also sad. My son Milhelm is not here. And my beautiful Katrina can only be with us in spirit. I miss her so much. You cannot believe how much." As he spoke remembering their years together, thinking of his lovely bride at their wedding, with joy at the birth of each child, Abraham's eyes welled up. "You were such a beautiful baby, Iskandar, and like your sister and brother, very good children. I'm proud of all of you. He reached to embrace his youngest son, so grateful for his arrival. "I love you so much, Iskandar," he whispered. "You have your mother's eyes and her smile. This is a wonderful, but bittersweet day for me, my son."

As other family members gathered around the room, Alexander obligingly responded to Uncle Mike's request, "Tell us about your trip from Beirut, Iskandar. You stayed awhile in Marseille like your father, didn't you?"

"Well," he began, "the trip was very hard and, like many of the passengers, I got sick a lot. But I enjoyed Marseille."

"Did you bend over the railing like your father did?" He laughed out loud, as did Abraham remembering his own painful voyage when he got sick so many times.

"One day when I was at the rail, sick with my friend Butrus, a member of the crew pushed Butrus, pointed at his feet, and yelled, 'Clean it up you dirty Arab!' I got mad. Butrus is my friend, and I couldn't restrain myself as I punched that crewman on the jaw. He hit me back. He was about my size, but I didn't care, so I hit him again right in his face. He looked at me with wide open eyes, staring at me, shocked. Then I said, 'Don't you ever call my friend a dirty Arab. We are as good as you, whatever you are, and don't you forget it.' Then I pushed him down and told him to clean it up himself!"

"But you were taught not to fight, my son."

"Yes, *Biyee*, and I do not. But that man insulted my heritage and I will not allow that in my presence. I'm sorry, but I cannot."

Uncle Mike said, "You did right, Iskandar. It's very hard to be quiet when someone insults your family. But we must do our best to show we are peaceful people. Now, let us speak about our lives here in Boston. My wife, Sara, and I own a store on the corner downstairs. We sell clothing, shoes, and notions to our community. We have worked hard together, every day but Sundays, and now we own our building. It takes time, yes, but we think in terms of family, not just ourselves. Everything is possible in America, *Insha Allah*, if it be the will of God."

Mike continued, now elaborating to the gathering as much as to Alexander, describing life in America for the immigrants, and how many had successfully dealt with it in their new country. "We have a large Syrian community here in Boston, one of the oldest in America. You know, don't you, Iskandar, Syrians have been living here in Boston since the 1850s. We even have a thriving Syrian-American Club here, and it grows every year! Like the Irish, the Jews, and the Italians, we formed our own neighborhoods. In that way, we know all our neighbors, go to the same churches, speak the same language, eat the same foods, and live the same traditions. Some have shops. Others work in the mills. It is good. Still, one-by-one, some leave for other places in America."

"Now," Auntie Amal interrupted, "the women tell me that many young men and young couples are moving to a place called Detroit in Michigan. They can earn a lot more money building automobiles for Mr. Ford."

"Yes, "Uncle Mike added, "I have been told the same thing in the store. They say the best jobs are in Detroit these days. I also heard of one cousin who started as a peddler in Dakota, out west, selling to the Indians and now owns a store. Another took the train to California near Los Angeles. They came from the Bekaa Valley, and are now doing very well farming and growing potatoes. Most are clothing shopkeepers or food merchants. We are everywhere…in small towns or villages in other states like Texas, Louisiana, Ohio, Mississippi, Georgia, Illinois, and Michigan. Some even left here to go to Cuba, Puerto Rico, Honduras, Brazil, and still others to Canada. We are all over America, even though there are not so many of us. But more are coming now that the war is over. It has not been easy for any immigrants. But we survive as we must." He paused, and now, looking directly at Alexander, pointed and said, "And so will you, Iskandar, so will you. It is your destiny to succeed here in America."

Abraham then interjected, "But for me and for Iskandar, I think our best future is in Florida. Soon, too, perhaps Milhelm will join us."

Finally, Alexander could no longer hold back, so he spoke of Marseille. "*Khali* Hanna asked me to give you his warmest wishes, *Biyee*. He treated me very well. We visited many times. He gave me the use of an apartment for six weeks and my new friend Butrus and I shared the room. *Khali* Hanna is so nice. He has a beautiful lady friend named Daniella." Tentatively, he ventured to the precipice. "She has a beautiful daughter whose name is Madeleine." Pausing in thought, sensing no positive response, he paused because he could go no further.

"Butrus met his father in New York as I met you, and his plan is to go to California where his father has established a small farm in some valley there. He told me it is very fertile like the Bekaa."

"That would be the San Joaquin Valley; it is very productive," spoke young Edward, the teacher-to-be. "They feed most of the western communities from there."

"That's the name Butrus said. 'San Wakeen,' or something like that," responded Alexander with a smile. "I must learn English as fast as I can, otherwise it will be so difficult for me. Going through immigration was a nightmare," he explained, still speaking in Arabic.

"Sara," Mike directed to his wife, "send one of the boys to get Salim. Tell him Iskandar is here and to come visit with us."

Mike turned to Alexander, "Iskandar, Salim has been anxiously awaiting your arrival. Since he arrived two years ago, he has been eager for you to come. He wants to introduce you to his lady friend. She's such a nice girl. Her name is Julia. We are all very happy. She's from a good Orthodox Syrian family like us. They arrived in Boston in 1905 from Damascus. She has many sisters. Perhaps one of them is for you." Mike laughed as he put his hand on Alexander's shoulder.

Alexander felt the conflict in his stomach. He felt more certain than ever that they would never understand his love for Madeleine.

"Salim works in the shop downstairs. He should be here in a few minutes. Now we will eat, *fudulou*, honor us,"

The group moved to the dining room table, a blessing of thanks was said, and before dinner was served, the first plates of the *mezza*, the cluster of appetizers, were passed around. After their dinner of lamb meat on a skewer, *laha mishweh*, beans and rice, *lubya oo riz*, and of course, *tabouleh*, *zeytoon*, olives, and *khoubas*, pita-like bread in which they wrapped almost everything instead of using forks and knives, the women cleared the dishes and gathered with the rest of the family to visit and relax in the living room. The men sipped their *arak* and exchanged stories late into the night. This was a time of re-bonding. They were family. Cousins came and went all afternoon and evening. The house was crowded for hours. It was very much like home in Douma where everyone's friends were relatives, an extended family reunion where every person had a turn to speak, even the children. Family was paramount in their lives.

"*Mahrharba*, Iskandar!" Salim almost shouted in happiness as he entered the room with arms wide open to hug his younger nephew. "How good it is to see you here. I have waited for this day for a long time. Let me see you! You have grown so much!"

Alexander smiled. "And so have you, Salim. Remember, you are only two years older than me!"

"Yes, Iskandar, and don't you forget it!" They laughed and embraced each other, kissing cheeks.

"Ah, Salim, I hear you have a lady friend. Wonderful!"

"Yes! Her name is Julia Shaheen."

Alexander glanced at his right hand and realized he was rubbing the gold ring on his little finger.

"Now then," replied Salim, moving quickly, said, "we must spend time together here in Boston before you and your father must leave. I want you to meet Julia. You will like her. She is wonderful, the eldest of seven children, four sisters and two brothers. One of her sisters, Helene, could turn your eye. She is just fifteen, but she's a beauty and will soon become the right age for marriage."

"I will be happy to go with you to meet Julia, Salim, but I must go to Florida with my father in less than a week."

"Well, then, Iskandar, we must agree to visit each other as often as possible."

"You are right, Salim. I must beat you at *towleh* at least a few times every year!" Laughing, he slapped Salim on the shoulder. "How else am I going to hear you sing your romantic love songs? Is that how you wooed Julia?" He laughed again.

"After all, you are the best singer in all of Lebanon!"

"Of course I sang to Julia, Iskandar. I even sang to her father, the *khoury*, the priest, because I fell in love with her and wanted her and her family to love me back!" he smiled proudly.

During the seven days following, they spent every day together. Each night during their week's stay, Salim entertained the family playing his *oud*, singing his original romantic songs of love. Alexander savored them even more having met the girl Salim intended to marry, and fantasizing about Madeleine. Evenings were devoted to family gatherings filled with singing, dining, and dancing. It was a joyous reunion for Alexander.

On Sunday, they all went to church together. That morning Alexander first met pretty, fair-haired, Syrian, English-fluent, 15-year-old, Helene Shaheen.

"*Ahlein*," spoke Alexander as he looked at the pretty, blue-eyed, shy teenager.

"*Ahlein*, hello," was her shy, smiling response to this handsome 18-year-old who had just arrived from the Lebanese mountains.

"He's kind of cute," Helene confided to her sisters later, "but he is dressed like a country bumpkin. He's okay, I guess. I do like his eyes. And he is nice."

Forgetting that Madeleine was just sixteen, Alexander later whispered to his uncle, "She's very nice, Salim, but she's so young. She's only fifteen years old, and I am on my way to Florida. I don't know when I will be back to Boston. Maybe a year. We will see. *Insha Allah*."

"I think Helene likes you, Iskandar," whispered Salim as they walked back home from church later that evening. "In fact, I think her whole family likes you. Of course, it helps that you are my nephew," he smiled, slapping Alexander on his shoulder. "And you're not ugly!" Sam laughed at his own joke.

"How could I be ugly and also be your nephew, Salim? Helene is pretty and nice. We shall see. There is a lot of work to be done before I can take care of someone else beside me. I have no money, no home, no job, nothing. I am not able to think about a serious relationship at this time. Besides…" he stopped himself before he spoke further about Madeleine. He realized even more that he must not now bring up the subject of Madeleine, Marseille, and his love experience. That would only go from Salim to Julia to Helene and to her parents. They wouldn't want to have anything to do with him if they learned of his liaison with Madeleine. So, reluctantly, he had to change the subject and not mention these things. But he constantly thought of that beautiful evening on the hill overlooking the Mediterranean Sea gazing down at Madeleine's lovely face as they lay on the soft grass…remembering how her beautiful, long hair caressed her shoulders and flowed onto the lush green grass around her head…remembering her passion as they made love. Too often, he caught himself rubbing her ring with his thumb as it circled the small finger on his right hand. He smiled for a moment…thinking… staring into space, remembering.

"Iskandar! You haven't heard a word I said. Where is your mind? You almost walked into that street corner lamppost! Are you blind?" Sam gripped Alexander's arm as he abruptly pulled him to his side. "Where are you, Iskandar?"

"Oh, Salim, I am so sorry. My mind was somewhere else. It's not important. I was just thinking," he replied with an embarrassed smile.

"Well, you had better look while you are thinking, my friend."

"You have electric lampposts here, don't you? In Beirut, they are still gas lamps."

"Well, Iskandar, it is 1920, isn't it? America advances very quickly. Look at all the electric trolleys full of people, and the automobiles. There are very few horse-drawn wagons near the city anymore. And now, we are nearly home. What do you think? Do you want to go to the picture show with us? It would be good for me. I cannot take Julia alone. If you go too, then Helene will go, and the four of us can have a good day. Julia told me that she would like to see the new Mary Pickford's film titled Pollyanna. Helene and Julia love the silent picture shows with the organ music accompaniment that makes them even more exciting!"

"What is a picture show, Salim?

"You'll see," Salim smiled "You and Helene have to go with us or we can't go, just the two of us in a dark theater! Maybe we'll stop for ice cream after. Would you like that?"

"What is ice cream, Salim?"

"Oh, Alexander, you have so much to learn about America. You will love ice cream. And you will love America!"

"Then let's get the girls so I can see a picture show, and taste ice cream!

After a full and tiring week in Boston visiting cousins, Abraham and Alexander boarded the train for Florida with their luggage, baskets of food for the journey, and two blankets. "*Allah ma'ak*, 'Brahim. *Allah ma'ak*, Iskandar. Come back soon. We will miss you!"

Uncle Mike, Uncle Salim, Julia, Helene, and at least a dozen cousins, aunts and uncles were at the train station that Monday morning as Alexander and his father stepped onto the metal steps leading up to the open air rail car that would be their temporary home via New York City, Atlanta, Tampa, and finally Kissimmee.

"All aboard!" the conductor yelled.

Work is to build a house with affection,
even as if your beloved were to dwell in that house...
Kahlil Gibran

CHAPTER 13

Kissimmee, Florida

The trip south to Kissimmee, Florida was long; yet, the sights were unbelievable to Alexander. "This is my new land. It is so different, so big, *Baba*," he exclaimed to his father sitting on the aisle seat next to him on the train's wooden bench. The 2,000 miles of cities, towns, and thick forests whizzed by. Traveling day and night, the train ride took nearly a week. Auntie Maha had packed a food basket for them, but after two days, most of the provisions were gone.

"*Baba*, it looks like we have eaten all the *kibbee*, *hummus* and *Baba ghanoush*," Iskandar said to his father after digging through the basket, pulling bags and bowls out, eagerly looking for more food. "I'm hungry, *Baba*."

"We'll be alright, son," Abraham replied. "I forgot you are a growing boy. At eighteen we eat much more than when we get older. I'll ask the conductor if there is food on the train and if there is a store at the next stop where we can purchase some provisions."

"Can we get food each day when we stop?"

"Yes, son, that's how I ate when I came to New York to meet you."

Luckily, the rail car wasn't full. "Northerners usually come south for the winter, Iskandar, not when it's hot in the summer. Looking around the car, he said that first evening, "We can each sleep on a bench. We'll use our coats for a pillow and the blankets we brought with us.

It was early summer, and a few flowering trees were still in bloom. Alexander marveled at the lushness of the rolling, wooded American countryside, its beauty, and the size of his New World. He stared out the window all day, everyday. The early summer weather was beautiful; cool air blew into the train through the open windows onto his face, blowing his hair to the side. Sometimes, Alexander would stretch his arms and head outside to feel the wind as the train moved along the tracks, "clickety-clack, clickety-clack," at twenty miles an hour. So fast, thought the young immigrant. His father, sitting beside him, watching Alexander's youthful enthusiasm, enjoyed the trip even more than he dreamed he would...because his son was with him.

Alexander told his father the story of the snowstorm on the mountain, Milhelm's rescue, Katrina's rubbing his feet with olive oil for many days, the villagers' suffering, the capture and release of Salim, the starvation, the locusts, the end of the war, and finally, the freedom under the French after the war. He wondered if he should ask the question he and Milhelm had asked themselves many times: "Why didn't you come for us sooner when *Imei* was still alive?" But he felt that it was too soon to ask and would be insulting and too painful for his father to discuss.

Abraham, in his deep, resonant voice, used all the evenings to tell his son of his life in America.

"I decided there would be more opportunity in the southern frontier of Florida, not Boston, which is industrial and most of our people work in the mills. It gets very cold there in the winter too. I preferred a smaller village and fewer people where it is warm much of the year. They say it is healthier there for many people who must leave the cold in the north because they suffer from consumption or pains in their bodies like arthritis. The winters are very mild and pleasant. I like it in Florida."

Wondering about his father's life, Alexander asked, "How did you find enough people to sell your goods? How did you do all this, *Biyee*? You had no family, no friends."

"It has not been easy, son. For several years, until only three years ago, every week, I rode the train eighty miles to Tampa and Tarpon Springs with my suitcase of notions our cousins in Boston sent to me. Then I walked back along the railroad tracks, selling at each house along the rail route, sometimes miles apart. It was exhausting and difficult because I could not speak English. I was embarrassed too much to speak."

Iskandar interrupted, "*Baba*, what is it you sold along the railroad? You called them notions. What are notions?"

"Ah, forgive me, my son. Notions is a word that describes many small things, like kerchiefs, sewing kits, needles, threads, buttons, garters for stockings, ribbons for ladies hair, earrings, things like that. I carried these things because they were not heavy and I could carry many of them. And, it took little amounts of money for my customers who were mostly women at their homes. They never had much money. Their husbands kept most of it, or put their pay in the banks. So, notions worked best for me. And it was easy for Uncle Mike to ship them to me."

He stopped for a moment, thinking, and continued with, "I still speak English badly. I wish I could sometimes speak to my customers in my native language, but there is no one here who will understand me. That's why it was so nice to be in Boston on this trip, so we could speak in Arabic. It was so easy," he smiled.

Then, thinking of the days behind him, wanting his son to know, he said, "I would open my suitcase to display my notions. When the people chose something they liked, I would show with my fingers the cost. Ten fingers was ten cents, one finger was one cent. As long as I sold something during the days I walked, I was happy. I always tried to make sure the people liked me. I am a large man speaking a foreign language, so I think I scared some of the children in the beginning. By trade, I am a stone mason, a home builder; I had to learn to be a salesman, and it is important to make sure everyone is comfortable with their purchases. I loved to dance, laugh, play cards and *towleh* back home. But, of course, it is not easy to do that here. Your sister's father-in-law is nice, but except for him, I am alone. I prefer to be with other people. In Kissimmee, I am sometimes called a 'gentle giant' because I am so friendly with everyone. I argue with no one, Iskandar. That is good advice, for we are strangers here. And some think of us as 'different.' That will be a new and maybe painful experience for you. It is a strange feeling to be thought of as different."

Then, he continued, "Some days I only sold enough to earn ten cents. The suitcase was heavy, but I had to do what I had to do. I had no money, but I believed in myself. I endured whatever I had to do to save enough money to bring you, your mother, and Milhelm to join me."

"I walked ninety miles each trip. It took me several days. And when it was dark, I slept on the tracks, using the rail as my pillow so I could hear if a train was coming. That way I wouldn't get lost. People were friendly, but since they couldn't understand my language, I could not sleep in their homes, or even on their porches. Of course there were no public rooms, and I had little money. Sometimes I sold my notions to the Indians near the swamps, and sometimes, the cattlemen would buy my goods. I slept in the village under a house many times to stay warm in the winter, and to be safe. But, of course, there were animals everywhere, and mosquitoes. My God, the mosquitoes were so thick that I had to cover myself with rags." Gesturing with his hands, he exclaimed, "Sometimes I had to chase a snake from my sleeping area."

Alexander listened intently to the stories with respect and wonder. He felt sad as he listened to his father's sacrifice and hardships. It seemed to him that his father's life was much more difficult here than it would have been in Lebanon.

"*Biyee*, did it ever get better for you?" he asked.

His father explained, "When the war in Europe grew to involve America two years ago, I could not go back to Lebanon, but business got better; so much was needed. In 1916, during the war, I used my savings to buy a house in Kissimmee for $400. I paid for it over the years. I added a few rooms on the second floor, and that's where we will live. It is a good home situated near the railroad, an excellent location. I opened my store on the first floor at the street and named it A. Thomas

Company. Maybe now I will change the name to A. Thomas and Son. What do you think?" he asked his bewildered son, rhetorically.

"Before the war ended," he continued, "I purchased another building, then another, and I now have three buildings. I rent and collect money from my tenants. That is an important lesson, Iskandar. Save your money and buy land. I choose not to give my earnings to the bankers. This way, I can see and touch what I own. Money does not come easily. I also own a vacant parcel of land where I bury my extra money. They call it 'banking in the field.' It is safe there because no one knows where it is. Soon I will show you."

Alexander listened carefully to his father's words, feeling enormous pride at what his father had accomplished under incredibly difficult conditions, taking them all in, and thinking eagerly how to begin his new life in America.

Abraham continued his counsel in Arabic, "It was only this year that I saved enough money to send for you and Milhelm. I can never forgive myself for not finding a way to send earlier for you boys and your mother, Iskandar. My son, for several years it was almost too difficult for me. I nearly went back to Boston to be with family. I am not a young man anymore, and I had hoped I would be able to send for you, Milhelm and your mother much, much sooner, but it was not possible.

"I was heartbroken when I received word from Elias that your mother, my beloved Katrina had died. I could not eat for days. I cried alone in my shack, missing all of you. Only later did I learn of the famine, the horrible locusts, the war, and those terrible Turks. I had no way of knowing what was happening to you and everyone in Douma during those days. Very few in Douma are accustomed to writing letters. Even so, there was nothing I could do. I felt so helpless. It was so painful and lonely for me." Pausing, he looked up and continued, "God helped me through those terrible days. And now you are here with me. But not Milhelm. When will I see Milhelm again?" Looking up, he sighed, "Only God knows."

Abraham and his son grew closer during the trip. There was so much to say, so much to describe. They talked late into each night, sometimes sleeping with their heads resting against each other, snoring together or listening to the snores of the other passengers. There were many stops along the way to their final destination of Tampa...Philadelphia, Charlotte, Atlanta, and Jacksonville.

"*Baba*, sometimes the other passengers stare at us."

"My son, they don't understand what we are saying. We're speaking in a foreign language. But they mean us no harm. After all, I don't understand most of what they say."

"It's the children who come and stare at us that make me uncomfortable, *Baba*. There are so many running down the aisle, yelling sometimes."

"Well, we will be at the next stop soon, *Biyee*," Ibrahim replied, calling his son the same as Iskandar called him, part of their culture, "and since it will be Charlotte, North Carolina, a large city, we can get more food and we can bathe and rest for a few hours. Maybe we can look around so you can see the city. Would you like that?"

"Last stop, Tampa!" yelled the conductor. "Time to get off, Mr. Thomas." He shook Abraham's shoulder to awaken the man and his son.

Abraham wiped his face, leaned back, stretched, and looked out the window. He spoke to Alexander who was just waking up a bit uncomfortably to the warmth and humidity of coastal west Florida.

"There is a large Greek community near Tampa, my son, called Tarpon Springs where we can get a room at the Inn. They have good places to eat, and a fine orthodox church we can attend. The Greeks are known for their large fishing fleet. They dive for sponges here and are the best sponge divers in the offshore waters. Tampa is a much bigger city than Kissimmee, with a busy port where large ships come from all over. There are many Cubans there. Cattlemen from Kissimmee, Bartow, and other towns near where I live, drive their herds here to Tampa, and ship their cattle to the markets in Cuba."

Getting off the train with their bags, Alexander eagerly looked around, fascinated by the sights, and the strange mixture of languages spoken — Spanish, Greek, English. He smiled at the newness, the unfamiliar, not understanding a single thing. His father pointed the way, saying, "It has been a long, tiresome journey, *Biyee*. Let us go find something to eat at a restaurant I know."

They arrived at the Aegean Sea Restaurant owned and operated by Stanos Demetriades and his wife Lydia, Greek immigrants and friends.

"Ah, Stanos!" exclaimed Abraham. "Meet my son, Iskandar. He has just arrived."

Stanos, setting the table near the front door, wiped his hands on his white apron, smiled and extended his hand. "Well, Iskandar, we have been waiting for you. Your father speaks of you all the time. Welcome! You must call me Stanos, Iskandar."

Alexander, returning Stanos' welcoming smile, reached out to shake hands.

Abraham interjected, "And now that he is in America, his new name is Alexander."

"Then you are both welcome here, Iskandar and Alexander." He laughed at his own joke. "Come inside. I will set a place for you. We have many foods you may find familiar, perhaps just slightly different from in Lebanon, but very much the same. Would you like rolled grape leaves in olive oil? I know you will enjoy Lydia's baklavah!" he said, smiling.

After their early meal, Alexander, relishing the new sights and wanting to walk around, wandered along the dirt road where hundreds of round, light brown sponges hung in huge stretched nets to dry.

"They are beautiful, but so strange," commented Alexander. *What do they do with them?* he wondered. He was fascinated by his first view of the turquoise waters of the broad Gulf of Mexico, the sponge and fishing boats, and the nets strung out to dry.

"We will come back here often," Abraham said to Alexander. "They are just like we are. Greeks and Syrians eat the same food, dance the same, and attend the same church and pray the same. I feel at home here with Stanos and his family. They are our kind."

After his first night in Florida, Alexander and Abraham left Tampa early the next day, taking the train to Kissimmee, nearly three hours to the east. It was a warm, sunny day in May, but heavy, dark clouds were building in the south, signaling the start of the summer rainy season. Evaporation from the Everglades and swamps to the south created their seasonal cycle of pounding heavy rains, winds, and then, evaporation by the hot sun providing more clouds, then rainfall for the miles and miles of grassy pastures. And the cycle continues.

As Alexander rode the train eastward from Tampa, he spent most of the ride still gazing out the window, watching the flat grasslands and pine forests of Central Florida flash by him. Nothing he saw reminded him of anything he had ever seen in his entire life. It was all so different, so flat, so green. And the smells of the region, including cattle manure, and decaying swamps were so strange to him and obnoxious in places. Although the area was infested with mosquitoes and stinging horseflies, Alexander and his father were safe in the rail car as the wind passing him kept them at bay. Mile after mile was mostly piney woods, palmetto fields, grasslands, and, occasionally, swamp lands and a gently rolling, grassy countryside.

Iskandar commented, *"Biyee*, it feels humid here, more so than Boston and Douma. Why is that?"

"There are many swamps here, son, and lots of water areas. They and the frequent summer rains keep this area humid. It is dryer in the winter.

They could see thousands of small cattle grazing in the open pastures and men on horseback. "The men are rounding up the scattered cows," said Abraham. "This land is filled with cattle. There are so many, they say, that it is one of the largest producers of beef in America. We are in the middle of a new American frontier that has a wonderful future. People are moving here from the cold winters in the north. Already, since I came here in 1912, the population of Kissimmee has tripled! Yes, even here there were natives, "Indians" they call them, the first Americans."

As Alexander watched the open countryside pass by, he said aloud to his father, "What a great, large country. I want to find my destiny here. I will seize every opportunity to better myself. I am anxious, *Baba*, to get started, to fulfill my destiny of success, adventure, and wealth. I want to learn all I can from you. I don't ever want us to be poor again!" And, he added, "I want to prove to you how much I appreciate what you had to endure to save enough money to bring me to America."

"Iskandar, our faith is our destiny. You must believe that with God's guidance, it will come true. So, my son, believe it, have faith, and it will happen. But be patient, especially with yourself. It doesn't come easy. It requires hard work, very hard work. And you must be careful, for there are those who will try to take what you have."

"As I told you when you first arrived, I have arranged for you to be taught by a tutor so that you can learn the English language, to speak it well, to write it, and to learn to think in English. That way, you will have an easier life than mine. That is my hope, my dream for you. I do not want you to be embarrassed or feel like an outsider, different from the other people, as I have had to feel. This is very important, my son. Each generation must make it easier for the next, as you will do for your sons one day."

True to his nature, Alexander's head was full of emotional eagerness to get started. He felt like a young horse who wants to run across the field, yet is being held back.

Alexander felt his weight shift, leaning slightly forward as the train began to slow down, signaling the approach to the Kissimmee railway station. "Kissimmee!" shouted the conductor in his dark blue wool suit with a railroad badge on his breast, and small brimmed cap walking briskly down the center aisle of the passenger car. They could feel the train buckle and sway as the arched steel brakes began to press against the smooth steel wheels. The train finally stopped abruptly in the middle of Broadway, the town's main street. Shops with wooden sidewalks lined this busy dirt street, the main access to the world, the railroad running down the middle. Broadway became the major commerce center of the region, especially serving the cattle industry, its employees, the railroad west to Tampa and then to the north, and the cargo barges south from Kissimmee to Fort Myers in southwestern Florida.

Abraham, still speaking in Arabic, looked at his son and said, "We must leave the train now. We'll go to our store over there."

Alexander liked the sound of "our store." As they reached the end of the car and stepped down onto the dirt road, Alexander turned his head and looked back at the railroad car and smiled. He rubbed her ring on his small finger, silently imagining she heard him announce his arrival in Florida…America. He whispered to no one, "I am here, Madeleine. I am fine and soon I will come for you."

*You work that you may keep pace with the earth
and the soul of the earth...*
Kahlil Gibran

CHAPTER 14

1920, Abraham, the Rail Peddler

By 1920, Kissimmee was an active frontier cattle town located in Central Florida on the north shore of huge Lake Tohopekaliga, which fed into the Kissimmee River, a majestic winding, well-flowing, wide river that meandered southward across the flatlands, through hundreds of thousands of acres of pastureland and piney woods, to Lake Okeechobee to the Caloosahatchee River, southwest to Fort Myers, finally emptying into the Gulf of Mexico. At the city's lake shoreline, busy docks sported supplies brought in by small steamboats up from the Gulf of Mexico. Because of its location, Kissimmee was one of the busier Florida towns of the late 1800's and early 1900's. Henry Plant, a former Standard Oil partner, brought his railroad from Jacksonville to Tampa with a spur to Kissimmee by 1883, at least ten years before Henry Flagler, a fellow Standard Oil executive, under the same franchise agreement with the state of Florida built his rail line south from Jacksonville along the east coast to Palm Beach and, later, Miami and the Keys.

When Abraham Thomé-Thomas Chalhoub, Alexander's father, arrived in Kissimmee in 1912, he found an area in transition from a single dirt road, remote frontier cattle village to a town with promise of better things to come.

In 1920, Broadway, a vibrant commercial dirt street, was lined on both sides with mostly two-story red brick or earth tone stucco shops with apartments above, some with a boardwalk or porch jutting below. Occasional wood framed clapboard single story homes and white pinewood frame two-story buildings with shops dotted the street. Plant Railroad tracks ran down the middle of the street. The present population of 2,700, nearly three times that of Douma, promised to grow more.

Cattlemen dominated the area since the early 1800s. Most of the Kissimmee families relocated from the southern states of Georgia, the Carolinas, Tennessee, and Alabama after the Civil War. Deep-seated Southern traditions and prejudices persisted since most of North Florida, "Dixie" in culture, consisted of cotton plantations, and pine forests still dominated by stubborn slave owners. With loyalties seeded in the Confederacy, Federal troops continued to occupy Florida's northern tier after the Civil War. Segregation remained unchanged.

"I like the size of our small village," Abraham pointed out to his son as they walked along earthen Broadway toward his shop. "Most of the people are friendly," he smiled, recalling a few faces, "yet, I must say, a few are not very tolerant of newcomers, Alexander, especially of new immigrants like us." Lines appeared on his forehead as he recognized two of those unfriendly "locals" riding horses just ahead. "Watch out for some of those rough young men on their horses, Alexander. They can be rude and insulting. But," he admonished, "try to avoid trouble. This is their country, and we are new here. We must find a way to get along with everyone."

"It looks nice, *Baba*, but where is the *souk*?"

"This is the *souk*, Iskandar, all of Broadway is the *souk* here. The shopkeepers are good people too, like in Douma."

During the eight years when Alexander grew from a boy of ten to a man of eighteen in Douma, Abraham worked in the Kissimmee area, first as a very poor, itinerant rail peddler, now as a small vendor-shopkeeper. These experiences had humbled him. And while he was not intimidated by the rough and wild cattlemen who descended on this cattle town on weekends at the end of their cattle drives, he found his life more pleasant by staying away from them.

"Son," Abraham said to Iskandar the morning after his arrival as they sat together at the small table in their bare kitchen, "it is best to live in the village. I'm sure there are some good cattlemen, but some are biased against outsiders. Let me tell you of one bad experience with cattlemen. Early one morning I took the train to Tampa, my suitcase filled with notions, and as I walked back, I sold my wares first at the houses of people who knew me by then. After, I began the long walk for several miles across the wide pastureland filled with cattle and few houses. As I walked, two young cattlemen…actually, boys younger than you…raced toward me on horseback. As one steered his horse up against me, he yelled, 'Get out of here, you foreigner! We don't want you here!' The other steered his horse close and snatched my suitcase, opened it and dumped all my goods on the ground.

"I got angry and almost grabbed one of them, but the other pulled his whip and struck me across my head and back. It hurt — a lot — making me very angry! But when I saw the other boy pull his pistol from his holster, I stopped. I knew he would kill me if I fought back. Although I was upset and afraid, I remembered why I was working so hard at everything — so I could bring you, Milhelm, and your mother here. At that moment, I feared all was lost."

"But what could you do, *Baba*? You were all alone!" Iskandar, inhaled, showing concern.

Abraham continued, "Just then I heard another cattleman racing toward me. He fired his gun. I thought I would surely die. But the new cattleman was older.

He rode right up to the three of us, shouting to the two younger ones, 'Leave the man alone!' He took out his whip and whipped the boy who whipped me, yelling, 'How does that feel, you son of a bitch?' To the other boy, he ordered, 'Put your gun away! Now both of you get out of here and get back to your jobs!'

"After they rode away, the older cattleman got off his horse, helped me up and looked at my head and back. Then he helped me collect all my goods and repack my suitcase. That's when I realized there were bad and good cattlemen. So, son, be careful, especially of the younger ones.

"The next week it happened to me again. I got whipped by the young cattleman who treated me so bad before. I wanted to pull his whip and whip him. But he pulled his gun and aimed it at me. All because I'm different. He warned me to leave and not come back.

"That's when I began looking for a space in the village. The snakes and mosquitoes, and other animals, made my life on the railroad difficult and painful. I didn't want to have to deal with angry cattlemen too!"

"That's a story I won't forget, *Baba*. You really have suffered here, haven't you? This almost sounds worse than the Turks. Maybe it's not worth it."

"Son," Abraham said softly as they stood in the doorway of the store and watched the cattlemen herding their cattle down Broadway, "Big John Sommerland, who owns a big ranch here, told me everyone in America came from somewhere else. First, he said, were the Spanish. Then the English came, then Scots, French, and Germans. I know the Syrians and Lebanese began coming to America in the 1850s. Of course, most of us didn't know exactly where America was, but once we got here, we loved the freedom to come and go. And," he added quickly, "many of the people that came years before us don't want any more immigrants. They want America to stay as it is. That is why they have a quota on immigrants allowed in the country. And that is why many Syrians, Lebanese, Greeks, Italians and others had to go to South America and Canada. We were lucky. Still, there are those who forget their families came here from somewhere else too!"

"I don't know what life is like in South America, *Biyee*, but I am very happy you and I were allowed into The United States! It's the freest and best nation on earth, in spite of those who are prejudiced against us! We will eventually be accepted just like everyone else."

Abraham paused and took a sip of his coffee.

"It takes time and many experiences, both good and bad. Iskandar, as you already know, bad things happen in this life. There's no way to avoid all of them. The important thing is how you respond to them. You must always be determined, yet kind. Be your own person. Of course," he added with a smile, you can be your own person after I, your father, have taught you more lessons. You are still young and innocent of the difficult new world you find yourself in.

"Iskandar, when I came here, there were mosquitoes and stinging flies everywhere. Some ladies wrapped their arms in rags soaked in kerosene to keep the mosquitoes and other stinging flies off them. One customer told me one day, as she was fanning herself with a palmetto branch, that there were so many mosquitoes here, especially during the summer rainy season, that what we now call Orange County and Osceola County were one county long ago named Mosquito County! But, she told me, when tourists began coming here in the dry season during the winter, the state split Mosquito County into two new counties.

"We depend on tourists here, son. They help keep me in business. I will take you to the saloon that has Chief Osceola's death mask on display. He is a big tourist attraction here."

"Who is Chief Osceola?" Iskandar inquired.

"He was an Indian chief who played a major role in the Seminole Indian Wars. He was actually born Billy Powell because his father was white and his mother of mixed race, but mostly Indian. He chose an Indian name when the whites tried to take the Indian lands. He was finally captured and died while in prison. He was very famous here.

"Cattle ranching is also big business in Central Florida and Kissimmee is best known as a cattle town. Besides the tourists, the cowboys are my biggest customers. I've done a little research about the area hoping to understand the people better. I found out that in 1884, only thirty-six years ago, Florida's Governor Bloxham contracted with Philadelphia heir Hamilton Disston to drain the swampland of central and southwest Florida, including making the waters navigable from Kissimmee to the Gulf of Mexico in exchange for an option to buy four million acres for twenty-five cents per acre. Disston's goals included draining much of the land to attract new settlers and farmers to Southwest Florida to buy his lands at a handsome profit. The region of Central Florida is second only to Texas in cattle production because of its enormous, uninhabited pasturelands and plentiful lakes. Thousands of these wild, roaming cattle are mostly descended from the small, spindly Spanish cattle deposited hundreds of years ago in St. Augustine on the northeast coast of Florida. More than one hundred years later, Hernando De Soto, a Spanish explorer and conquistador also left cattle and hogs in the mid-1500s when he landed in the Tampa area. Since the mid-1800s, they've been tended by rugged cowmen all over the vast open range of Central Florida. It was a hard, but adventurous way of life for these men, most of them around your age. And those were the only jobs available to them after the war. Few older men beyond their forties could endure the hardships, and usually quit, returning to a more sedentary life.

"Son, there are people here like Mr. Sommerland, a tough, weathered man, yet very kind to me. He will treat you fairly. He is a good man. Just be careful who you choose as your friends. Work hard, never quit, never give up, and don't worry. He told me it would be wise to buy land, and so, I think in time I will do more of that. He is very different from the young cattlemen who have not yet learned the responsibilities and lessons of life.

"Big John Sommerland came into my store one rainy day, and we talked for several hours. He is among the largest, most successful and most respected ranchers around here. He owns more than 160,000 acres of open lands part palmetto, huge groves of thick pine trees, and part grasslands and 16,000 head of cattle. He told me that because of so much palmetto, wetlands and pine forests, he can raise only one head for each ten acres."

"One hundred and sixty thousand acres? *Baba*, how many hectares would that be? I'll bet he owns as much land as all of Lebanon! He is really like a king, isn't he? And he owns 16,000 cows? That's more than Lebanon and Syria's combined. I want to see this man!"

"That would be over six thousand hectares. Alexander, I learned much about this region from Big John. There are opposing views here among the people just as there are in Lebanon. However, the Lebanese have religious differences, and here, the differences are because of the strong feelings between people of the North, the Yankees, against people of the South, the Confederates, all a result of a war during the 1860s between the northern and the southern states, which included northern Florida. The use of slaves on the plantations in the South was a major cause of the war."

"That's very sad and complicated, *Baba*, but to outsiders, Lebanon's religious differences, mostly between Christians in the north and Muslims in the south, would seem complicated too."

"Oh it's complicated alright. Kissimmee and this area were mostly a Southern culture until nearby St. Cloud on "Little Lake Tohopekaliga," only five miles away, was settled by retired Yankee Civil War veterans from places like Illinois, Ohio and Michigan. This created sharp and interesting contrasts between the citizens' behavior of both neighboring communities. While they tried to get along, they each have their loyalties and do not really mix."

Because of the Confederate heritage of most cattlemen and their cowmen, rarely, if ever, did the major ranchers of Central Florida ship their cattle to northern markets, preferring Cuban markets to the Yankees. After the end of the Civil War in 1865, during the years of Reconstruction, and for years after, there was still a lot of simmering anger and frustration over the abusive Federal occupation during those Reconstruction years.

"Big John told me that for decades, the cowmen continued to be free spirits, living on the range, branding, herding and moving the cattle. Today, their cattle drives end in Kissimmee as they herd hundreds of cattle down Broadway to the rail yards and river wharfs for loading and shipment. They ride into town on their horses pistols on their hips, rifles in their saddle holsters, lariats and leather whips tied to their saddle, and horn, and spurs on their boot heels and remain in town to have raucous fun in the hotels, brothels, and saloons late into the night. Sometimes, son, those cattlemen get very drunk, shoot into the sky, yell into the night, and frighten everyone with their fights and shooting their guns."

One day, Abraham took Alexander across the street to the hotel and bought him lunch in its restaurant. They sat at a table for four, and talked together. There were others in the room at nearby tables, and although they didn't understand what Abraham said, they found him and Iskandar interesting to watch. As Abraham began telling his son about the importance of the three economic engines of Central Florida, tourism, cattle and citrus growing, he expressed his belief that they all would grow significantly over the years. The two men at the table nearby recognized Abraham, came over, said hello, asked if they could join them, and sat down when Abraham gestured to the two empty chairs.

One man spoke slowly in English to Abraham, "I know you. My wife shops in your store, Mr. Thomas. I don't understand your language, Arabic, but my friend here from Philadelphia studied French in school. Do you speak French?"

"*Parlez-vous Français?*" asked Iskandar eagerly of the other man.

"*Oui,*" he replied with a friendly smile.

This made Iskandar smile too.

For the next hour, the four men conversed alternately in Arabic, French, and English, laughing sometimes at their errors and at how long it took to get an answer back in the correct language. With a lot of patience and effort, Iskandar learned a great deal about this new area that was now his home.

By the 1920s, the growing number of automobiles were hitting so many free-roaming cattle on the expanding roadway system of the region that "No Cows on the Roads" became the cause, since drivers were liable to have to pay for or replace the "prime" bull or cow the cattleman would claim had been killed. Even so, the cattlemen continued to drive hundreds of herds of cattle right down the middle of Broadway to bring them either to the rail spur for loading and transporting to the port in Tampa, or to the boat docks for shipment south to Cuba via the Kissimmee and Caloosahatchee Rivers to Ft. Myers., And, just like the other store keepers, Iskandar and his father stood in front of their shop on the wooden sidewalk to watch the horsemen move their herds down the center of Kissimmee's commercial main street. They created excitement, activity, and enormous amounts of flying dirt and strong odors of wild cattle and their "droppings."

Watching these cattle drives come down Broadway, smelling the cattle and their droppings as they were herded to the wharfs or the stockade at the rail terminal readied for shipment, and watching the cattlemen drive them, using their whips, yelling and whistling, were all new sights, smells and sounds for Alexander.

One Saturday night, Alexander watched from his father's shop as the younger cattlemen, weary from their cattle drive to the village, sought relief with whiskey and women, their desired recreation.

Alexander's attention turned to one very noisy, drunken group who were angrily bumping into each other as they left the bar, some staggering. A fight started in front of the A. Thomas and Son store. He wandered out into the street, curious to see what would happen. His slingshot was tucked in his pant pocket, garters on his white shirtsleeves, very different in dress from these cowboys but of the same age. A couple of the men turned to watch him venture toward the growing crowd. Ibrahim, looking out the store entrance, realized that a dangerous situation could quickly erupt and his naïve storekeeper son might be an easy target and fun diversion for the jeering cattlemen.

Just then, one of the young cattlemen, staggering from his liquor consumption, spotted Alexander in his foreign looking clothes, drew his whip, and, wanting to scare Alexander, cracked his whip within inches of his arm as Alexander turned to walk back to his store. Alexander's eyes went wide in anger as he spun around and grabbed the end of the whip. He had been toughened throughout his young life and wasn't about to tolerate an attack like those the Turks administered. He pulled the whip hard, bringing the unbalanced cowman to the ground. Then, tossing the whip down, he started to return to his store just as Big John Sommerland picked up the cowman, hit him in the face, and shoved him back into the crowd where he fell again.

"Sorry about that, Mr. Thomas," Big John yelled to Alexander and Abraham, "It won't happen again."

Alexander, bowed slightly toward Big John in thanks, then reentered the store for the night to avoid anymore problems and keep away from the fray. Just in time.

"I sez she's mine, Curly, now git!" one cowboy slurred as he shoved another man in the chest.

"Naw, I ain't leavin', Moe" he yelled back and stumbled forward as he drank greedily from his whiskey bottle.

"Yer leavin' and yer leavin' now!" Curly pulled his whip from his belt and struck the other cattleman across his back and arm, knocking the whiskey bottle out of his rival's hand.

"Now you've done it!" Moe yelled as he pulled his pistol, aimed it shakily at his adversary, and fired a shot, just missing his arm.

"Stop it, you idiots! Stop it!" yelled Big John as he drew his whip and struck the pistol out of Moe's hand. "Now either you both git, or I'll whip both your asses. We ain't havin' no shootin' here in Kissimmee. Y'hear? Now git! If you can't hold your liquor you don't deserve any woman. Y'hear?"

"Oh, alright, Big John," Curly replied, lowering his head, "yer right."

Moe joined in, "Ah'm sorry, Big John. Maybe we got carried away."

Then, like contrite little boys, out of respect and fear of Big John, they shook hands, realizing that was the only way Big John Sommerland would let them stay at the bar.

"Alright then," said Big John, "gimme your whips and guns. I'll keep 'em until we leave town Monday morning."

By 1922, hundreds of new visitors and settlers began to heavily invest in Florida land, significantly driving up prices. The "Roaring Twenties," introduced a period of easy money and the start of the Florida Land Boom. More and more settlers crowded into St. Cloud. At auction in New Jersey, for $50 they could buy a downtown lot, plus an option on the adjacent lot, and a five-acre parcel in the country. By 1925, those $50 lots and five acres unbelievably were worth over $10,000. Yankees were eager to flee the harsh winters in the north in hopes life could be easier, and they would overcome their "consumption" as their doctors described the various bronchial diseases, and many bought land with dreams of becoming rich.

"Iskandar," Abraham called as they worked the store's inventory, keeping themselves busy moving their wares around, presenting fresh items to their customers each day, "you will see in time, as the winter approaches, that newcomers and what they call tourists will add to the numbers in Kissimmee. It is like that in Douma, when Beirutis come to the cool mountains during the summer. And more and more come each year. The winter months are best for us in our business.

"But, son, you should also know that many are moving here to get away from their harsh winters because they are sick, and we must not get too close to them, yet we must always be kind and pleasant, for life is hard when you suffer from illness. Maybe today, Mrs. Willingham could come in. She always stops by on Fridays. Her husband is in bed at home. She said he has something called consumption. I think it's in his lungs. He coughs all the time, she tells me. It's too bad we don't have the flowers of Douma's mountains your mother gathered. She made a tea of seventeen different flowers whenever I got sick and coughed. It always cured me. *Allah y'rahamrah*. May she rest in peace."

"*Imei* did so much for all of us, didn't she, *Baba*?"

"Yes, my son, and I am sad now just thinking about her. She was and remains my only, most important love in my life. How I miss her so much."

Tears welled in the eyes of both father and son as they spontaneously sought refuge in an embrace.

"Life is good, son. But sometimes it can be very, very difficult, especially for immigrants, to continue. But we must always persevere, for to stop in sadness or self-pity is to dishonor your mother and our family."

Turning, he stepped to the front door and welcomed two well-dressed ladies glancing inside.

"Good morning, ladies," he smiled, offering a slight bow of welcome

"And good morning to you, Mr. Thomas."

"You are here early this year."

"Yes, we are," one replied. "Our husbands have decided to buy some land in Florida. Everyone in Chicago is talking about all the opportunities for investing here. Our husbands bought lots in St. Cloud last year, and already we've gotten an offer of 100% more! Can you believe it?"

The other woman spoke up, "It's so cold in Chicago during the winter, we'd rather be here, and so many people want to invest in Florida, our husbands say they want to get into the land ownership business early as possible. They're pretty smart, aren't they?"

"Do you think land prices will continue to rise, Mr. Thomas?" asked her friend. "We surely hope they do!"

"If I was a rich man, ladies, that is exactly what I would do. How long they will continue to increase is anyone's guess, but as long as people keep coming down here for more than just a short vacation, the more houses and land will be needed."

"We understand some people from upstate New York have already bought a large tract south of here. My husband told us they want to call it Lake Placid after their hometown where people go to ski in the winter. Have you heard that, Mr. Thomas?"

"No, I haven't, Madame, but I wouldn't be surprised. There have been a lot of new faces in town this year. They seem to be looking around for land to buy."

And in the sweetness of friendship
let there be laughter and sharing of pleasures…
Kahlil Gibran

CHAPTER 15

Wilbur McCray, Cowman

"Come, Iskandar, it is late. I am sure you are hungry." His father was standing in the bedroom doorway, relishing his son's presence after so many years of living alone. "You slept well, son. It is morning now. Come be with me. You were very tired from your long trip so I let you rest. Let us eat, *Baba*."

He rubbed his eyes with his hands and replied, "Huh? Uh, yes, *Biyee*, of course. It's time to begin my first full day of my new life." He pulled on his pants and buttoned them, pulled on his white, full-sleeved shirt, stretched his suspenders, and buttoned his sleeves at the wrists. Then, he stepped into his only pair of leather shoes. He washed his face in the porcelain commode, and joined his father in the modest kitchen.

"Sit down, son. I have bread, cheese, olives, and yogurt from Stanos. I don't know how Americans can start the day without *jibneh*, *zeytoon*, and laban," he smiled. "After breakfast, we will go to the store."

Alexander looked around his father's plain, yet functional shop, studying the shelves along the white plastered walls layered with notions and stacks of bedding and towels, and the bolts of cloth on the tables in the middle of the store. He noted that the pine wood floor and ceiling matched. Sparse lighting fixtures hung from the high ceiling. Multi-colored candies in glass containers brightened the counter near the front door where the store's books and a hand cranked cash register containing the money collected from the shoppers before they left the store.

Within an hour of their arrival that morning, an attractive middle-aged woman entered the store. Her long cotton print dress with a full skirt flowing to her ankles, and long, full sleeves emphasized her height. She pulled her brown hair up under a cloth bonnet with a large brim in the front to protect her eyes from the bright Florida sun. Early June in Central Florida, already very warm and humid, announced the departure of the last of the winter tourists who returned to their homes in the North. Kissimmee was left to its year-round residents, cattlemen, farmers, and a few new emboldened settlers.

Once inside the store, she folded her parasol. "My, Mr. Thomas, it surely is getting warm these days," she exclaimed, smiling as she fanned her face with a paper accordion fan. As she folded up her fan and slipped it in her satchel, she asked, "Do you have new goods from your trip?" She stood in the middle of the small store by a table laden with bolts of various fabrics, lifting the bolts with one hand, while holding the hand of her child in the other. "You promised me you would be bringing a surprise with you. What do you have for us?"

"My son is my surprise, Mrs. Andrews," said Abraham, smiling, speaking in his broken, heavily accented English and gesturing toward Alexander. "He just arrived with me from New York." Holding up three fingers, he said, "Three months from our village in Lebanon to Kissimmee. And, I have new goods for you to see. In a few minutes I will have them ready for you to see."

He turned to Alexander, motioning with his hand and speaking to Alexander in Arabic, "Iskandar, help me with these rolls of fabric and these boxes."

Alexander welcomed the opportunity to do something. He could only stand and watch all the time as his father conversed, ever so clumsily with his limited English, thinking, I have got to learn to speak their language here, and very soon.

After Mrs. Andrews viewed the goods and selected several yards of the new cotton cloth from one of the bolts, she reached across the counter to pay Abraham. "It's nice you are back, Mr. Thomas," she smiled warmly. "I will tell my friends of your new lovely things." Looking at Alexander, she said, "And I am sure your son will be popular here, especially with the young ladies." She whispered as she bent toward him, "My, he certainly is handsome! Bless you, Mr. Thomas. Perhaps we will see you both in church on Sunday?"

"We will do our best, Mrs. Andrews. Thank you," he smiled, almost saying, *Shookrun*, as he watched her walk to the door.

Mrs. Andrews stopped and turned back to speak over her shoulder after considering Alexander, "Oh! I nearly forgot. I looked into finding a proper tutor for your son, Mr. Thomas. I believe I have someone who would be perfect," she exclaimed, keeping her small daughter in tow, while glancing at Alexander across the store. Then, smiling, she said, "Abigail Sommerland has returned for the summer from FSWC, you know, the Florida State Women's College. It's in Tallahassee."

Abraham turned and spoke in Arabic to his son, "Tallahassee, another Indian name, is where the government is located, in the north. It is also where young women go to the university.

"I was just telling Alexander what you said, Mrs. Andrews. Please continue," he encouraged her, waving his hand in a cupping motion.

"Well," she responded, enthusiastically, "I'm sure Mrs. Sommerland has shopped here, and I believe you have met Abigail's father. He's known as Big John, a very important man in this entire region. He's a good man and his family is very well thought of all over this area. Oh! I nearly forgot to tell you, she continued, "Abigail has been studying French and Home Economics at the college for three years and just arrived last week. Next year she will graduate and receive her Bachelor of Science degree. She's very smart; she makes all her own clothing, teaches cooking, and home bookkeeping. I am certain she will be very good at teaching English to young Alexander. Since she knows Florida so well, perhaps she can also teach him about our cattle country and citrus industry, so he can learn about our ways in Florida and America. She can ride a horse as well as anyone too! Does Alexander ride a horse?"

Abraham, watching her lips while trying to understand all she said, listened intently. It was difficult, but Mrs. Andrews had learned over the years to speak slowly to Abraham.

"Well, Mrs. Andrews," said Abraham as he struggled with his English, "I have not seen Iskandar, uh, Alexander since he was ten years old, but he cared for the goat herds, and I am certain he can ride a horse. He was always adventurous. I do know that he was good in mathematics in school, and I am sure he will be a good student in English.

"I assumed his tutor would be an older woman or man, not a young girl, but she sounds well qualified and it is fortunate she studied French also, because Alexander speaks fluent French, Mrs. Andrews. Please tell Miss Sommerland that Alexander is eager to learn, and will be ready to meet with her as soon as possible. I am prepared to pay her what you asked, five lessons for five dollars each week. Thank you, Mrs. Andrews," Abraham confirmed as he bent at the waist in sincere respect.

"Perhaps, if you both come to church on the Sabbath, you will meet Miss Sommerland. Would you like that, Alexander?"

Not understanding a single word of the conversation, and too embarrassed to say anything, Alexander simply smiled and nodded his head at Mrs. Andrews as he watched her speak to Abraham, nodding to him while walking to the door.

"Sunday then. Good day, Mr. Thomas."

Turning to his father, Alexander said, in his native Arabic, "*Biyee*, I am useless without understanding what people say. I want to learn English as quickly as possible. It is so embarrassing, so strange. I feel like I'm not even part of the world here."

"You will be tutored this summer and begin attending the town school in a few months."

Near sunset, at the end of his first bewildering day, Alexander went upstairs with his father to his own almost barren room, and finally unpacked his meager personal belongings: an extra shirt and pants, a gift for his father of a carved piece of cedar wood from an ancient tree near the village, the mountain stone in his pocket, and his treasured sling from his suitcase. He delicately grasped the sling, pulled each of the two strands of leather, each a meter in length tied to the leather pouch in the middle, and set them on the cabinet next to the stone. The small stone was his reminder of his village and his youth. His tasks completed, he lay down on his small bed. For the few minutes before he fell into deep sleep, he fondled his gold ring, the ring Madeleine gave him that night on the hill overlooking Marseille.

He dreamed and dreamed…of Madeleine.

One day, Alexander ventured out of the store to see his new surroundings. He decided to walk down Broadway to get more familiar with the town of Kissimmee. The sun, already casting its warmth, made everything bright. Lavender clouds hung low in the blue western sky, typical of the early summer mornings. Early in the morning, shopkeepers across Broadway opened their stores, swept their walks, and hoped for their first customers of the day. Kissimmee's main street buzzed with activity.

He crossed the street, careful for the noisy, unpredictable automobile traffic, and looked back at his father's store where he saw the name above. Although it said A. Thomas Company in large letters, and beneath the name it said: Dry Goods, Hats, Shoes and Notions, Alexander found the lettering totally foreign to him. Even though he could read French, it was too different for him to understand. Everything he smelled and witnessed seemed so foreign in this new place. No cousins, no mountains in the distance, and no cedar trees. Even though he felt a moment of melancholy, his emotions turned to excitement as he watched traffic, both auto and pedestrian along Broadway.

As he walked the streets and wooden sidewalks, all he could do was look around. He could see the frame buildings, often separated by vacant sandy lots and scattered pine trees. The two storied buildings featured overhanging roofs protecting the people on the sidewalks from sun or rain as they came and went. The women mostly acted friendly to him, although some did not make eye contact, and as the ladies walked past him, he could sense the pleasant fragrances of perfume and talcum powder. Their fragrant smell reminded him of Marseille and Madeleine. They wore ankle-length dresses, wide at the bottom, with long sleeves, formfitting at the waist, and high-neck collars, fashions different from Marseille, he noted. Some carried parasols to block the sun. A few would smile at Alexander, returning his happy smile with a friendly, "Hello." He then said to each, with a slight bow of his head, using his French, "*Bonjour*," or "*Allo*," as he began to overcome his shyness. Men slightly nodded their head or tipped their hat brims, most neither speaking nor smiling, but amicably acknowledging this unfamiliar young man. He began to feel better about his new home and the people he would get to know in time. His emotions took off as he felt a new spring in his step. Many of the men who didn't speak to him wore their business suits, high-necked shirts with starched collars, ties, and straw skimmer hats. Others wore overalls or jeans and work shirts.

After he had walked past the five blocks of buildings in the busy center of town, Alexander saw in the near distance a few scattered white wooden one- and two-story homes with sandy yards and shrubs surrounded by a few shade trees, but mostly pines around the downtown area. Open land spread between and beyond the houses, and in the far distance, cattle grazed on the lush grasses of the open pastures and in the piney woods. The strong pungent odor of the cattle pervaded the town, their droppings a clear message to him that there were hundreds of cattle everywhere in the area. He continued walking down the dirt road even further until it became a path of wagon wheel grooves in the dirt leading into the grassy open lands.

He walked into an unfenced pastureland near the trees marveling at its flatness, so open, such a big sky, enjoying the slight breeze brushing his face, unconcerned that his dark pants, suspenders and long-sleeved shirt identified him as a shopkeeper.

A man on horseback galloped toward him wearing high-heeled boots with spurs at the heels, blue faded jeans and shirt with a faded red kerchief around his neck, and a wide-brimmed, sweat-stained, felt Stetson hat atop his head. Alexander focused on the man's eyes as he got closer and closer. Then, too close. The large horse brushed against Alexander, knocking him down. As he got up, brushing off his pants, he glared at the rider. He noted the man's deeply suntanned face with his prominent, straight nose, the scar across his eyebrow and on his left cheek, the demeaning scowl on his lips, and his long dirty brown hair that emerged from behind the large-rimmed hat and fell down the back of his neck. He watched the rider turn the horse and walk him back to Alexander so that the horse's head bumped him. Alexander quickly reached to the bridle and tightly grabbed the reins, now taking control of the horse's movements.

"Hey, storekeep'," said the surly rider. "You're a little outside your place, ain't ya?"

The sneer on his face deepened the knife scar on his cheek. Alexander could only stare back at him. He refused to speak.

"Better git outta here, storekeep', before you git hurt. These cows will go anywhere. And so does my horse," he laughed at his lie. He jerked the reins but Alexander tightened his grip as the horse spun his head violently, Responding, Alexander's shoulder muscles tightened, keeping the horse's head down in spite of the rider's efforts. He glared at Alexander's strange clothes and haircut.

"This is the place for cowmen, not storekeepers. You don't belong here, you foreigner," he hissed. "Git off these pastures! Now! the cattleman said as he waved his arm, pointed back to town and dug his spurs into the sides of the horse, causing Alexander to lose his grip, this time brushing hard against Alexander. The horse leaped, and then the cattleman rode off, laughing as he looked back at Alexander to make sure the intruder was on his way. Alexander watched, befuddled, angered and startled at the cowman's unfriendly behavior. He thought about his sling in his pocket, but remembered his father's stories and advice. He took notice of the coiled black leather whip tied to the saddle, the black pistol and holster tied to the rider's right thigh with bullets in his gun belt. The horse had a brand on its hip: TJ.

Alexander watched the cowman ride away. The man certainly talked different, looked different, and, he supposed, because he lived on the range and rarely bathed, smelled different. He smelled like *khudda*, manure, Alexander smiled to himself. Still, he was struck by the strange aggressive nature and appearance of this man up close; the twang of his speech, so different from the others' he had heard speak in town. The whip. And the gun. He shrugged, angry, but under control, turned, and walked back to town.

"You've been gone sometime, where did you go, Iskandar?" asked his father in Arabic as he entered the store.

"I walked down the street and to where I saw those animals we saw on the train. Out that way," he replied, pointing. "I met a man on a horse who wasn't very friendly. He spoke differently than the people in the town, Father, and he smelled different, too."

His father laughed and his face became a broad smile. "They are with the animals all the time; some even become like the animals. They sleep with them in the fields. I don't know when they bathe, but to me, they smell like *khudda*. I'd forget him. Most everyone here are nice. Don't worry about him. They're just rough people."

Alexander laughed again remembering his own similar thought. "He smelled bad and he was not nice. He acted like he was a Turkish soldier," he replied to his father. "I saw he had a rifle, a whip, and wore a pistol on his hip. Do they really need guns here? Are there many bad animals around here?"

Abraham nodded and explained as best as he could, "There are some wild animals here and big poisonous snakes too. Actually, there are many kinds of animals — panther, foxes, deer, bears, cougars, and in the wet areas, there are even wild pigs and large alligators. Some are dangerous. So, guns are sometimes necessary for them, Iskandar. But, there are times when the young men drink too much and shoot their pistols while they race down the street. Sometimes, they even shoot their guns at each other. It can get dangerous. You have to be careful. Some of those men are crazy."

"Do I need one?"

"A gun? Not these days. If you stay in town, you will not need one. Certainly I do not want you to wear a gun on your hip in town."

"Well, I brought my sling. I think I will carry it with me, and even practice later out in the field. I'm pretty good with the sling. I'll show you.

"I was thinking, *Biyee*, it's so hot here, I wonder why the men wear tight-fitting, heavy clothes. Wouldn't they be more comfortable wearing the loose-fitting abeyeh gowns like men wear in Lebanon? And I bet a kifeyeh on their heads would be cooler than those hats too"

"Maybe they would be cooler," Abraham replied with a smile, "but I think the cowmen would rather be shot than wear what they would call a woman's dress. And the shopkeepers have their own European culture. So, my son, don't get any idea of wearing an abeyeh or kifeyeh either. You would be so different and they would make fun of you. It's a good idea, but not one for us to consider," he said, laughing, but maybe just a bit sad too.

He soon forgot about his encounter with the cowboy and styles of dress, as he had more important things to think about…like learning English.

During the next several days, from dawn until dark, Alexander diligently tended the shop with his father. Some slow days they stayed in the shop until late into the night waiting for one last purchaser, while constantly folding and refolding the cloths and rearranging their goods. When he got bored, he would venture into the fields and practice throwing his sling. He could swiftly hit a rodent from 50 feet without a sound except the soft whirring of the rotating pouch overhead. He always held one end of the thin leather lanyard in his right hand by pinching it with his largest right ring and small finger against the heel pad of his hand. He then would pinch the opposite end of the other thin lanyard between his index finger and his thumb. With a stone or marble in the small pouch in the middle of the two lanyards, he would then quickly whirl the pouch over his head three times, taking careful aim, and release the single lanyard between his index finger and thumb. The three feet of lanyards would reach a very high speed at release. The stone could actually kill small animals, like rodents, snakes or rabbits. It could even kill large animals like deer or pigs when it hit the animal's head. "It is the same sling David used against Goliath," he often boasted.

Alexander was expert with the sling and could probably beat another man with a gun if they competed. He hit his target every time.

Wilbur McCray, whose family came to America from Scotland during the 1700s, was a kind soul, a friendly, self-assured popular young man in his early twenties who had no problem bridging the cowman-shopkeeper cultural gap. "I want a life that lets me be me," he would say. "Free to ride the range, sleep under the stars, and someday have my own herd."

One Monday, Wilbur rode his horse up to the hitching rail in front of Abraham's store. While he was in the store looking around for kerchiefs, he suggested to Abraham, "Mr. Thomas, you should stock Stetson hats here. There are a lot of people who would buy them. Right now, we have to buy 'em way down in Polk

County in Bartow, because there's no place in Kissimmee to buy a new Stetson. I think you ought to try them."

"*Shookrun*, thank you, Mr. McCray, that's a good idea. I'll look into that and see if I can find a supplier."

Wilbur turned to Alexander, thinking they were about the same age. "Is this your son, Mr. Thomas?"

"Yes, his name is Iskandar, uh, Alexander, and he just arrived from Lebanon. He doesn't speak English yet, but he will."

"I've got some time. I'll show him around," he responded with a friendly smile. He was wearing a wide-brimmed felt hat, and jeans like the other cowman Alexander had run into, but his face was kinder. His hair was light brown, his face and hands tanned and, Alexander noticed, he also was wearing those same kind of spurs on his boots' heels and a gun belt on his waist with the pistol's holster tied to his right thigh.

Wilbur beckoned to Alexander, "Come on, Alexander. Let's ride."

In the days that followed, Wilbur would come by the store, wave to Alexander to come outside, hook his arm under Alexander's and swing him up onto the horse behind him. The two of them rode around the lakeshore into the open areas and into the piney woods around the town, sometimes at a gallop, sometimes just walking, passing the hot, lazy summer days with Wilbur McCray playing the friendly tour guide. He became a weekly visitor to the store and showed Alexander the area by the lake and river, the boats, and the docks. He rode Alexander into the cattle pastures and taught him many things of local life. For reasons that were simple, Wilbur liked making friends with young Alexander. His grandparents were immigrants too, and he was well aware of the difficulties Abraham and his own father had faced. He was happy to find a young man his age, a newcomer to Kissimmee who wasn't a cowman but looked strong. He soon became a good and reliable friend for Alexander who looked forward to his visits. Alexander watched everything, noticed everything, and listened as best he could, became familiar with the area because of Wilbur. Wilbur loved the freedom of the open range and sleeping under the stars. He was willing to share his life with this new immigrant who apparently had talents but needed a friend to find his way in this very unfamiliar country.

"Want me to show you how to handle a pistol, Alexander?" Wilbur said to his new friend, standing in the piney grove, showing his gun to Alexander. "Lemme show you how to aim it and hit that stump over there. Think you can do it?" he asked as he pointed to a rotting pine stump, then fired his gun. Alexander jumped; he hadn't heard that sound since the Turks. Alexander understood Wilbur's instructions just by his hand gestures.

After trying unsuccessfully several times to aim the gun, frustrated but still confident, Alexander pulled his sling out of his pocket, placed a stone in the pouch and after three fast turns over his head, let the stone fly in a blur. Smack! The stone drove into the stump.

"Wow! That was something, Alexander. You sure make that stone fly. How'd you do that so quick?"

Alexander just smiled and shrugged his shoulders. He really could understand so little of what people said to him. But his friendly smile seemed to be adequate, maybe infectious, at least for now. Even though his new friend was good to him, Alexander still felt embarrassed that he could not yet converse with Wilbur. Much of their "conversation" was through hand signals, not speaking.

Then, Wilbur pulled his coiled whip from his saddle strap and swung it over his head. With a quick jerk, the whip tip reversed on itself and made a loud report: CRACK! Alexander simply stood and watched as Wilbur cracked his whip several times. "That's how we get the cows to move out of the pine trees, Alexander. If you don't git a cow out of the pines, they'll just circle a tree for hours until you give up. That's why we all carry whips. And that's why they call us 'crackers'." He laughed at his own comment.

One afternoon, Alexander bought a few handfuls of marbles from the hardware store next door, put a handful in his pocket, and left a handful in a dish on his father's store's counter. When Wilbur came by, he was ready.

They rode Wilbur's horse out to the piney woods to the stump. With hand signals, Alexander challenged Wilbur to see who could hit the stump the fastest. With Wilbur's hand hanging by his hip ready to draw his gun, Alexander likewise held the lanyards of his sling beside his leg. "Go," said Wilbur as he reached for his gun. At the same moment, Alexander whirled the lanyard. The bullet struck the stump just as Alexander's marble reached the same stump.

"What the hell? How'd you do that?" exclaimed Wilbur. "Damn! You're fast!" He slapped his thigh and bent over with laughter.

All Alexander could do was smile as he placed another marble in the pouch of his sling.

*You would know in words
that which you have always known in thought...*
Kahlil Gibran

CHAPTER 16

Kissimmee - Abigail

The following Sunday morning, Abraham and his son walked three blocks to church, joining a number of others on their way, some carrying Bibles. Alexander was wearing his good white shirt buttoned up to his neck, and a new coat his father bought for him at Joe Willingham's Men's Store, his friend's shop on Broadway.

After the service, they made their way outside the church through the after-service gathering.

"Good morning, Mr. Thomas. Good morning, Alexander. I'm so glad to see you here at church. And isn't it a beautiful day? My, but it certainly is warm," Mrs. Andrews said as she fanned herself and dabbed her forehead with her white kerchief.

Alexander smiled and nodded in response. He noticed that Mrs. Andrews' dress looked as fashionable as some he saw in Madeleine's mother's shop. Her pretty "Sunday" dress featured a bodice decorated with delicate white lace, cuffs similar to her high-necked collar, and a skirt patterned in cornflower and pastel blue flowers that flowed to her ankles. A straw bonnet with a ribbon tied under her chin covered her hair. Scanning the faces of the exiting congregation, she turned, smiled broadly, and said, "Just a moment, I see Abigail Sommerland now." She stepped a few feet away and waved her hand while calling out, "Yoo-hoo, Abigail!"

Alexander watched as she made her way through the gathering to a very pretty, fair young lady with bright blonde hair who had briefly caught his eye in church as the only person in the congregation of his age. She wore same style of dress and bonnet as Mrs. Andrews, but was taller and more slender. He liked her smile as she focused on Mrs. Andrews's eyes while she politely listened. Suddenly, Abigail glanced over her shoulder at Alexander and smiled broadly, coquettishly tilting her head to him as she continued to listen to Mrs. Andrews. Uplifted by Abigail's acknowledgement of him, and attracted to her friendliness, Alexander returned her smile with a courteous European nod of his head. Mrs. Andrews, aware of the tacit reaction between Abigail and Alexander, pulled Abigail's hand and they both walked toward him and his father.

"Good morning, Mr. Thomas," Abigail spoke with a very sincere smile as she gracefully extended her hand to Abraham. Then, tilting her head toward his son in a slightly flirtatious manner, continued, "And you must be Alexander." She smiled again, extending her soft hand, palm down, looking into his eyes.

"*Bon matin, enchanté*," Alexander responded, in French, returning her smile.

Surprised and impressed, her interest piqued, Abigail responded with an even wider smile, "Oh my, you speak French. *Merci*."

Mrs. Andrews interjected with a smile, "Alexander, I am pleased to introduce you to Miss Abigail Sommerland. She has agreed to be your English tutor for the summer, until she returns for her senior year at Florida State School for Women in Tallahassee. Isn't that nice? It so happens that she has studied French there and that should be helpful to you both. Abigail is very popular in this county, and proven herself to be an excellent horsewoman as well. Why, I believe all the men in town stop what they are doing when she walks or rides by!"

"Shall I call you Alexander?" Abigail demurred softly in French, looking teasingly into Alexander's eyes, her voice reminding him of Madeleine.

"*Oui, Mademoiselle*," he replied, a bit nervous, but happy finally to be able to converse with someone, as he returned her smile, noting her large blue eyes with long lashes, and her face framed by long, wavy blonde hair that caught the sun's rays beautifully. Her high cheekbones gave her an exotic look.

"When can you begin?" she inquired. "Tomorrow?"

Seeing his father nod, he eagerly replied, "*Oui*."

"Early tomorrow then," she said. "It is cooler in the morning." Turning to Abraham, she queried, "Can he come to my home at nine o'clock, Mr. Thomas?"

Abraham responded, "Absolutely, Miss Sommerland, he will be there. He is very anxious to get started on his English lessons. He is a good student, and, I am sure, will progress rapidly, especially learning from you. You are very kind to do this for Alexander."

"It will be my pleasure, Mr. Thomas. He looks like a fine, young man, and will make a wonderful addition to our community. I am also sure the young ladies in Kissimmee will be happy to meet such a handsome young man. I will do my best." Then turning back to Alexander, she smiled directly at him and continued in French, "Soon you will be speaking excellent English. Tomorrow then, Alexander," "I will expect you at nine o'clock in the morning. You know my father's home, don't you, Mr. Thomas?"

"Yes, I do. I will show him today. And thank you, Mrs. Andrews," Abraham said, looking to his friend with a slight bow.

"*Au revoir, Mademoiselle*," smiled Alexander to Abigail as she, now flattered, stepped away with Mrs. Andrews, tickled to be spoken to in French by a handsome young man. Then, turning to Mrs. Andrews, Abigail whispered, "He's very charming, isn't he?"

As the women walked away, Abraham asked, "She is a very pretty, young woman, wouldn't you say, Alexander?"

"She's very nice," responded Alexander to his father in Arabic as he fondled his ring, remembering Madeleine's beautiful wide smile, longing to receive a letter from her.

After what seemed like hours of standing among others, uttering not a word, Alexander finally whispered to his father, *"Baba,* this has been a wonderful morning, but I am hungry. Can we go home now?" Alexander wanted to write a letter to Madeleine and anxiously looked forward to leaving the reception where everyone else but he was chatting with each other. It frustrated him just to watch in silence.

"Yes, my son, I'm glad you met your tutor. She's younger than I expected, but she seems to like you and is very smart I am told. You've met her father, Big John. Her mother is from a prominent, wealthy family in Philadelphia and she is very cultured socially, I am told by some customers. They say that Abigail, a tomboy in her youth, learned the finest social skills from her mother as she matured. She looks a lot like her mother."

Then, he added, "Son, I'm a bit tired, let's go home now. I think I'll take a nap after lunch."

"Maybe I'll do the same, *Baba,* but I want to write a letter to Milhelm and tell him how wonderful Americans are, especially in our village of Kissimmee."

As soon as they returned home, they ate lunch, sharing Syrian goat cheese, olives, tomatoes, bread and fruit, much like the midday diet in Douma. Afterward, Abraham quickly went to bed for a nap, and Alexander went straight to his small wooden desk in his bedroom and immediately began writing his letter, in French, to Madeleine:

> *My dearest Madeleine,*
>
> *How I miss having you in my arms. Today I went to church for the first time with my father. I met some wonderful people. They were very nice to me and I am really beginning to enjoy experiencing my new home. My father's store is good and I help him there. I am saving every penny so I can return to you. Everyday I think about you, remembering your beautiful face, your soft lips, and your voice. With love, it seems agony must come too, for I am in agony, my love. At night, I fondle your... our...ring as I lay awake, praying for you and for the day we will be together again.*
>
> *Have you received my letters yet? I look for yours everyday, but have not received any. Please, Madeleine, please write me soon. It would be wonderful to hear from you. Until then, know I love you with all my heart and always will.*

Je t'aime, mon amour,

Iskandar

After he finished his letter to Madeleine, then read it again, tears of love welling in his eyes, Alexander sat back for a few minutes, thinking of his love still in France without him. He knew he would never stop loving her and would be hers forever. Americans, though good to him, would never replace her in his heart. Love and agony were his most present emotions.

After a few minutes more, he reached for his pen, wiped his eyes, and began his letter in Arabic to Milhelm, his brother in Douma, still away from his father, his sister Leila, and brother. He felt very sad for that, and began writing:

Dear brother Milhelm,

Biyee and I just returned from church. He's taking a nap now, and I will rest after I write you. We are both tired as we work in Baba's store many hours every day but Sundays. Today at church I met my English teacher that Biyee arranged for me. I wish you were here to take the lessons with me. Leila and her family live about thirty kilometers from here in Orlando. I hope we can visit them next Sunday. Our village, or town as they call it, is bigger than Douma, and a busy place with many cattle in the region. They are brought here by cowmen for shipping to Cuba and other places by rail and barge. We are in the center of the state of Florida in the southeastern part of America. The people here are mostly from northern European parentage, the land is very flat and filled with cattle pastureland. Biyee believes the future here is very bright, but we both miss you very much and wish you were with us. Someday soon, we hope, we will all be together again. We hope you are feeling well and happy with your decision to remain in Douma. You would certainly miss the mountains, the snow, and the cedars. There are none here. And no olive trees or vineyards. It is truly different. It is getting very warm now that summer is upon us. It's even warmer than Beirut and southern Lebanon.

I pray for you everyday, and Biyee and I speak of you all the time. Be well, my brother, and please write to me soon. We love you, Milhelm.

With love,

Your brother, Iskandar

Let your ears thirst for the sound of your heart's knowledge.
Kahlil Gibran

CHAPTER 17

Abigail: Alexander's Tutor

"Good morning, Alexander," Abigail welcomed him at her door as he walked up the steps to her porch and front door, trying out her stilted French to impress Alexander. "You are here exactly at nine o'clock." She continued, returning more comfortably to her native English, and with a grin and shrug, "I'm glad you are not late, and I'm glad you didn't come too early. Ladies are never supposed to be ready too soon," she smiled sweetly. "It makes them look anxious." She spoke now as the teacher of social graces. Cupping her hand to her mouth, she laughed, while educating her student. "Oh, I think I gave you a secret. Do come in. We will sit in the dining room and begin. I have books, paper, and pencils."

Not understanding her words, but interpreting her friendliness and directions, Alexander followed Abigail up the few steps into the beautiful Sommerland home, larger than any home Alexander ever saw. He marveled at its size and beautiful furnishings. Although modest in its design, he admired the white clapboard siding and large open wrap around porch, and the large windows. He was impressed the house was two stories with tall, decorative dormers providing sunlight to the rooms on the second floor. Tall oak trees shaded most of the residence and grounds.

"*Hillou*, beautiful, *magnifique*," he exclaimed as he looked around Abigail's fabulous home.

He recalled his humble, stone, two-room home in Douma, and his father's sparse rooms above the store. Now he had an American reality to dream about and hope for.

During the first bewildering but challenging week, Alexander met with Abigail at her home for his basic English lessons. Five mornings each week thereafter, Alexander diligently arrived promptly at nine o'clock, and sat down at the dining room table opposite her. He studied intently and stayed focused. The lessons consumed a full hour devoted to elementary steps in learning the alphabet, then on to identifying pictures and words, or simple phrases like: "See the horse, house, store, street." His early conversations were stilted, clumsy and difficult, but when he stumbled, Abigail, quite patient with him, smiled to minimize his embarrassment. Sometimes, upset with himself, he would blurt out something in Arabic or French, causing her to laugh. He appreciated her sense of humor and her patience. It kept him from becoming too frustrated. And he admired her when she laughed.

Alexander concentrated on learning as fast as he could and so he listened to her every word, carefully watching her lips as she formed words. His growing respect for Abigail helped to accelerate his learning process. He liked it when she tilted her head and when she would look at him out of the corners of her beautiful ice blue eyes, sometimes cheering him, happily applauding with her hands, and sometimes showing a quizzical look when he erred.

"Good morning, Alexander. Today, the beginning of our third week, we'll review all that you have learned."

"Bon," Alexander quickly replied with a grateful smile, happy at his progress, pulling from the stack of elementary books, the one with names matching pictures of structures, animals, fauna, and just about everything printed that Abigail had gotten for him from the library.

"I'll point at pictures, then you say the correct word. Okay?"

It was very much an exercise that first and second graders repeated day after day in the public school, but the recitation accelerated since Alexander had already studied diligently the night before. He had completed his schooling in Douma, though in Arabic and some Russian as he was taught by the missionary from Russia. He liked being with this very pretty and charming young woman who kept his lessons from being dull.

As the lessons progressed, they began spending more time together. Abigail, enjoying her teaching and Alexander's eagerness, extended the lessons to two hours. So concentrated on the subject matter were the two, now sitting side by side, that the sessions began to stretch to noon.

The repetitious exchange of Abigail pointing and Alexander responding became a pleasant game for the two young adults. They easily laughed together as Alexander might occasionally mix-up or confuse the words.

"*Towleh*, er, table," he said as she pointed.

She laughed. "No, Alexander. That's a chair. This is a table," pointing to the opposite page."

"Oh. *Shookrun*...uh...sorry."

"How about this?"

He hesitated for a moment. "That's a bicycle."

"*Oui*, yes! Exactly right!" She laughed as she patted his hand, becoming friendlier and more familiar each day.

"You are making good progress, Alexander. But let's stop now. We've been at this for three hours. Time for us to take a break," she declared, looking at the wall clock about to chime twelve o'clock.

"Excuse me," Mrs. Sommerland interrupted with a smile as she stepped into the room, wiping her apron with both hands, "would you two like to have lunch?"

At welcomed breaks like these, Abigail would speak to Alexander, first in French, and later, more and more, slowly in English.

"You are going to help me improve my French, Alexander, as much as I help you speak English." As she laughed, Alexander felt himself noticing how really pleasant and kind she was. And beautiful too. He couldn't help but grow to like her. They were becoming good friends as the weeks passed by. Abigail, twenty years old, was a bit more than two years older than Alexander. But that didn't seem to be an issue with either of them.

Sometimes, they would take breaks and walk in the gardens behind the house. They strolled together so Abigail could point at the trees, flowers, houses, and automobiles in the street teaching Alexander the names of everything in sight, trying to expand his vocabulary and inventory of words.

One day after a lesson, Alexander was pleasantly surprised when Abigail carried a tray of chicken salad sandwiches, fruit, and lemonade to a wooden picnic table on the back patio. Her mother watched from the window as they sat next to each other, almost touching. Speaking in French, Abigail told Alexander all about her life at Florida State College for Women in Tallahassee. She spoke of the campus and the fact that only girls attended there.

"Boys only can attend the University of Florida in Gainesville," she remarked. "Imagine all those girls in Tallahassee and all those boys so far away, yet so close. Sometimes," she laughed, "some of the boys drive over in packed cars and come to our campus to meet new girls. They come on Saturdays and take girls out dancing. It's a lot of fun," she laughed. "Don't tell my parents, but sometimes I go out on Saturday nights with a group of girls so we can see the boys, and dance." She hastened to add, "I never was alone with a boy. That wouldn't be right, would it? Only with groups."

Carefully choosing his words to make a sentence, he spoke haltingly in English, "I am glad…you are my tutor…Abigail…and I thank you…teaching me English," he said as he shook her hand and looked in her eyes, surprising himself a bit at how appealing touching her felt to him. He also noticed that Abigail, at first indifferent to his touch, reacted warmly, sometimes smiling demurely, sometimes even turning her head toward him. Her demeanor reminded him of Madeleine.

"Would you like to go for a ride on horseback, Alexander? I can show you some of the area around Kissimmee. We have nice open pastures, piney woods, rolling hills, and some beautiful lakes."

"I would like that very much, Abigail," he replied, thinking she might be offering to ride right then. "Can we do it after my English lessons one day?"

"What a wonderful idea," she diplomatically responded. "After your lessons, we'll have two horses saddled, and ride over to Lake Joyce. There's an ice cream store there. It will be fun. Next week, Alexander, how about Monday?"

"Yes," he responded eagerly, "I would like that."

That weekend, Alexander wrote a long letter to Madeleine describing his lessons, how much he was enjoying his new life, and how much he missed her. His love for her was still very strong, and it showed in his letter. While his letters were in French, he wrote a few words in English, hoping to impress Madeleine with his new knowledge. Each letter always ended with the words, *je t'aime, mon amour.*

> *My dearest Madeleine, my life here is getting better each day. I work at the store from daybreak preparing for the day, learning all I can about our inventory and business from my father. Then, always just before nine, I walk to the Sommerland home for my English lessons. Miss Sommerland, who is older than I, is a really good teacher. I work hard those three hours, and study in my room at night. There is little to do here in this small village, so I have most evenings to prepare for my instruction. I have a new friend named Wilbur, a cattleman. He is teaching me all about this area, cattle-raising and riding horses.*
>
> *My father goes to bed right after dinner, depending on what time we close the store. I'm able to save some money so that soon I'll have enough to come to Marseille and bring you here.*
>
> *I miss you, chérie, and hope soon I will receive your letters. Je t'aime, mon amour.*
>
> *Iskandar*

Your friend is your needs answered...
Kahlil Gibran

CHAPTER 18

The Cottonmouth Encounter

"That's enough English for today," Abigail exclaimed, already dressed in jeans, boots, and faded blue shirt. "It's Monday, and I promised you we'd go riding together today," Abigail smiled. "It's time for you to learn to ride a horse if you're going to live in Kissimmee! I've had two horses saddled up for us. I'll ride the bay, and you can ride the Appaloosa, she'll treat you right."

"I can ride a horse. Let's go look."

Alexander's first ride in a western saddle was really exciting. Back home in his village, he had, on occasion, ridden a horse up and down the mountain path, but his horse, "Toufeh," was an older, slower Arabian, and knew the path well. Those days, he rode on a makeshift saddle of wood similar to those used on camels, or, sometimes, bareback with only a blanket thrown over the horse's back. His horse always walked. He never ran his horse.

Abigail spent the afternoon happily riding with Alexander, at a walk at first, teaching him, and coaxing her new friend. "Hold the reins lightly. Let her go." She led them from the family stables through the piney woods, out onto the pasture about three miles, then down the gentle grassy slope to the lake on the family farm Big John had built, as he enjoyed saying to others, "with only my bare calloused hands."

"Now, let's sit over there by the lake for awhile, Alexander," she told him while she pointed to the shoreline. "We'll take a rest."

He was concentrating on guiding the mare with his thighs and the reins, so he just smiled and laughed, as he was concentrating, hoping to learn rapidly how to ride in a western saddle for the first time. He enjoyed riding horseback with Abigail, and wanted more opportunities to be with her, to learn every American way he could.

Each morning Alexander looked forward to his arrival on Abigail's front porch precisely at nine o'clock, where she would meet him at the door with her lovely smile and greet him in deliberate English, "Good morning, Alexander. And how are you feeling today?"

"I feel good, Abigail," he would reply with a smile, more confident and bold in the English greeting she had taught him, as she opened the screen door, inviting him in.

She would lead him into the parlor where they could sit opposite each other he on the armchair with the high back, she on the settee. They would go through verbal lessons for the first hour.

"Come sit by me, Alexander. We must now read together for awhile." She patted the settee next to her. He was always a bit shy and nervous to sit so close to her, but when he did, their hips might accidentally touch, sending a pleasant feeling through his body. And if she brushed his hand with hers, he would feel a bit embarrassed. He was still shy in spite of having been with Madeleine, but that was different. She was younger than he. But Abigail was older. Even as he felt happy with Abigail, and complimented that a 21-year-old woman student from a university enjoyed being with him, he was also aware of this sense of reluctance, as though he might betray Madeleine's trust. He liked Abigail, who was here, but he considered himself near betrothed to Madeleine, who was six weeks away by rail and ship, and from whom not one letter had been received in all the weeks since he left Marseille.

Alexander's English abilities improved more and more, and everyday his confidence increased.

After reading together in the parlor, tutor and student moved to the den and sat at her father's desk where, again, they would sit next to each other in separate chairs to practice writing, at first the alphabet, then names, then sentences. Alexander laughed with a sense of great accomplishment when Abigail taught him to print, then write in script his own name. He wrote his name twenty times, looked at the paper, put the pen down, sat back and smiled. "Thank you, Abigail. You have brought me to a wonderful place. Look! That is my name. I will show this to my father. He will be so proud of me. Now, I will show you how I write my name in Arabic. Watch."

"Oh, Alexander, your Arabic lettering is beautiful. And you write right to left. Isn't that interesting! And with French, you can now write your name in three languages!"

There were times like this when Alexander's background would enter their conversation. He would tell Abigail of his village, his ancient heritage, his mother, and how important these things were to him.

One day he wanted to tell her of his ancestry, sometimes breaking into French as his English was still a bit stilted at times, "The Phoenicians, my ancestors, traded and settled throughout the huge Mediterranean Sea, Abigail. All the way past Gibraltar, even to Britain. Imagine. Sailing ships so far away, even 2,000 years before Christ. We like to boast that Hannibal of Carthage was of Phoenician heritage. He defeated the Romans, you know. And though I am an immigrant here in America, I have an ancestry equal to any. And I am just like them. I am willing to become like other people here, to work hard, trade, and become a successful American. That is my destiny. That is why God brought me here." He smiled as he proudly explained his heritage.

She reached out to touch his hand, smiled warmly at Alexander, leaned over and kissed him on his cheek. "Your English is getting better and better. You only made a few mistakes, telling me about your ancestry. I am so proud of you, Alexander. You have done very well with your lessons, and it has only been, let's see, eight weeks. Goodness, how time has flown by! Only four more weeks and I must leave Kissimmee to return to school." She frowned at the thought. "There are so many more things I want to teach you." With that, she smiled and looked at him with a sense of accomplishment.

He looked sad at her news, reaching to his cheek and touching with his fingers where she kissed him. As he looked into Abigail's eyes, returning her stare, he felt tempted to hold her. But he knew he couldn't. She had become his special friend, and he had grown fond of her. Every time Abigail complimented his latest achievement and gently touched him, or smiled warmly at him in approval, he felt appreciated and his self-esteem became reinforced.

But, any attractions felt toward Abigail paled as soon as he returned to the store or to his room, where he immediately resumed thinking about Madeleine and how much he missed her. *One letter. Just one letter is what I need. Where are they?*

He knew Abigail liked him even though he was an immigrant and different. She was from a prominent and important family, so cultured, and accepted everywhere. As a consequence, he felt reluctant to make any advances, no matter how innocent.

Sometimes, when Abigail's mother would interrupt with sandwiches, or to announce noontime, he would catch her looking at him with a rather stern look, which he interpreted as disapproval. He'd observed other men rising when a lady entered a room and decided that was what was bothering her, so today, he stood when she entered the room. That brought a slight nod and a smile.

"Abigail. I need to also learn about your customs and *ce qui est poli* or *courtoisie*.

Do you think you could teach me that?"

She immediately began to teach him new customs, greetings, slang, and behavior. He studiously watched Abigail's gestures and listened carefully to her every word. She even taught him to sit properly at a table, keep his elbows off the table, and utilize the fork instead of wrapping food in bread, as was the custom in the Near East.

Alexander's days all that summer were spent with Abigail in the mornings and afternoons, and evenings with his father in the store where he worked long hours, and then studied his lessons into the late hours of the night. He knew that working at the store with his father gave him a sense of purpose, slow as it seemed, to become the independent person he wanted to be.

During the slow summer months, on some days, he and his father might have realized only a dollar in sales. But unless it was needed for food, it was deposited in their "bank in the field."

Abigail and Alexander enjoyed the days before she would have to return to FSCW in September for her senior year. After the lessons, they often shared lunch, sometimes on the back lawn. Horseback riding also became part of their daily activity. He was quickly becoming a very good horseman thanks to Abigail's advice and encouragement and his rides with Wilbur.

Alexander loved to watch Abigail who could ride a horse as well as any cowman in the region. He learned that when he wanted to ride fast, he must dig his heels into the horse's sides, rise up off the Western saddle and, with bent knees, stand in the stirrups and lean forward. He shared her love of having the wind blow in his face. She showed him how to rope a calf, tie it up, and cut cattle from the herd. She would yell to Alexander, "Watch me and do as I do!"

"You are so good!" he would exclaim with pride.

One day, late in August, Abigail raced Alexander on horseback across the wide pasture, through the piney woods to the largest lake on the family's ranch outside of Kissimmee. She laughed all the way, waving to him and yelling, "Catch me, Alexander! Catch me!" And while Alexander laughed as he trailed behind, trying to catch her, her bay was just too fast. The wind was cool on their faces on this typically hot afternoon. The sky was overcast with large gray rain clouds building, causing a strong cooling breeze ahead of the rain. He loved racing her on his Appaloosa.

Alexander, now keenly aware that their time together was drawing short, realized he likely wouldn't see her until Christmas, and then only for a few days. They would not again have much time together, he knew, as she would graduate next year, and then what? These thoughts caused Alexander to notice her behavior even more carefully. She, in turn, was becoming more bold with him.

They finally reached the lake and dismounted. Together, they flopped down on the grass, resting, touching slightly, and laughing together as they lay back side by side looking up at the cloud-filled sky, her light blonde hair cascading over her shoulder onto the grass.

"That was fun, Alexander. It's always fun being with you. You're probably the best friend I have. You Lebanese…Phoenician!" She laughed aloud at her candor and smiled warmly as she reached for his hand. "You are a wonderful, kind young man. I'm glad we have become such good friends. Most American men have difficulty being friends with a girl. I'm glad you are not that way. I hope we're always friends."

"Abigail, you are so good to me. I cannot express to you how happy I am hearing your words. America is such a wonderful free country, and I have so much to learn. You have taught me how to become an American, and how to speak English properly. I also hope we stay close friends for a long time. You must know that I am determined to be successful here, and maybe soon own my own land, raise my own cattle, and establish myself. I need friends and help to get there. And so, I am grateful to you."

He stood up to relieve the tension that was building inside him. He still wasn't sure of his place and didn't want to overstep his bounds.

"I need to stretch my legs. I'm going to walk down to the water."

Looking back at Abigail, he slowly walked away and gave her a small wave of his hand. She had risen on her elbow and followed him with her eyes.

As she watched Alexander stroll through the tall grass along the lake's shore, she sat up, reached to her feet and pulled off her boots and socks. She loved the feel of the cool grass between her toes as she slid her feet through the grass, then lay back, arms outstretched.

She kept watching Alexander, now perhaps thirty feet away near the water's edge, as she slid her toes back and forth in the grass. Alexander searched around and found a gathering of stones. He grabbed a handful and put them in his pocket. Then he pulled his sling from his back pocket and pulled the leather strands together. As he wrapped one strand around his last two fingers on his right hand and pinched the end of the other strand between his thumb and forefinger, he placed a stone into the pouch. The weighted pouch by his side hung nearly to the ground.

He spotted a ripple in the lake, quickly whirled the pouch over his head three times, and let the stone fly. Almost in an instant, the stone struck the water's surface exactly at the ripple. He smiled at his accuracy.

"Nice shot, Alexander," Abigail called to him. "How do you do that so fast?"

He laughed, accepting the compliment. "I have been using the sling since I was five years old," he called back. "When I watched over the goats in the mountains, I had to protect them from predators. I once hit a hawk in flight when I was fifteen," he boasted.

As he turned to walk back toward where Abigail was sitting, near the water's edge, feet outstretched nearly to the rushes, wiggling her toes in the cool grasses, his eyes searched the area for another target.

The deadly cottonmouth moccasin snake watched with its beady eyes as the bare pink toes wiggled before it in the grass. With a flash of its forked tongue, the viper sensed flesh. Its keen eyes dripping from the lake's waters as it emerged, slithering through the grassy rushes in the shallows onto the harder shore line, now focused on the movement of Abigail's slender toes. The snake had found its meal, its prey. It slowly moved onto the higher ground, inch by inch, never moving its head from its target, its entire body pressing against the grasses, moving inexorably toward its nourishment. As it drew within striking distance, mere inches from Abigail's bare toes, it began its coil by bringing its entire body directly behind its tapered head.

The snake's forked tongue silently, rhythmically, flicked again and again, searching the air for the scent of its very tempting target. Hardly a leaf of grass moved as the mature moccasin slinked along the ground. The forked tongue flicked one last time as the entire five feet of sinew and muscle, held together by a series of bone and ligament, was poised to lash forward in an instant. It would engulf its prey in its hyper-extended mouth, sinking its fangs filled with deadly poisonous venom into flesh not of a young rodent, but of Abigail's toes.

"Don't move, Abigail!" Alexander suddenly yelled, interrupting her reverie. He quickly placed a stone in the pouch and almost as a blur, swung the pouch over his head, once, twice, three times, and with a whirl let the stone fly. Thud! The stone flew true to its target, as he knew it would, striking the viper in the head, instantly killing the reptile only a few inches from Abigail's feet. He ran toward her.

"Oh, my God!" Abigail screamed, staring at the very large, lethal snake. She leaped up and ran to him, frightened, with both arms outstretched. "You saved my life! That was a big and dangerous cottonmouth. Thank you. Thank you."

She embraced him tightly, wrapping both her arms around his neck, shaking at the realization of what might have happened. "Oh, my God, Alexander. That was so awful." Now, more emboldened and yet still very frightened, Abigail spontaneously kissed him on his lips.

Then, pulling her head back, she cupped his face in her hands and brought her face to his. She could not help herself as she excitedly kissed him deliberately and firmly on his lips. He held her and enjoyed her lips on his, but could not return the kiss. He felt wonderful, but very reluctant to respond to her embrace.

After a few minutes, she stepped back, and more calmly said, "Wait until I tell my father what you did. He will love this story, Alexander. You are my protector. I love you!" She was still shaking as she exclaimed her gratitude.

He was stunned by her demonstrative affection. They spent a few minutes looking down at the now immobile, dead five-foot reptile.

"I think we should ride back to my house now, Alexander. I'm a little nervous," she whispered in his ear as she hugged him once again.

He picked up the snake and tied it up with a rope and attached it to the saddle. They rode their horses side by side, first walking, then breaking into a canter for awhile. Smiling at him affectionately, she pulled up close to him, reached over and clasped his hand while mouthing the words, 'thank you, Alexander.'

Alexander, trying to better understand all that had taken place, sat tall in his saddle, proud that his mastery of the sling from his homeland had saved his friend from certain severe pain, if not death. He recalled Abigail's response, her embrace and genuine affection. The thoughts empowered Alexander. This was a big day, an important day in both their lives, and he understood the strength of the affection.

"Mother, I've never seen anything like it! Look at the size of that snake," she exclaimed as Alexander dropped the snake on the porch. "I think that with his sling, he could beat any cowman in Osceola County with a pistol. He is so sure of himself in his modest way, and yet, he never misses his target. He saved my life, Mother. I want Daddy to see the snake."

"Oh dear, I worry so much when you go out into the country. Alexander, could you take that snake out back? I'll show her father later."

Alexander was working at the store the next afternoon, rearranging goods on the table at the front of the store, when he heard someone calling his name.

"Alexander, come here. I want to talk to you, son." The deep, masculine voice came from a tall, muscular, broad-shouldered, middle-aged man standing in the shop doorway. He was wearing a large grey Stetson hat low over his face, deeply creased and tanned from the harsh Florida sun. His faded blue shirt was wide open at the neck, unbuttoned at the collar; sweat marks spreading from under his armpits. On his hip was a silver pistol in a black well-used holster. His jeans were worn, faded Levi's as were the jeans of most cattlemen. His wide leather belt with an embellished large, tooled oval silver buckle stood out against the deep blue of the jeans. Alexander surveyed the man in snakeskin boots still wrapped by the spur straps at the ankles. He knew who was standing there in the doorway, and he knew he had to be absolutely respectful to this man, a recognized man of power and wealth.

"Yes, sir, Mr. Sommerland."

"Big John, son. All my friends call me Big John. C'mere, son. Let's talk."

Alexander walked toward this big man several inches taller than he and likely forty pounds heavier than his own one hundred-ninety pounds. He had a broad chest that filled the shirt and a slight paunch that hung over his buckle.

"What you did for my daughter, Abigail, is right important to me." He spoke firmly in a deep Southern drawl as he reached out and put his large, calloused hand on Alexander's shoulder. "I appreciate yer killin' that danged cottonmouth. That's a bad ass snake that coulda killed her. I do believe you saved her life, son, and for that, I'm mighty grateful."

Alexander was immediately overwhelmed. He shrugged, a bit embarrassed, nodded and said modestly, "Yes, sir. I only did what another man would do."

Big John stared into Alexander's eyes, so as to hold his total attention. His face very serious. "I'm not so sure of that, son. Young man, if you ever need anythin,' and I mean anythin,' you jest come over and ask. You jest come on over t' the house and see me anytime, y'hear?"

Alexander stammered, "Yessir, Abigail's a good friend, sir, and she has taught me so much. I would do anything for her."

"Well, son, from what she says about you, the feelin' is mutual. You know, she's mah girl, mah only daughter and she's right important to me. Nah, she's the most important thing in my life. And I am so grateful. D'ya understands what I'm trying to tell you, son? You gotta good dad, Alexander. I like him a lot. You both are good people, and we need good people here. So, I'm tellin' ya, come see me, son. You know where we live. Mrs. Sommerland told me to tell ya, don't be a stranger. An' don't let me down, y'hear?"

"Yessir. Abigail is giving me lessons tomorrow, so maybe I can see you then."

"Right, then, I'll see you tomorrow," he replied as he turned to walk out of the store. As he did, he perfunctorily raised his right hand above his shoulder, not looking back, as to conclude the visit. That was his style.

*And in the sweetness of friendship,
let there be laughter and sharing of pleasures…*
Kahlil Gibran

CHAPTER 19

Christmas at the Sommerlands

Abigail left for college in Tallahassee three weeks later. The same week, Alexander was required to enroll in the first grade in the local town school just a few blocks down the main street.

"Do I really have to go to school with six year olds, Father?"

"That's the law, son. Just do your best," his father shrugged. "Maybe you'll learn English faster that way."

"Aw…" Alexander complained.

Within eight weeks, he attended the first grade through the eighth grade in the same building. The teachers were understanding and realized it was futile to hold him back. He didn't enjoy school very much, since he was much older and bigger than his classmates — at nearly six feet tall. With nothing in common with his classmates, who were mostly under the age of ten, and with twelve years of schooling in Lebanon, he advanced quickly, especially in English and mathematics. His concentration centered on American history, American government, and a few other subjects like biology.

With Abigail gone, his boredom grew. He was ready to venture out before Christmas. *It's my time to begin* he decided.

"I want to go out on my own, Father. Will you help me?"

"So soon, son? What will you do?"

"I want to open my own store before the winter season and sell goods you do not sell. I believe I can do well with furniture, clothes for cowmen, shoes, hats and jewelry for the ladies. And for the tourists, perhaps oranges and grapefruit, and local novelty crafts to ship back home as gifts." Remembering all that he had seen while riding with Abigail through her father's lands and massive herds of cattle, he added, "One day I want to own some land and raise cattle like Big John Sommerland. Boldly, he asked, "Will you lend me $500 to get started?"

"You are in a hurry, aren't you, son?"

"Yes, sir, I am! After all I am your son, aren't I?" he smiled.

By Christmas, Alexander's small store on Broadway opened and word spread through the hotels, the docks, and at the cattle corrals. Tourists began arriving by train from northern cities, and the street filled with more shoppers, including ladies in their latest fashions from New York, Philadelphia, Pittsburgh, Detroit and Boston. Dress hemlines were beginning to rise to mid-calf so sales were picking up as women wanted to be fashionable and not wear the Victorian floor length cotton dresses of the past. The ladies needed fashionable sun umbrellas, and the men liked his inventory of hats. While Alexander initially ordered from his father's suppliers, more and more traveling salesmen and manufacturers' representatives stopped by his shop with their catalogs. Alexander eagerly reviewed the catalogs, looking into new opportunities, and ordered on consignment all that the companies would permit. He ventured into ladies' shoes, which, he found, were a bonanza. It seemed every lady needed at least several pairs of shoes while men would wear the same boots or shoes for more than two years. He stayed open from seven in the morning until nearly midnight six days a week. He worked very hard, and studied at night, but he was intoxicated by his opportunities, his freedom, and his mission to save enough money to somehow return to Madeleine. Still, almost everyday the absence of a letter from her gnawed at his stomach. When he looked to the postman with sorrowful eyes and watched him shake his head, he almost felt sick. It's been five months! He felt awful and was bewildered at her silence.

During that autumn season of 1920, both Alexander's and his father's stores prospered. They deposited their growing earnings in their "bank in the field." With their Spartan lifestyle, it cost little or nothing for them to live. Their expenses were minimal, including rent on his store, ethnic foods, biweekly train rides to Tampa to see friends or to Orlando to visit Leila, Alexander's sister, and her family. There was little else. There were no taxes to pay, no insurance premiums, no gasoline, for they did not yet own an automobile. So, except for their meager personal expenses, and paying cash for their goods for sale, their income was saved and deposited every Saturday night after closing. The immigrant's visceral, most personal concern for security was too difficult to set aside.

"When you come from the poorest, oppressed land to make a new life, son, you cannot forget ever that it can all be taken away in an instant. An immigrant remembers always…everyday…every minute, that there is no one to help if he fails. He cannot afford to fail. All depends on his willingness to take responsibility for his life and his family's life. He must try harder than others, save more, not waste any time, and not spend his money on foolishness. Abraham often spoke to his son of his near obsession with his frugality and sense of financial insecurity.

"You must never look back and say I wish I had worked harder."

"But, Father, we work as hard as we can," Alexander interrupted, almost frightened at his father's words.

"You must save everything you can. I knew bringing your mother, you and your brother would always be up to me. No one else. There are no cousins here… no one to help. So I saved every penny. I spent nothing on myself. Sometimes, I gave a little something to your sister to help her. But I waited too long for you and your mother, Iskandar, and I am so sad I did."

"Why did you wait so long, Father?" he pleaded, hoping for an explanation that would salve his wounds.

"I did the best I could, my son. Still, my heart aches. You must work very hard, have a better life than mine, and make certain your children have a better life than yours. Do you understand, my son, what I am telling you?"

Alexander understood. And he would remember. He thought about his father's predicament and remembered he could not bring his own wife whom he deeply loved to America. He tried to think of how he would manage to bring Madeleine here.

Abigail returned to Kissimmee to celebrate Thanksgiving and, a few weeks later, for the Christmas holidays. During Thanksgiving, her father bought a new 1921 Ford Model A coupe for her senior year gift. It was considered the "hottest," "the cats meow," the best car for young people in America. Of course it was black, like all Fords. When Abigail drove into Kissimmee mid-December, she stopped first at the sidewalk in front of Alexander's store where she hopped out of the car sporting a scarf around her neck, a ribbon in her hair, and stepped onto the boardwalk. With a great big smile, she shouted into the store, "Hi ya, Alexander! Whatcha' doin'?" She spoke like she was still at college with her girlfriends.

Alexander was on a stepladder reaching for the Stetson hats he kept on the high shelves with the ladies bonnets. He turned at her welcoming voice. "Hi, Abigail!" he shouted, releasing one hand to wave to her and, almost losing his balance and falling off the ladder. "Be right down." When his feet touched the floor, Abigail noticed a familiar clicking sound.

"Are you wearing boots, Alexander? You rascal!" She laughed out loud. "Come here and give me a hug. It's Christmas, Alexander!"

"It's so good to see you, Abigail! You look wonderful." He smiled, feeling his affection for this lovely creature, his pretty friend. "I've really missed you," he nearly shouted with pleasure.

"Listen, Alexander, I just drove in from Tallahassee. I haven't even been home yet, but I wanted to see you so bad! So, why don't I go on home, and if you don't have any plans, come over to the house for dinner with my momma, Big John and me." Then rushing out, she called out over her shoulder, "See you at 6:30. Okay? I'd better get home now. Momma's waiting."

Alexander eagerly closed his shop early, went home, still above his father's store, freshened up, and combed his hair in the middle the way all the young men did that year. He put his straw skimmer on top of his head, and stuck his head in the store downstairs to see his father.

"Hello, *Biyee*. How do I look? I'm going over to see Abigail. She invited me to supper."

His father, smiling with pride, said, "Go see your friend, son, and have a good time. This is the first time you or I have been invited to dinner in a home of someone so prominent, so enjoy it. I'll take the train to see Leila. I miss her so."

Alexander nearly ran all the way down Broadway, then one block south where he stopped, wiped his brow, and gazed on the grand Sommerland home, admiring his friend's lawn, flower beds and trees. "I am so lucky," he said to no one, with a happy grin on his face as he briskly walked toward the Sommerland front porch, and bounded up the four steps to the door. From the minute Big John opened the front door, stretched out his hand of welcome, Alexander felt on top of the world.

"Thank you, sir, for inviting me. It's so good to see you again, and especially wonderful to see Abigail and Mrs. Sommerland."

Just then, Abigail nearly ran to greet him with a big hug. "Thank you for coming, Alexander. We're all so proud of you and what you've done in such a short time! And listen to your English."

"Thank you, Abigail. You look so pretty tonight, and, as always, make me feel welcome here."

"Come sit down, son," said Big John as he sat in his favorite chair on the porch. "Mrs. Sommerland's gittin' supper ready. I want to tell you that Abigail's mother and I are really impressed with your progress here in Kissimmee. I mean, you coulda just stayed at your father's store, but you had bigger ambitions. And, you've shown me a lot goin' to those school classes with children. I'm not sure I coulda done that, and I know none of my cowmen would ever do that. But you are sure workin' hard to get ahead, aren't you?"

"Mr. Sommerland, as my father taught me, I must do three things: become a true American in every way, take full responsibility for my life, and make sure I provide a better life for my children than I had. And that's why I'm working so hard, and learning as much as I can. And I owe your daughter so much for teaching me not only how to speak, read and write English, but also for teaching me American ways of thinking and doing things."

After dinner, as Abigail walked with Alexander to the porch, her arm in his, she whispered to him, "My daddy wants you to come over on Christmas Eve after church. He says he wants to talk business with you. I think you should say yes, Alexander. Besides, I'd love to have you be with me on my favorite evening, Alexander. So please come for dinner."

At seven o'clock on Christmas Eve, Alexander arrived early as requested.

He stopped at the walkway to the Sommerland home and could see the brightly decorated Christmas tree through the large living room windows. Abigail was in her holiday dress with red and green ribbons in her hair. As he considered his own future plans, he smiled and stepped onto the stones leading to the steps and up to the large front door with that familiar oval vertical window framed by dark oak.

He swung the doorknocker with its clack-clack and waited as he had so many mornings during the summer.

Now it was Christmas Eve, and Abigail had invited her "special friend" to join her, her mother and Big John for dinner.

With anticipation, Alexander waited at the door, carrying a wrapped gift for Mrs. Sommerland and wondering what Big John wanted to say to him. He was happy tonight and excited about Abigail's invitation.

Tomorrow he and his father planned to take the train to Orlando and see his sister Leila, nephew, and niece, and his boastful brother-in-law. Christmas is for family.

After dinner, Big John asked Alexander outside to sit on the front porch in the rocking chair facing him. With his pale blue, almost transparent eyes, Big John leaned forward toward Alexander and placed his thick hands on his knees.

"Son," he spoke slowly in his drawl, as though there was no one else in the world. "I'll get right to the point; I don't like wastin' time." Quickly moving on, he looked straight into Alexander's eyes, a tad intimidating, and continued, "I owe you, and I want to do something for you."

Alexander, drawn to this man with great respect, his eyes bright with anticipation, leaned forward so not to miss a word, unsure of what was coming next in this unfamiliar situation.

"I like your daddy, and I like you. And I know my daughter likes you a lot. She wants to be your friend for a long time. I'd also like to see you stay in Kissimmee." Then pausing, sitting back with a serious look on his face, he announced, "Here's my proposition."

Alexander watched Big John and listened intently, having no idea where the conversation was going. Big John was very focused. Earlier, Abigail had urged him to accept whatever her father was proposing.

Lowering his voice, he spoke softly, "Mrs. Sommerland and Abigail are very important to me, and I'm obliged to you for saving Abigail's life. I know what a cottonmouth can do to someone, and I've seen the pain their bite can bring.

"Now it's Christmas Eve, a time when we all feel good. I've seen how hard your dad has worked since he came here. He's honest, and his word is gold. I admire what he has accomplished here in Kissimmee. An' I've watched you, son. You are the same way. You work harder than any young man I've seen. And you're important to Abigail. I do believe you are good friends, and I want you to stay friends."

Big John continued, leaning toward Alexander as he described his family's life in Kissimmee since the Civil War, and how he had bought his first land from Hamilton Disston, had amassed 160,000 acres of pasture lands, more than 16,000 head of cattle, and 5,000 acres of citrus land over at St. Cloud just five miles to the east.

"That Mr. Disston, now he knew how to do business. He got the Governor to hire him to drain all the swamps in this part of Florida back in 1884. Disston connected Lake Tohopekaliga with East Lake Tohopekaliga over in St. Cloud." He laughed. "I hear that when he opened the gate, East Lake Tohopekaliga dropped eight feet! Scared the hell outta everybody, too, I'll tell ya. And then, he opened up the Caloosahatchee River down to Fort Myers; that made shipping cattle to Cuba easier and opened up a helluva lot of pastureland too. Why, if truth be told, Hamilton Disston made Florida's cattle industry. That man got an option from the state to buy four million acres for twenty-five cents each. With a little help, I bought my first 10,000 acres from him in 1895 for fifty cents an acre."

Alexander watched Big John's lips carefully, trying to understand his every word, picking out most of the familiar sounds.

"That's the price I'm going to charge you, Alexander. Here's my deal. I'm offering to sell you 5,000 acres at my cost price, and I'm throwing' in five hundred head of cattle too. Now, that oughta get you started, son. And I believe Abigail will give you a hand when you need it. After a few years of grazing, you should be able to start shipping your own cattle to market. Until then, you gotta watch your herd and protect your land."

By the time Mrs. Sommerland stepped onto the porch announcing dinner, Big John had completed his offer to Alexander. Both men were smiling broadly. Big John reached for Alexander's hand to shake on the deal.

It took Alexander a pregnant moment to fully understand what had just taken place and he had difficulty disguising his surprise. He was amazed such a generous offer would ever come his way, especially after having to work so very hard for every penny. To be certain he fully understood what was being offered, he memorized the figures so he could write everything down on paper when he got back home. He was thrilled at his good fortune. Five hundred cows and bulls! We will never be hungry again!

Noting Abigail's smiling face in the window as she nodded her head urging him to accept, Alexander, overwhelmed, but without hesitation reached out his right hand with a nervous smile and said, "Big John, I can't refuse your excellent and very generous offer, so my answer is yes, sir, and thank you very much. But I think I'll need a few years to pay you, and I'll need your guidance. I'm really new at this. But you have offered me a wonderful opportunity. I accept, and I'll do what ever I must to earn your confidence, sir."

"Good. Take two or three years, son. I'm in no hurry. What with those politicians up in Tallahassee, I expect I'll have to start payin' taxes on all this land anyway. Looks like the days of the open range will soon be over. My cattle are all over three counties now. Too many cows gittin' hit by them dang automobiles. So, it won't be long before we'll have to fence our grazing lands, and that's gonna cost me a lot of money. In a way, you're doin' me a favor." He smiled. "I'll git you a survey of what you're buyin', and by spring, we'll have it fenced for you. You can pay me back for the cost of the fence. By then, you better have a man run the operation for ya and git you a brand registered. Wilbur McCray is a good man; I'll let you hire him from me. He told me about the day you showed him how you worked that sling. Little did I know at the time how valuable to me that talent of yours would be."

"I like Wilbur very much, sir. He's my good friend and I will need his help. I have a lot to learn about owning land and cattle, sir," Alexander interjected, smiling and nodding as he listened to Big John describe his generosity.

"Good, son. But I'd stay away from T.J. Hatfield and cowmen like him. T.J. is always angry it seems. He's a bad one. His family came from to America from Germany, I think. They have good solid character, but I wouldn't trust him if I was you. He doesn't take kindly to immigrants. His family was involved in the Native Party back in the late 1800s when they fought…and I mean fought…hard to keep out immigrants. They want America to themselves. So be real careful of T.J. and his family, Alexander. Now," he continued after a thought, putting his hand on Alexander's shoulder, leading him to the door, "let's not keep the ladies waitin.'"

"I'll stay away from that man. I already learned that. I don't want any trouble."

Abigail met Alexander at the doorway to the dining room with a warm, happy embrace. "Merry Christmas, Alexander. I'm so happy you are here tonight. Let's sit down for dinner and drink a toast to your new ranch!" She had known exactly what her father was going to do, and that made her very happy.

All through dinner, although it was delicious and smelled so good to him, Alexander could hardly eat. He was startled at his good fortune while also sharing this wonderful evening with such a prominent family.

After dinner, they visited awhile before the ladies started cleaning up. Alexander could hardly restrain himself. He nearly ran to his home to tell his father what had happened.

"Five thousand acres and five hundred head of cattle, *Biyee*! I will pay him $2,500 over two, maybe three years. Can you imagine what this means to our lives in America, *Biyee*? I love America!" Then, thinking of his mother and Douma, his terrible hunger as a child, he exclaimed, "I will make sure we are never hungry again." Oh, how I wish *Imei* and Milhelm were here!

Abraham embraced his son and whispered, "Merry Christmas, Iskandar. Your mother and I always believed you would have a special future. God has blessed you, my son. The Sommerland family is very generous and good, and they care. But remember, I am your father and you are my son. We must not forget our Lebanese heritage and our culture. The Sommerlands are good people, but they are different from us. We must stay with our own kind." Then he became silent for a moment, mulling over what had just happened, and unable to suppress his immigrant's sense of caution and fear, continued, "Now you will have to protect and care for God's gift to you. It will be a big responsibility, and there will be others who will want what you have. They will be jealous and angry. So, be cautious and safeguard your new treasure."

Not totally understanding, and perhaps a bit naïve, he considered his father's admonition. Then, Alexander looked at his father with utter respect and pride. "This would not have happened, *Biyee*, were it not for who you are and what you have taught me. Mr. Sommerland has great respect for you, *Baba*. We are so fortunate."

"*Baba*," Abraham responded, "what we are and how we live will determine what happens in our lives. You have a long and good heritage. Be proud, and someday you will be able to help someone as Mr. Sommerland has helped you." Father and son embraced warmly, having been struck deeply by the good fortune that had come their way. "And now, my son, you are going to have to work very hard to raise those cattle, protect your land, make it more productive, In that way, you will prove Mr. Sommerland correct and wise to offer you this wonderful gift."

Alexander, looking around their sparse and humble home, noticing the simple pinewood dining table, two ladder pine chairs, and a single reading lamp, began considering what all this could mean to them. "Perhaps one day we might have our own home, like true Americans. Maybe even as grand as Big John's house," Alexander said quietly.

They both prayed to the Lord with thanks that night, grateful for the blessings they were receiving.

Abraham sat quietly, pondering the impact this event would have on his son's thinking and future. And his role in his son's days to come.

Your children are not your children.
You may give them your love,
but not your thoughts. For they have their own thoughts....
Kahlil Gibran

CHAPTER 20
1924, The Florida Land Boom: Alexander's Dilemma

In early 1924, Abraham and Alexander, like those throughout Central Florida, began witnessing the second year of the most incredible real estate "Land Boom" in Florida's history. Open pasture land and pine forest land valued at fifty cents an acre until 1915, and 75 cents per acre in 1920 had shot up to an incredible $20 per acre by 1924.

Some Florida tracts, even into 1925, were bought and sold several times in one day! "America is amazing," the local people told each other as they watched. These were heady days when Alexander stood at the door of the shop and watched the frenzy of speculators on Broadway negotiating hurriedly, buying and selling. He was both befuddled and excited...torn between being amazed at what he saw...and wanting youthfully and anxiously to join in it. The Land Registry office was just a block from his store. He was sorely tempted, watching the endless lines of buyers registering their purchases.

"Don't you think we should be buying more land, *Biyee?*" asked impetuous twenty-two year old Alexander. "Everyone says to buy land now, not wait until later."

"No, my son, we mustn't get involved in this very emotional buying spree all the tourists are participating in. They're buying everything in my store. Yours too! They're buying automobiles, fancy clothes, land and more land. Son, I have devoted myself to working more than twelve hours a day since I came here. You must realize we dare not touch our bank in the field at this time. Remember, do not buy when everyone else is buying, and don't sell when everyone is selling. It is not wise to do so in business dealings. Besides, no one in our Thomé or Chalhoub families has ever sold our land in Lebanon. It simply is not in our culture to speculate on land."

"But, *Biyee*, much of the money in our bank is mine, and I think I should invest in more land."

"Iskandar, don't talk like that! That money is for our future. We share our bank in the field. One day, we may need that money just to live. Do not think of it as yours or mine. It is ours. Don't forget that and don't let me hear you talk like that again! Haven't you noticed the big ranchers with all their lands have not sold any of their holdings? And they aren't buying more now. There's a good reason. Prices are too high. Prices are increasing so fast because there is not much land available. And, another thing, Big John told me that buyers are not paying much cash, just five percent, like stocks on Wall Street. Ninety-five percent is borrowed from the sellers. He told me that Wall Street buying is completely irrational. That people believe there is no top! He says this situation cannot last long. And I agree."

These disagreements occurred each night at their dining room table, sometimes growing into heated arguments.

"You have enough now, Iskandar. You have cattle, 5,000 acres of land, and a few lakes. Maybe one day you can buy a building and own your own store. But now, son, it's time for you to forget about getting into this craziness. Be patient. It is now time for you to consider getting married and having a family. You need to think about this. Listen to your father!"

That night, Abraham beckoned to his son as he sat in a chair at the table. "Sit with me, son."

"Iskandar, you know I only want what is best for you. Your mother and I hoped our children would have happy lives one day with their own families. If we were still in Douma, it would be easier to understand. But here in America, especially with no other Lebanese or Syrian families nearby, I fear you will leave our culture and either become an old single man or marry an American girl who won't understand our ways. I believe completely that you will have a happier life if you choose to marry someone of our kind…a Syrian girl."

"*Biyee*, I know you only want what is best for me, but I fell in love with a wonderful French girl in Marseille and I want to marry her!"

"Iskandar, listen to me. I'm sure your friend in France is nice. But it is better that you marry in your religion, your culture, so you will avoid the difficulties that you will face if you do otherwise. And while I am also sure Abigail is a kind and beautiful girl, she too will be advised by her mother the same way you are by me. I am certain Abigail's parents want what is best for their only daughter. Even though they respect us and are grateful to you for saving her life, they want her to marry her own kind also. It is best. As the Bible says, 'Always seek to be in equal yoke with your partner.' You will see."

Interrupting, Alexander blurted, "But I have not said I want to marry Abigail, although I think she would be a perfect wife for me…" his voice trailed off as he rolled his "Douma stone" in his fingers, something he always seemed to do nervously when he and his father talked about his personal life and his views of America.

"We are immigrants, Iskandar. We are considered different. Be aware of that. The Sommerlands are more understanding about this than most people, but still, they too want the best for their daughter as I do for you." Abraham, watching Alexander fondle his ring, looked up, paused, caught his breath and spoke firmly. "Iskandar, it is for your own good that I insist you marry a good Syrian girl of our religion. She will bring you healthy children, cook for you, love you, and support you." Then looking around his Spartan apartment, Abraham swept his arm in a circle before him and admonished, "Look at our house. It is bare; it is not what an American woman can accept. We accept it because we came from less than this, but want more. A Syrian girl will understand. She will make it pretty, warm and comfortable just as your beloved mother did in that small stone home I built for her. Marry someone like your mother, Iskandar. We can find one like her in Boston. Of this I am certain. Forget this infatuation with a girl in France."

"I don't love some girl in Boston. I love Madeleine and want to go back and bring her to America."

"What is happening here, my son? Why do you get so angry with what I wish for you? Listen to me. Do what is right. You can learn to love the proper woman."

"But, Father…"

Alexander stood and angrily stepped away from the table where he had listened to his father's plans for him and went across the small room, his back to his father who stayed seated, watching his son pull away, not willing to be convinced that this proposed marriage arrangement was in his best interests.

Alexander got so infuriated with his father's adamancy that he stormed out of the apartment, went down Broadway, and literally ran away. He was gone an hour, trying to get rid of his frustration and anger.

The next morning, after a restless night, Alexander met with Wilbur to ride out to the herd.

"Wilbur, I'd like your opinion about something."

"Of course, Alexander. What about?"

After a moment of thought as they stood near their horses, he began, "Well, Wilbur, I met a wonderful girl in Marseille on my way to America, and we fell in love. I mean, Wilbur, we really fell in love. We declared our lifelong love and that our destiny would only be fulfilled with each other."

"So, what's the problem, Alexander?"

"Well, Wilbur, first, she's still in France and I'm here. I'd go to her as soon as I can afford to go, but you see, there's a big problem. Although I've written her at least once a month since I left Marseille almost four years ago, I have never, I mean ever, received a letter from her! Her name is Madeleine and she is my true love. But I don't even know where she is. It's been four years, Wilbur! My father is insisting I find a good Syrian girl, marry her and have a family. But I don't know any girls like that. There aren't any around here."

"Four years is a long time to not hear from someone. Maybe she's found someone else. What about that pretty Abigail Sommerland? I know she likes you, and it looks to me that you like her too."

"I can't give up. We made a commitment to each other. The biggest problem is that my father feels very strongly that I should marry my own kind, and that Abigail's parents feel the same way. Yes, I really like Abigail a lot, but I don't think she can marry me anyway."

"Oh, Lordy, Alexander, you do have a bit of a problem. Lucky for me my folks don't care who I marry, when I marry, and if I marry. And I don't see me bein' a daddy for a long time anyway."

"What should I do, Wilbur?"

"Danged if I know," he replied, after stroking his chin, thinking, rolling a cigarette and lighting it. "I jes' don't know, my friend, but I'll sure think about this."

Over the next several weeks, Alexander's future remained a painful issue of contention for him and his father, to the point of creating significant tension between them. Their body language became more separated, almost adversarial.

In spite of his differences with his father, Alexander stayed totally committed to his work. With a $500 loan from his father, Alexander rented a small store down Broadway about two blocks from his father's store, and across the street. Slightly smaller than his father's store, it had the same wood floor, ten foot ceiling, a storeroom in the rear, and a glass front so he could exhibit his latest goods. The first floor store, part of a free-standing two-story building, belonged to Mr. Nathan Anderson, a friend of his father's who decided to retire at the age of seventy-four. "I'm jes' tired, son. I've been at this store six days a week fer twenty years. After my wife died last year, I decided to take it easy an' spend my time fishin' over at the lake. I'll stay livin' upstairs fer awhile. Maybe one day you can buy the whole building so's I can move down to Miami an' be with my daughter."

It didn't take Alexander long to get his store open. He was as anxious as a thoroughbred horse out of the starting gate. After cleaning out the shop, he painted the walls with a bright yellow glossy finish that he thought would entice the ladies of Kissimmee, recalling Madeleine's mother's courtier shop with its colorful appeal to the upper class women of Marseille. Then, he loaded his tables and shelves with the latest style bonnets, ready-to-wear dresses, and shoes from New York. He did not stock cloth bolts like his father. He added men's Stetson hats, boots and other accessories for the cowmen. Out front, he displayed local fruits, including bright oranges and grapefruit. He made a big sign with bold red letters on a white background stating: "Send your family and friends a package of Florida sunshine. Only $1.98 plus shipping."

Due to the fortuitous timing at the beginning of tourist season, the only Broadway store not painted white and his aggressive sales flyers, Alexander's shop turned a profit within weeks.

Women shopping along Broadway, enticed by his flyers, his sign and window treatments, came into his shop curious and, flush with new money, eager to buy. Compounding his father's friendliness to customers, Alexander's enthusiasm attracted more than his share of tourists and shoppers.

Alexander bought and exhibited everything the manufacturer's reps would sell him on consignment.

Sales at both Thomas stores increased substantially; their earnings multiplied as they did for most of the other merchants in the region. Alexander's life, beyond his personal longings, was liberating and prosperous.

By 1924, wealthy investors and Northerners looking for opportunities flooded the entire region. In nearby Lake Wales in Polk County, Blue Mountain Development Co. began building a resort of homes.

"It's plain crazy what's goin' on, Mr. Thomas," Big John Sommerland said to Abraham one day on the sidewalk in front of the store. "Everybody's gone plumb crazy, I tell ya. Soon, I do believe, someone's gonna pay a price for all this, and I don't want it to be us. Debt is not good. We're going to cut back soon. I suggest you and your son think about that."

"I agree it can't last, Mr. Sommerland, it can't last. But it's getting tempting to sell something, isn't it?"

Alexander devoted his waking hours to his store, his cattle, and his land. Wilbur was put in charge of the cattle and the pastures. He closed his store during the hot, slow summer months all day Wednesday and Thursday, and at noon on the other work days.

During the winter harvest months, he changed his fruit display daily so it wouldn't spoil. It was easy to drive over to St. Cloud and pick up his daily needs.

Sometimes, early in the morning, Wilbur would stop by the store with Alexander's new horse in tow. They would then ride out to visit his growing herd of cattle, talking as they rode.

"Tell me, Wilbur, what brought you to Kissimmee? In the beginning I mean," Alexander said, gesturing with his hand. "Where did your family come from?"

Wilbur responded, without hesitation, "Well, I'm told my family first came during the late 1700s from Scotland near the Isle of Wye. My family, like most poor folks, had a small flock of sheep as tenant farmers. The land wasn't rich and fertile and they had short growin' seasons. Times got bad. Really bad for my family. The Anglican English persecuted the Scots who were Presbyterian, and my family was surely Scot and Presbyterian." Stopping to think a moment, he continued, "Like a lot of people, my family thought there was freedom and better opportunity in the Colonies. That, my good friend, is when this America was just gettin' started, y'know My folks, like most Scots, came to Philadelphia. My family was still poor and couldn't make it in the city, so they went west to the frontier in western Pennsylvania."

"Poor like us?" asked Alexander.

"Yep, just like you and your Dad were," Wilbur replied with a knowing smile. "Just like you."

"You know, it seems like most immigrants coming to America are poor, or trying to escape some army, famine or something bad. They seek freedom and opportunity. It's the only place in the world like this, isn't it? After the war, I decided to come here and really be free."

"Seems to me, "Wilbur nodded, "the only difference between you an' me is when our families came to America. That's the way I see it anyhow."

"How about T.J. and his family?" asked Alexander. "What about them?"

"I think, Alexander," Wilbur said, rubbing his three-day-old beard with his free hand, "I think they came from England originally, or maybe Germany in the late 1700s. I'm not sure. But I do know his family was already in New York when all those Irish started coming here in the 1800s after the Civil War. His people hated immigrants real bad. They killed a bunch of those Irish and called 'em bad names. They thought they owned America and nobody else had the right to be here."

"I think he doesn't like me for the same reason," Alexander shrugged.

"Yep, that's likely, and I'd sure be careful of T.J. He can be mean. And don't you wear a gun, Alexander. Best not or he'll see that as your challenge and come after you cause you don't use a gun so good yet."

"I know. He doesn't bother me. I just do my work. But I've got my sling. And I'm not afraid of him."

"Yeah, but he's jealous of you an' how good yer doin.'"

After an hour of walking the horses, they reached the gate to the pasture as they pulled the horses to a stop.

"Whoa," called Wilbur to his steed.

"Whoa," followed Alexander as he leaned back, pulled his reins equally, and pushed his feet forward in the leather stirrups, just like Wilbur had taught him.

"Well, Alexander, let's have a look and see what's happenin' with the herd." Wilbur leaned down and unlocked the gate's latch. Then, resuming his position in the saddle, kicked his horse with his heels, leaned forward, squeezed his thighs, and entered the fenced pasture through the gate opening, then took off at a gallop. With Wilbur watching, Alexander followed close behind. They first checked the fence line each day, then rode into the herd.

"The grass is growing richer everyday, Alexander, and with this good weather, sun and rain, we got our shares of calves. They're breedin' all the time. Our bulls have been right vigorous," he smiled, "and there's plenty of young heifers here to keep 'em busy."

Looking over his growing herd of cattle roaming the green grasses with the new calves prompted Alexander to lean back, press his stirrups forward, come to a stop, sit squarely in his saddle and ponder. He smiled gratefully, more than a little amazed at how far he had come.

"As I look at this herd with you, I see the lush green grass, and realize this belongs to me. I am amazed, Wilbur. And I'm grateful you are by my side."

"I'd say, lookin' at this growin' herd, these pastures and your store, you're doin' right good, Alexander."

"And so are you, Wilbur, because if I do good, you do good." Then, shifting in his saddle with a new thought, he asked his friend, "When do we go to Tampa again?"

"I reckon we're about ready," replied Wilbur, as he pulled a small bag of tobacco from his left breast pocket. Then, as he sat in his saddle, his feet secure in the stirrups, looking over the herd alongside Alexander, he pulled out a packet and rolled himself a cigarette, then slowly licked the edge and rolled it tight and slipped it between his lips. "Want a smoke, Alexander?" he asked as he placed the bag and packet back into his left breast pocket, making sure the bag strings hung over the pocket's lip.

"No, I don't think so. My sin is *arak*," he smiled, waving his hand in the air. "Thanks anyway."

Riding out to inspect the herd in the early morning hours became a twice weekly ritual.

"I think," Wilbur paused, looking over the herd, "I think," he repeated typically for emphasis turning his head to the herd, "that we can afford to cut out at least a hundred head and send them to Tampa's yards next week. We don't want to take too many yet; a hundred's about what we can deliver. And," he added, "prices are gettin' higher all the time. But I think thinning the herd's good, so they don't eat up all the grass. See them yearlings over yonder? Well, next fall they'll be bigger and by then the prices'll be even better."

Then, Alexander, anticipating Wilbur's next thought, picked up with, "Maybe we ought to plan on two hundred in the fall then?"

"Yep, that's what I'm thinkin.' Now, let's have a look at some of those calves. See if any are sick or got worms. Can't have any get the others sick now."

After several hours of checking individual cows, yearlings and calves, the two returned to the gate where Alexander rode through and Wilbur remained inside the fence. Waving over his shoulder as he looked back at his employee and friend, and his growing herd, Alexander kicked his heels in his horse, smiling with pride, and headed back at a fast canter to town and his shop eager, anxious, and grateful to the Sommerland family.

Your children are the sons and daughters of Life's longing for itself. They dwell in the house of tomorrow which you cannot visit.

Kahlil Gibran

CHAPTER 21

Kissimmee - Secrets Shared

On alternate Sundays, Alexander and his father took the morning train to Orlando to visit his sister, Leila and play with her children, Maha and Nabil.

On other Sundays, they attended services at the Episcopal church in Kissimmee, aside from the eastern ritual, basically, but not quite like their own Antiochan Orthodox church. Other Sundays they took the train to Tampa and visited with Stanos and Lydia Demetriades and other friends in Tarpon Springs. At their Aegean Sea Restaurant, they visited with friends over glasses of ouzo, so much like anisette based *arak*, feasted on familiar foods of Greece, and simply enjoyed their day of rest and companionship.

He exchanged friendly letters occasionally with Abigail. She encouraged him to write her saying it would improve his writing skills in English. He realized he was getting better and better at writing and thanked her for that. And he found that by writing letters, telling his friend about goings on in Kissimmee, he was sharing more and more of his feelings with her.

In February, she wrote that she would be coming home during the approaching spring holidays. When she arrived on a Friday afternoon in March, she drove straight over to Alexander"s store.

"Hi, Alexander! I'm so happy to see you, she said giving him a hug. I can't stay very long, I have to get home. My mom is waiting. Let's make plans to go out for dinner tomorrow night."

"I'd like that a lot, Abigail. How about we go to the fancy new restaurant at Mr. Plant's new hotel? My customers say it's real nice. The food is good and they even have cloths on every table. Quite high class they say, so the wealthier tourists dine there often. What do you think?"

"I think that's a wonderful idea. That will give us more time to talk. Let's celebrate your new ranch! And there's something I want to tell you."

"Is six thirty good for you? That will give me time to close the store and wash up."

"That's perfect, Alexander."

The next day at six thirty, Abigail drove to Alexander's store. She was all dressed up in her finest dress, her hair drawn up in a twist, and she wore a small amount of lipstick. She smelled as beautiful as she looked.

"Abigail! You always look pretty, but tonight you are beautiful!"

"Come here, Alexander, and give me a big hug! I've missed you a lot!"

"It's wonderful seeing you again, Abigail. I've missed you too. I think all of Kissimmee misses you. But I've missed you a lot! Now, let's walk to the new hotel and enjoy a nice dinner."

"That's good idea, Alexander. These days a good girl doesn't enter a restaurant or hotel alone. That's why it was best I come to your store, so we could walk together to the hotel."

"How do you like my new suit, Abigail? It came from New York. I decided to add some things in my store, and a few ready-to-wear men's coats and suits are part of my inventor…"

"Inventory, Alexander," she giggled. "That's a word I didn't teach you! And that's an important word in your business." She hooked her arm in his and said, "You look very handsome! Now, let's go to dinner, Alexander. I'm really looking forward to tonight."

"Me too, Abigail. There's something I'd like to discuss with you."

They turned to enter the huge, richly decorated new hotel.

"This is some fancy place, isn't it, Abigail?" Alexander exclaimed as they both marveled at the décor of the high-ceilinged, exquisitely furnished lobby.

"Wow!" Abigail whispered to him. "My mama told me this place was the finest hotel Mr. Plant ever built in Florida! He must have spent a fortune on this. Let's see what the restaurant is like," she said as they walked arm in arm to the entry where the well-dressed maitre d' watched them approach his station.

"Two for dinner, sir?"

"Yes, there are just two of us," he replied nervously as the maitre d' picked up two large menus. "This way please."

As they followed him to their table, Abigail whispered, "My parents took me to a place like this once and they taught me some things. Watch and do as I do."

Seated, she carefully placed her cloth napkin across her lap. He followed her example, wondering for a moment why he didn't place the napkin's corner inside his collar to protect his tie and coat.

She smiled, leaned toward him and whispered again, nodding toward an uncorked bottle sitting in a tall, silver footed urn alongside the table across from theirs, "They serve wine here, as you can see. Now there's a procedure you need to know, Alexander."

Abigail helped him select a wine, then coached him quietly, "Take a sip of the small amount of wine the waiter pours into your glass, taste it, and if it's good, nod to the waiter with a smile and tell him it is good. He will then fill our wine glasses, mine first."

Throughout the dinner, Abigail touched his hand as she corrected anything he might find unusual or perplexing.

"Use the smaller fork for the salad," she whispered.

"You are so good, Abigail, and formal American dining customs are so difficult. Thank you for not letting me embarrass myself. I'll learn fast, but it is very different than what I've known."

After their main course arrived, Alexander grew quiet, pondering, and, with more than a bit of trepidation, cleared his throat and said, "Abigail, there is something I want to share with you. This is very personal and I know I can trust you. I've wanted to tell you about this for a long time. But I've been so confused."

She watched him lower his eyes as he debated within himself where to start and what to say.

"On my way to America, Abigail," he began as he reached out to touch her soft hand, "I met a wonderful young girl in Marseille, France. She was sixteen and I was eighteen. We fell deeply in love and knew we were destined to be with each other forever."

He went on in great detail to describe Madeleine, their mutual love, their adventures in Marseille, and how broken-hearted they were when he had to board the ship to America.

"That's beautiful, Alexander. Everyone wishes they could have that kind of love sometime in their lives. I know I do, and my sorority sisters feel the same way. But please continue, Alexander. There must be more."

"Well," he added in a soft voice to keep their conversation private, "I've written many, many letters to her during these past four years."

"That's lovely, Alexander. You are a warm, loving person. That's why I treasure our friendship so much."

"Yes, but," he continued, almost tearing up from disappointment, "I have not received even one letter from Madeleine all this time. I don't know what to think. I'm not even sure she's still alive or in France anymore. But, I must tell you, she's still very much in my heart.

"And now, Abigail, my father keeps urging me to find a good Lebanese girl, get married and have a family. He believes I'll be happier if I marry someone of my own kind, as he describes it. I'm getting depressed about it. You are the nicest thing that's happened to me since I came to America, and I'm beginning to feel drawn to you more than just a friend. I mean, we've spent so much time together, and you have been so wonderful. But I don't think your parents would want us to become more than friends. And I know my father would be opposed to it, for sure."

"Oh, Alexander, I'm so glad you told me about Madeleine. I do understand, but I don't understand why she hasn't written you. That doesn't make any sense to me. But, you know, I think your father is just like Mama and Daddy. They keep telling me I'm getting too old and that it's time for me to get married. They too, tell me I should find a man who is like us because I'll be happier that way.

"Well, dear friend, I too have something to tell you because you are the only person I trust enough to share my true innermost feelings. I mean, you saved my life, Alexander. I told everyone at school how you killed that big old cottonmouth just before he was going to strike my foot. They couldn't believe you didn't use a gun! That you actually used your sling from Lebanon! They all want to meet you. You are very important to me, almost as important as my parents, but my mama is very clear about what kind of man I'm supposed to marry. And these days, Alexander, we young ladies are bound to follow our parents rules, aren't we?"

"Maybe young men too, Abigail. Sometimes, I think my father and your parents say the same things. Maybe we are all that different anyway."

"Alexander," she said quietly, "I have to tell you that during this past semester I met a young man. Actually, he's two years older than me. He's in law school now at Florida State College for Men in Gainesville, and will take the bar exam soon. He's Episcopalian like me, his family is wealthy and prominent in Tampa, and he's even said one day he wants to be governor of Florida. His name is G. Hamilton Smythe III. His football buddies call him 'Ham.' Ugh, I don't like that nickname." She spoke as if she was reading her textbook, without her typical joy and delight. Then, she lowered her head as she continued, "But last summer, when you and I were spending so much time together at your lessons, having fun riding together all the time, and we were becoming very close friends, my mama believed we were getting too close and she got upset. Now, Alexander, I don't need to tell you how much my daddy and mama respect you and your father, and how much they like you, but when it comes to their feelings about who their only daughter marries, well, I have to tell you, when she sat me down before I went back to school, she explained in great detail what my prospective husband should be. She even wrote down a list and gave it to me. So, I kept my eyes open for someone who would please my parents, and Mr. Smythe fits all their requirements. He should make them very happy, Alexander."

As he listened to Abigail tell her story, he watched her eyes. He felt her hands as she reached out to his. He also felt a sadness for her as her eyes moistened. She was not happy about her situation any more than he was trying to satisfy his father's demands. He sensed his feelings for Abigail were growing much stronger than simply friendship and always would. He knew too that she cared much more for him that simply as a friend. He believed, even though neither mouthed the words, that in most ways they loved each other, but caught in a situation that convinced them they could never marry as long as their parents felt so strongly opposed. Tears welled in Alexander's eyes as he watched Abigail lower her head so he couldn't see her tears.

They were sharing their most important, secret feelings with each other, with no reluctance. It was a poignant moment for both.

He automatically tightened his grip on her hand. "Oh, Abigail, I am sad for both of us. I don't know what to say or what to do. I do want you and me to be close friends for the rest of our lives, and maybe, as I've always been told, 'Have faith in the Lord. He loves us and He will provide.'"

"Alexander," she sniffed, "can I come visit you in your store tomorrow? I really want to talk to you some more."

"Of course, Abigail. Please come by. Can we go horseback riding together too? We can ride out and see my growing herd you and your family gave me. Would you like that?"

*Even as love crowns you so shall he crucify you.
Even as he is for your growth, so is he for your pruning...*
Kahlil Gibran

CHAPTER 22

Abigail's Dilemma

"Hey. Alexander! Let's go for a ride!" Abigail's upbeat mood permeated the morning air. Alexander reacted with a smile to see her ebullience, especially after listening to her divulge her inner anxieties resulting from her mother's demands that she marry "someone like us."

"I'll be ready in a minute, Abigail, just let me close up the shop."

Both jumped in her car and she drove to the stables where they saddled and bridled their respective favorite horses, the bay and the Appaloosa.

"Come on, Alexander! Show me your herd of cattle. I'm so excited."

Abigail spurred her horse who leapt into a gallop almost immediately, then watched Alexander follow suit, quickly galloping behind her. As he pulled alongside, she went into a cantor, then a walk so they could continue their conversation from the night before.

"I do care so much for you, Alexander," she said as he pulled close.

"And I like you so much, Abigail. I mean, I really care about your happiness. I think you're not very happy about your mother's requirements for a husband, but do you think you could eventually love your Mr. Smythe? He does seem to have excellent credentials."

"Oh, Hamilton is basically a good person, Alexander, and I suppose he'll make a good husband, but I'm not sure. I've heard that occasionally he gets drunk, and sometimes he acts like a rich spoiled brat."

"Has he ever hurt you?" Alexander asked quickly, deeply concerned for her welfare.

"No, but I did hear some bad things from his frat brothers."

"Like what? What is a frat brother?"

"Fraternities are sort of like lifetime social clubs for men. At FCFW, we have sororities, which are similar organizations for women. Everyone in a frat is proud of his fraternity. Same with the women. I'm in a sorority called Delta Delta Delta, or Tri-Delt for short."

"Isn't that Greek?"

"Yes, smart guy," she laughed. "They do call all of us Greeks because of our names.

"Anyway, Alexander," she explained as she brought her horse to a stop along side Alexander, "one of his brothers whispered to me at a party that Hamilton treated a couple girls he dated pretty ungentlemanly. And that worries me."

"Hmmm, I see what you mean, Abigail. No man should treat a woman badly. Certainly not you! Do you think that those brothers could be jealous?"

"I don't know," she frowned. "I guess I'll have to find out when I see Hamilton back at school. I think he's planning to propose marriage to me when he gets his law degree and I've graduated. My mother would like me to get married this fall when it's cooler here."

"Omigosh! That soon, Abigail?"

"Yes," she replied with a worried look that Alexander hated to see.

In late June, Abigail returned to Kissimmee. After depositing her belongings at home, she drove to Alexander's shop on Broadway.

"Alexander," she exclaimed happily as she stepped into his store, "come here and give me a big hug!"

"Hi, Abigail, it's great to see you! You're a college graduate now, aren't you?"

"Yes, Alexander, after four years of lots of study, hard work, and, I must admit, a lot of fun sometimes. Whatever, I have my degree!"

"And how about Mr. G. Hamilton Smythe III?" he asked, curiously.

"Oh, yes," she answered, lowering her head slightly and speaking in a softer voice, "last Saturday night, after my graduation dinner, Hamilton did ask me to marry him, telling me he loved me and offering me a very large diamond ring."

"And?" Alexander asked impatiently.

"I told him I was very fond of him and would give him my answer tomorrow."

"You mean you are making him wait five days for your answer?"

"Alexander, I wanted to think about it, and speak with you and with my parents. This is such a serious decision for me, of course."

"What are your thoughts about this commitment, Abigail?"

"My mother, especially, is very excited. My dad hasn't voiced his opinion yet. I have to admit that Hamilton has treated me quite respectfully. He seems sincere and his family background impresses my mother. What do you think, Alexander?"

"Abigail, I think, since you ask, both of us must respond to our parents' wishes. We should respect and love our parents and, as it is said, we must honor them.

Maybe they are wiser and correct and you must give yourself to your heritage. But, I'll say this, Abigail, I really don't like not being able to follow our own hearts. My father really makes me mad about this!"

"Alexander, I suppose you're right. I'm sure that marrying Hamilton will make my parents happy because his family is very wealthy and prominent. Also, if I think about it, he's a good guy. We do have similar views of life. And he says he loves me."

"That's it? I suppose that's all good, and perhaps in time you'll grow to love him. Whatever happens, Abigail, you can always count on me and our friendship."

As Abigail dismounted her horse, she beckoned to Alexander to do the same. Standing together, Abigail gave him a warm hug and whispered, "Thank you, my dear friend." Then, she cupped his face with her hands and kissed him softly on his lips.

Alexander's emotions collided with each other. He felt a deep sense of loss, realizing for the first time that Abigail would soon be someone else's wife and not able to be as close to him as in the past. Yet, he felt a great sense of relief for his special friend as she looked forward to her wedding.

Attendees at Abigail's engagement party at the new Kissimmee Regal Hotel, Henry Plant's finest, included friends of the Sommerland family, cattle families, political leaders, friends of the prominent Smythe family, and, much to their own surprise, Alexander and Abraham.

Hamilton, an only child, became formally introduced to Kissimmee society and all who knew the Sommerlands.

While the invited guests circulated, congratulating Big John and Mrs. Sommerland, the Smythes, and the two honorees, Abigail watched Hamilton across the room at the bar with his fraternity brothers.

"Look at Hamilton!" she said to Alexander. "You'd think he could stay sober tonight of all nights."

"Does he usually drink a lot at parties?"

Rolling her eyes, she nodded yes. "Stay near me, Alexander, please," Abigail said softly. "Hamilton has had too much to drink. He's done this at school, but I begged him not to drink too much tonight. I'm furious that he is misbehaving now of all times. I need you to be close but I don't want him to get jealous. I want the two of you to be friends."

"Sure, Abigail, I'll always be nearby. And thank you for inviting my father and me. This grand party reminds me of parties we have in Douma all week long before weddings. But there, the bride and groom's families host parties in their homes. It's all about family and traditions. The whole village plays a big part of the courtship. Two people may decide to get married, but many in both families get to know and approve of both people and their families. They really have to spend a lot of time getting to know in detail the character of the prospective spouse before they approve the wedding plans. How long have your parents known your fiancé?"

She giggled at his innocence as she replied, "Only a week. He and his parents arrived last Sunday for a few days."

"You mean your parents just met the Hamiltons a few days ago? Your culture is very different than what I grew up with. Do you really know this man, Abigail? Do Big John and your mother know his character, his background?"

"Hey, Abigail," Hamilton slurred loudly as he struggled to walk toward where she and Alexander stood, the overindulgence of alcohol clearly evident. He waved a half empty glass at them as he moved away from a group of his college buddies raucously laughing and drinking at the bar. "Whatcha' doin, darling?" He put his hand on her shoulder, too heavily, claiming his fiancée. "And who is this foreigner here with you anyway? And that one right over there?" he asked sarcastically, motioning his glass toward Abraham, standing nearby.

"Hamilton!" she responded, shocked at his pejorative labeling of her friend. "This is Alexander Thomas, my dear friend, and that gentlemen standing over there is his father."

"Your friend? He sure looks...urp...like an Arab or somethin' to me. Why are they here? They don't belong with us Americans!"

"Stop, Hamilton! Don't insult my dear friend and his father. They are my guests and you are way out of line!"

"But, Abigail, they don' look like us and they don' belong here!"

With that, Alexander watched Abigail's face turn red from embarrassment as she gritted her teeth. She raised her hand to slap Hamilton's face. Alexander quickly reached for her cocked arm. "No, Abigail. Don't slap him here. It will embarrass your parents, and we must always honor them."

"But I want him to apologize to you now! Hamilton, if you truly love me and want to marry me, you will apologize to Alexander this very minute. And to his father too! I mean it!"

At that moment, Big John approached Abraham, standing near the couple and listening to the confrontation. "Hello Abraham, my dear friend," he said in a booming voice, wearing a proud smile. "Are you having a good time? I'm mighty proud you and Alexander are with us tonight. You know how much the missus and I respect you two. Thanks for being here. I know Abigail's grateful too."

"Thank you, Big John. We're very proud to be here, and consider Abigail and your family our very dear friends too."

Hamilton's angry loud retort to Abigail abruptly interrupted their conversation. Big John turned toward Abigail with fire in his eyes.

"Abigail," he said loud enough for those nearby to hear, "Do you need my help?"

"No, Daddy," she said, tilting her head upward, smiling for the benefit those watching, "I think all is under control. Hamilton is about to sincerely apologize to Alexander and his father for what he just said. Maybe you should bring Mr. Thomas over here so all of us can witness Hamilton's apology."

Alexander saw the anger in Big John's eyes as he ordered his potential son-in-law, "If I was you, I'd hurry up and do what she says, Hamilton. Now!" he added in a deep, stern voice that those who knew him, understood his daughter's wishes must be obeyed immediately.

Big John whispered to Abraham, "That boy is lucky I didn't bring my whip!"

"He is very lucky, Big John, and he needs to change his ways or Abigail could have problems in the future with him."

"Ah'm going to have a talk with him before the wedding. He'll get my message, I can assure you."

Noticing the slight commotion, Hamilton's parents crossed the room and joined their son as he lowered his eyes from Big John's disapproving look, bowed his head to Abigail and contritely apologized to her, Alexander, and Abraham. They graciously accepted the apology, noting the number of guests gathering around them, murmuring among themselves. As the orchestra resumed playing, the engagement party resumed albeit with a cloud of mixed emotions.

Wedding plans resumed after Abigail and Hamilton resolved their issues, and the marriage took place in September as planned.

After Abigail's wedding, Alexander began rethinking his personal life.

"If Abigail can move on with her life and be happy, so can I," he said to his father.

"She made a beautiful bride, son, and she'll always be your friend. And, yes, I think that in years to come she'll agree that it is best to marry someone with a similar upbringing. That solves so many problems."

"And, *Baba*, they are both Episcopalians, though I doubt Hamilton attends church. I must admit I miss her."

"Yet, son, she lives in Tampa, not far away, and her family is here. You'll see her again."

"She certainly had a grand wedding, didn't she, *Baba?*"

"Oh, yes, a completely filled church, overflowing with flowers, and everyone happy for the couple."

"Imagine, twelve beautiful bridesmaids in elegant gowns and twelve handsome groomsmen in tuxedos."

"There are similarities and differences between our ways, Iskandar. Their service is much simpler than ours. The Orthodox wedding lasts much longer, and to me, has more meaning. The dance of Isaiah is so important to our wedding as a pledge to God."

"They don't include that at all, *Baba*."

"I mean no disrespect, Iskandar, but I like our service very much. When your mother and I married, it was so meaningful, an ancient ritual. And one day you too will experience that holy sacrament, filled with meaning."

"And I think when you go through such a long ceremony, you stay married," Iskandar said as he laughed along with his father who agreed with the humor.

"Their style of wedding ceremony might be simple, but the dresses, tuxes, and flowers looked very expensive! And the reception outside under the tent! Wow! Big John must have spent a fortune!"

"You see, son, our cultures in that way are truly different. Trust me. You'll be happier with your own kind. A good Lebanese-Syrian girl won't expect so much. You'll see when we get to Boston and you are with Salim."

Well, Alexander thought to himself, with Abigail no longer in Kissimmee, and still no letters from Madeleine, I'm going to Boston to meet my future wife. With that thought, he sat back and smiled broadly at his father who understood his son's change of heart.

Late in the fall of 1924, Alexander went to Boston with his father to visit relatives. After four years, he had not received any letters from Madeleine. He often wondered what had become of her and why she hadn't answered his letters. His father stayed with Uncle Mike, while Alexander stayed with Salim and his wife Julia. The purpose of his visit was to see the family, to be sure, but more importantly it was to find a wife, a companion, and, in time, the mother of his children. To Alexander, remembering his culture, this was appropriate.

He had finally received a letter from Hanna in Marseille saying that Daniella and Madeleine had to go to Paris because of "personal family reasons," and that times were difficult in Marseille. He didn't really understand what Hanna was telling him, or more importantly, what Hanna wasn't telling him. But at least, after so long, he now knew that Madeleine was alive…personal reasons? Did she get married? Does she have children? Is she ill? Is her mother ill? There were so many questions but he never received any correspondence from Madeleine. So, Alexander felt he had to stay focused on his own life and bring his attention to the present. Nevertheless, it remained an emotional struggle for him.

"Eat your dinner, Iskandar." Julia spoke, still referring to Alexander by his Arabic name. "My sister will be here in a few minutes, and you have been picking at your food. Are you not well?" Alexander looked up and abruptly stopped thinking of Madeleine. Julia and he spoke for a few minutes more until they were interrupted by a knock at the door. Salim went to the door and ushered Helene into the sparse but comfortable dining room.

Alexander stood, and spoke, "Hello, Helene, I'm glad to see you again." In that first moment, he saw a pretty young woman, fully blossomed, no longer the young girl he met when first he came to Boston. His eyebrows rose as his eyes widened, seeing her as a fully developed young woman.

"You have really grown up since we last saw each other. You were only a little girl. Now, you look wonderful." Helene was dressed in the fashion of the day: a clinging chemise that draped over her winsome figure, reaching to just beyond her knees. Her shoes, he noticed, were very fashionable with pointed toes and t-straps across her feet. She wore a pretty ribbon in her hair. He knew she had dressed her best for their meeting, just as had he, to make a strong first impression and get on with the formalities of a proper courtship.

Helene smiled coquettishly, "I was just fifteen, Alexander. Now I am nineteen, a woman." She posed for him, hands on her hips, smiling confidently, turning so he could see her figure. "It's nice to see you too after such a long time. You must like Florida. Uncle Mike says you and your father are very successful. He told me that you have your own store, a cattle ranch, and are buying an automobile. That's exciting."

"Oh," he laughed and replied, pulling his hands as though riding a horse, "I also own a horse and a bicycle!"

Helene laughed with him, impressed by this successful, handsome, determined, yet modest, young suitor with a sense of humor.

Alexander and Helene visited for several hours that evening in the parlor with Julia and Salim, properly chaperoned, as Alexander spoke of his experiences in Florida. "I learned a lot from the Sommerlands," he began as he told Helene of all his cultural advances and of learning English with Abigail as his tutor. He spoke of his cattle ranch, Big John and Mrs. Sommerland, and their daughter, Abigail, carefully avoiding saying anything beyond his platonic friendship with her.

Helene, in turn, described her life to Alexander. She worked in the textile mill in Boston like most young women, had completed high school, and would likely continue working in the mill to help the family's finances, not considering college.

Julia, in an effort to tempt Alexander, exclaimed with a smile, "Two men have come here to meet Helene! They asked her to marry them in the past year. Can you imagine? One was from California; his name was Butrus. He was nice, but Helene didn't think she was meant to live on a farm in California. It's so different and so far away. Another came here from Toledo, Ohio. They were both looking for a wife, for sure. They wanted to find someone their age, of their religion, and Syrian. Helene didn't like them enough, so she said no."

"You said 'no' to two suitors?" he asked, turning to Helene, befuddled. "What would you say to me? That is, if I were to ask?"

"Hmmm," she demurred, smiling, "I'm not sure yet," as she turned her head away coquettishly, with a wink at her sister. "You'll have to ask to find out,

Iskandar," she teased.

Her confidence made Alexander want her more. His feelings for this lovely young woman grew stronger each day. After all, he was in Boston for a reason.

Alexander knew he was on a mission, determined even before leaving Kissimmee that he would find a bride in Boston. He didn't really know even one single Syrian girl in Florida. But in Boston, there was a large — in fact, one of the largest — Syrian communities in America. And he knew he had something to offer, including his business success, his tenacity, his resilience and his willingness to accept a challenge. He did find Helene attractive, although she didn't stir his emotions like Madeleine had. But, she was pretty; she was Syrian; she was Orthodox Christian, and her family certainly accepted him and his father. So, he knew all was well, and perhaps Helene would be the means of fulfillment of his destiny. After all, marriage and children were a large part of where his life must go. So, he decided to do whatever it took to sell Helene on the idea of marrying him during his four-week stay. As a result, Alexander spent a lot of time with Helene, Sam, Julia, and the family.

Madeleine's lack of response to his many letters had finally convinced him to move on and seriously consider another woman.

By the end of the summer visit, Helene had indeed turned down his first proposal, like she had done to her two previous suitors, instinctively knowing how to make sure her man really wanted her, but in the end, she finally said yes to Alexander's more convincing second effort, making him very proud and happy.

At the right moment, he had reached into his pocket and pulled out the two-carat blue diamond ring he had bought from his supplier, Syden and Company, when he knew he was going to Boston. On that important evening at Salim and Julia's house, in their living room before dinner, with Salim's encouraging nod and hand motion, Alexander nervously stepped across the room, and stood before Helene. Mustering all his courage, he looked into her eyes as she gazed into his, clearly excited and flattered. He carefully kneeled onto the floor. Then, reaching for her hands folded in her lap holding a rose bud, he whispered so softly she could barely hear his words, "Helene, will you marry me?"

Then, in that pregnant silent moment, as she looked at him without responding quickly, realizing the importance of what all this meant, Alexander got even more flustered. Before she could reply, remembering she had already turned down his clumsy first proposal, and two other suitors, Alexander blurted out, "If you say 'yes,' I will build you a big house! I will buy you a horse and your own saddle! And…"

"Iskandar!" she laughed, "yes!" Then, hearing her own loud laughter, she quickly covered her mouth and giggled silently. "I will marry you because you are too funny to let go! I think you and I can have a good life together, but don't worry about getting me a horse and saddle. I'm a city girl. Remember?"

Still holding her hands, Alexander stood up and pulled her to him very relieved, very happy. "Yes," he said, "yes, Helene, I will be a good and faithful husband to you. So let's get married right away and then let me take you to Kissimmee!"

"Kiss…a…me," she laughed. "What a name! Is that what you do down there? Just kiss…a…me all the time?"

They all laughed together at her joke, dissipating any lingering tension and drawing the entire family into the laughter so that everyone nodded, knowing that this marriage would last a long time.

Alexander and Helene were very soon married at her family's Antiochan Orthodox church before several hundred family members and close friends who witnessed the ritualistic one hour ceremony, which included a performance of the Song of Isaiah while wearing crowns of their bonds with God. Marriage was a means to continue his life's destiny, have a family and a life-long companion.

He recalled his father's admonition. "You can learn to love her later."

Helene liked Alexander very much. She would whisper to Julia, "He is so good-looking, and I think he will be kind to me. I don't think we will ever go hungry; after all he has lots of cows. And," she laughed, "He's very funny!"

These realities were the most important considerations; love and passion would come later.

These were times of family naiveté and joy, so their post wedding days were filled with family gatherings, dancing, dinners and celebrations. Perhaps because of Helene's innocence and shyness, they didn't consummate their marriage for a month, not until after they had arrived back in Kissimmee.

Helene discovered a totally different world. *What have I done?* she asked herself.

*Joy and sorrow are inseparable. Together they come,
and when one sits alone with you at your board,
remember that the other is asleep upon your bed...*
Kahlil Gibran

CHAPTER 23

Hardships: 1926-1941

Within a year of Alexander and Helene's arrival in Kissimmee as a married couple, costs of everything began rising. Realizing that his very attractive bride would not want to stay in the upstairs apartment with her father-in-law for long, Alexander quickly invested in a large parcel for the two of them and built a beautiful Victorian home for Helene in Kissimmee on the west shore of Lake Tohopekaliga, fulfilling the promise he made that evening in Boston.

He admired the Sommerland home so much that he used it as a model for Helene's new house. He designed the house with five bedrooms, because he fully intended to have several children, including an extra room downstairs for his father, just in case.

In the spring of 1925, Helene bore a healthy and beautiful son, Michael. Alexander felt a sense of completeness. His baby son's giggles blocked out any thoughts of Marseille.

"I have a son," he repeated every day to his wife. "If a man has a son, he will live forever, it is said. I now have a son who will carry on my name...my legacy. All that I do everyday will be for my son. My life is dedicated to him. He is my life." Alexander began to fully believe he had indeed found his destiny with the birth of Michael.

He spent almost all day, every day, particularly during the busier winter months, at the store, and for several hours into some early evenings on horseback with Wilbur searching for his cattle on the open range. He focused on working to insure that his family's life was secure, but began carving out more time for Helene and Michael. There was no such thing as "working too hard" to Alexander. He worked long hours with his characteristic sense of responsibility, tenacity, and even stubbornness. "I will do whatever it takes, *Baba*," he would often say to his father, "to provide a better, easier future for my family than you and I had. If it takes working twenty hours a day, I will do it."

But too, he was often home for lunch with Helene, as they grew closer and closer, depending on each other to make their lives full, and as warm and happy as possible.

"My son, Helene," he'd say proudly as he played with Michael, fascinated by their incredibly perfect creation.

"Yes, Alexander. We have a beautiful son, thank God," she always responded lovingly as she watched her husband hold Michael aloft, making him laugh.

They laughed a lot together, especially as they shared the life of their son.

But Alexander's fortunes changed quickly, due to conditions beyond his control. The severe hurricanes that swept through central Florida in the summer of 1926 caused havoc, death and economic ruin. But the 1928 hurricane shocked the entire community of Kissimmee with its intensity. Cattle were swept away by wind gusts of over one hundred fifty miles per hour. And heavy, unprecedented blowing rains flooded the Kissimmee River basin, killing thousands of cows and steers, including hundreds of Alexander's herd.

During the "Boom" years of 1925 and 1926, Alexander had built a small hotel, and lost his entire investment when the 1928 hurricane came so suddenly. His builder had left town in the night, leaving Alexander to pay the suppliers and workers in addition to his payments to the builder only days before. As a result, he paid for his new store and hotel twice. Another expensive lesson learned. He was devastated and miserable about it.

"We lost the money and the hotel, leaving us very little to pay even the property taxes," he lamented to Helene.

Speculators defaulted on their loans like dominoes, many disappearing in the night, leaving the region in economic devastation. Land values plummeted to as little as $1 per acre in just two years. While Alexander and other cattlemen and citrus growers of central Florida still had their lands, their cattle and their citrus trees, the market for beef and citrus completely evaporated, prices fell dramatically every day, and everyone suffered economic ruin. Alexander's fate was no exception. He too was on the financial ropes. He became distressed, yet stayed determined. There was little or no business at the store; no one had cash, and only with bartering of goods and services did the people survive.

The Land Boom became the Land Crash.

In October of 1927, Helene was in her last month of pregnancy with their second child. Alexander worried how he could afford to feed another child.

"I do hope it's a girl," she would write to her sisters in Boston. "My son has been a wonderful gift from God, and he makes Alexander so proud. But, I'd like a daughter for myself," and, teasingly, she would add, "so she can take care of me when I grow old. A man stands taller when his wife bears a son, for he will soon be able to help him with the ranch. But I wish for a daughter."

Helene had been the second of eight children whose immigrant parents were very spiritual, always gaining strength from their prayers. They steeped their children in the core beliefs of Faith, Faith, Faith and trust in God. Being the daughter of a priest, Helene knew what it was like to live on very little income.

In mid-November 1927, during the worst of times, Helene bore Alexander a beautiful dark-haired daughter they named Helena.

Alexander and Helene found joy in their two children, treasuring their smiles, giggles, and love, but suffered economically along with everyone else in the small community of Kissimmee. Business was much slower, nearly evaporating. Days became longer and longer. A malaise overcame most people of the region.

"Sales at the store have dropped so much. No one is buying. Sometimes I wonder why I even go there, Helene."

"We must have faith. We'll make do, my husband," she consoled him. "These difficult times will only make our family stronger and allow us more time together."

"I hope you are right that in time this will pass, Helene," Alexander replied optimistically, as they comforted each other. "We must be thankful for what we have. These are terrible, terrible times, but I am doing my best, and we will be fine," he assured his loyal, loving wife. At least our home is fully paid for, so no one will take it away."

Later, in a quiet moment, he confided with her, "Even now, we are experiencing a new problem. There is a fruit bug ruining all the citrus. They call it the Mediterranean fruit fly. We may lose our entire harvest this year and have to destroy much of the groves…it's always something and it seems to just get worse."

Helene gripped Alexander's hand and reminded him, "Our faith will sustain us. Just do the best you can."

"All we can do is fight these things and endure. These are bad times, Helene, but the locust infestation in Douma was worse. If I survived them, I can survive anything. And we will."

A few years earlier, Alexander had followed the advice of his mentor, Big John, and began crossbreeding his growing herd with the newly arrived Brahman bulls that the Stewart family in Bartow, and large rancher Bud Parkins, had brought to the area from India by way of Texas.

"The Brahman breed can handle the heat and any lack of water during the dry months better than our cattle. They're larger by far, add more weight faster than our cattle, and are resistant to the Texas Fever Tick," Bud Parkins had told Alexander.

"They sure look strange with that hump on the back."

Will Stewart down in Polk County was a strong advocate of crossbreeding with the Brahman breed. "I'm convinced, Alexander," Stewart had told him during one of Alexander's visits to Bartow, "that you'd better get your cows with my bulls and get ahead of the rest. You ought to get a few cows too. It's a wise decision. Take a few of my bulls and get going, son." He added, almost as a throwaway statement, "I'm gonna build the best darned Brahman herd in the country. That's how strong I feel about this breed."

"You've sure been good to me over the years, Mr. Stewart. I do appreciate your help."

"Yeah, I'll have a couple of trucks sent over with, say, six bulls and a dozen young Brahman heifers. You're doin' the smart thing, son."

Within a few years, Will Stewart, known as one of the finest, most honest ranchers in the region, did indeed build the best quality closed Brahman herd in America. Alexander knew Stewart's word was gold, that he was a good Christian man and could totally be trusted. The word on him was spreading across America's cattle country. In time, even the Argentines began arriving in Bartow to partake of the excellence of the Stewart farm breeding bulls.

Thanks to his listening to Will Stewart's advice and crossbreeding his herd with Stewart's Brahman, Alexander's herd soon grew not only in number, but in size, quality, and value. Each head gained more weight and required less water. Back in 1920, before Alexander owned any cattle, the Texas Fever Tick had struck the area killing thousands of heads of cattle. Those few herds that were at least one-eighth Brahman crossbred were spared. He was now protected if and when the tick returned.

But, even worse conditions were to come during the 1930s Great Depression with plummeting demand for beef in the Northern markets. Alexander and the other ranchers suffered once again.

Alexander sold a minimum of cattle at depressed prices, working instead to save his herd and improve its breeding with Brahman bulls and cows, and improving the quality of his pastures. He did what he could to clear his land of scrub and obtrusive palmetto to make his land more productive, always looking ahead.

"We're not getting anything for our cattle these days anyway, with beef at almost give-away prices," he said to other ranchers when they met at the Cattlemen's Beef Market. "I'd rather just keep them in the pasture, and improve my breeding with the Brahmans until prices increase. And they will one day. This can't last forever."

"You are always the optimist, Thomas," one of his colleagues responded.

Some began to believe these economic conditions could get even worse and maybe last forever. But Alexander, like the Stewarts, the Parkins, and the Sommerlands, never gave up on the cattle business. They found solutions, determined to hang onto their land and precious herds. As terrible conditions grew worse across the country, Alexander always found an inner strength.

"You know, Big John," he said optimistically, one day as they were all sharing drinks of whiskey at the hotel bar, "It's always darkest before the dawn."

"Yep, Alexander, and don't forget," Big John said, smiling, jabbing his elbow into Alexander's ribs, "it's always darkest before the end too." When he laughed sardonically, everyone joined in, nervously laughing at this not so funny reminder. There was comfort in being with their friends during these moments when they weren't suffering alone over their dismal books.

Some large landowners did make it through the early darkest days of the Great Depression, but many who were over-extended, lost their lands, tens of thousands of acres, literally hundreds of square miles of pastureland, to the counties and state governments for ad valorem taxes. They had no money to pay for anything, even property taxes. One rancher lost over 15,000 acres of land for only $200 in taxes. He simply could not put $10 together and the government would only accept cash. He nearly committed suicide. Others, scared and depressed, simply gave up and left the region for good.

*Your children are not your children.
You may give them your love, but not their thoughts."*
Kahlil Gibran

CHAPTER 24
The Great Labor Day Hurricane of 1935

As conditions worsened, Alexander did not feel the need to be in the store every day. Consequently, he spent more and more time with his family, taking his young son, Michael, fishing in the lake in their small boat, and hunting in their fields for small game. He loved teaching his son as much by example as by his words.

"Michael, we must always take care of our land and our cattle. And you must learn to hunt, master a gun with care and learn to respect it. Wilbur will teach you how to use the whip."

"Oh yes, *Baba*," Michael replied eagerly. "I want to learn all those things."

"One day, son, you and your sister will own all this. Your mother and I won't live forever and you, as the man of the family, will operate all these businesses. You must learn everything I do. That way, you can provide for your own family someday."

Alexander's heritage, as he knew it, looked to future generations so they had opportunities to live even better lives than did he. He recalled his own father's guidance and wisdom.

Abraham enjoyed spending time teaching his grandson, often saying proudly, "You are just like your father, Michael."

Michael helped his mother in the garden…working each day "to make Dad proud of me." He was especially proud when his vegetables ripened and he could bring them into the house. "Do you like my tomatoes, *Baba*? I'm bringing in lots of beans in a few days. I want to help Mom."

Helena, a playful child, loved teasing her parents who doted on her all the time. Alexander marveled at his daughter's playful nature, her charm, and her sense of self-responsibility. She helped her mother fold the laundry, and assisted her in the kitchen while learning how to prepare the Lebanese foods.

As the children grew older, attending school, Helene began spending more time in town, volunteering at their church and helping Alexander in the store, always certain to be home by the time the children arrived from school.

"Good mornin', kids," Wilbur said to Michael and Helena, opening the back screen door into the kitchen. "Your daddy asked me to watch over you two today. Why aren't you in school?"

"It's Labor Day, Uncle Wilbur! There's no school today," they laughed in unison.

"It's a beautiful day! Sunny and bright!" He looked around, "Where are your folks?"

"Daddy's at the citrus plant over in St. Cloud, and Mama's at the church doing volunteer work."

"So," he said, helping himself to a cup of coffee, and sitting down at the breakfast table, watching the two youngsters finish their breakfast, "what would you like to do today?"

"We want to go riding with you," Michael yelped, gleefully.

"Can we, Uncle Wilbur? Can we?" Helena asked excitedly.

"Sure, and bring your whips and lariats with you. We'll be doin' a lot of ridin' looking for strays. You want to help me round up some strays?"

"Oh, yes!" squealed Helena. "That would be fun!" She sprung from her chair and jumped up and down, clapping her hands and laughing. "I love you, Uncle Wilbur," she exclaimed, hugging him, happy to be included in this adventure and feeling very grown up at age eight. "I'm old enough to help you, don't you think?"

"I know I can help too," interjected 10-year-old Michael. You've taught me so much. Wait until you see me crack my whip! I've been practicing."

"Well, OK, kids. Helena, you get your pony. Michael, go get your saddles and bridles on. I'll cinch your saddles tight when yer ready."

"Yippee!" yelled Helena as she ran out the kitchen door toward the stables. "Come on, Michael, let's get ready!"

"I'll get our rain hats and slickers, in case we need them."

Wilbur loaded his revolver into his holster and fastened his gun belt packing his Bowie knife into the belt. He then led Michael and Helena into the southern pastures and beyond into the open range. For the first couple of hours, Michael paced his horse to Helena's pony side by side as Wilbur instructed them on what they would do when they found stray cattle. "Stay close to me, and when we find some strays, stay calm and don't let them get between us and the pines. Never let them get between us and the Cyprus hammocks and swamps. We don't want them running away from us into the swamps or pines. It's too hard to get them out. And watch out in the cypress for those danged cypress knees!"

"What are cypress knees, Uncle Wilbur?"

"Oh, you know, Helena. We've seen them."

"I don't remember, Michael. What are they?"

"Helena," Wilbur interjected, they are part of the cypress root system and grow straight up from the ground, sometimes four feet high. They look like tapered candles covered with bark and can be sharp on the tops. Some are short though, and if there's water in the swamp, we can't see them. Neither can the horses, who could break their ankles if they step on them and maybe throw you off your horse. Avoid them, kids! They're dangerous."

"Oh!" exclaimed Helena, thinking about their threat to them, "Let's just stay out of the swamps."

They started cantering, now in the level flood plains of the Kissimmee River basin, trying to make up some time lost by their slow pace.

Despite Wilbur's advice, Michael wanted to break into a gallop. He looked to Wilbur, "Can I run for awhile? We haven't spotted any strays and we've been walking a long time, Uncle Wilbur."

"Can we, Uncle Wilbur?" Helena begged, "Just for a while. We won't go far."

I guess it's okay, kids, if you stay close. You can gallop for a few minutes but don't get too far ahead of me. And if you see strays, stop galloping. I don't want you to scare them into the pines or the swamps."

"OK, we won't," Michael yelled back as he kicked his heels into his horse's sides. "Let's go, Helena!"

"I'll beat you, Michael!" she yelled, giggling. But despite her eagerness and abilities, her pony simply couldn't keep up with Michael's horse who was galloping ahead toward a cluster of six heifers. Michael laughed out loud as he watched them stop their grazing, look up at him approaching them, and quickly break into a run to escape Michael as he came too close.

"Danged ten year old, I told him not to do that!" Wilbur yelled to no one as he kicked his horse's sides and leaped into a gallop. Michael," he yelled, "stop!"

Michael couldn't hear him. He was too far ahead. But Helena, now sitting on her still pony heard, then, cupping her mouth with her hands, shouted, "Michael! Uncle Wilbur wants you to stop!"

But Michael, impetuous as his father at his age, began to chase the cluster of cattle as they scattered, most heading for the nearby cypress hammock and swamp. As Wilbur rode up to Helena, who was waiting for him on her pony, he looked all around, including the sky to the southwest. "Look, Helena! Look at those thunderclouds. Where did they come from? There was no clouds jest a while ago! They're really getting dark. I think we'd better head back to the house. It's nearly three o'clock, and I don't like the looks of those clouds."

"What about, Michael?"

"I'd better git after Michael," Wilbur responded as he pulled his reins, turning his horse's head. Then, looking again at the billowing clouds growing steel gray, he kicked his spurs into his horse's sides and took off for the nearest edge of the cypress swamp where Helena pointed to where Michael entered.

"Dang fool," he muttered to himself as he raced toward the swamp.

"Michael!" he yelled, "Michael!" His horse reached the first shallow waters of the swamp, splashing water as he entered. "Michael! Answer me, boy! Where are you?"

"Over here, Uncle Wilbur."

"Where, Michael?" Something in his voice made Wilbur sense that Michael was in trouble. "Keep yelling so I can find you. We've gotta git outta here! Looks like the weather's gonna git bad!"

Just then, Wilbur heard Helena behind him, her pony splashing into the shallow waters.

"Uncle Wilbur, where is Michael?" she asked anxiously.

"I don't know, Helena. Where the hell are you, Michael?" he shouted out.

"Over here, Uncle Wilbur. I don't see you."

"Did you go deep into the swamp?"

"I chased the cows that I scattered, hoping to catch them," he yelled, "but they're gone now. They ran away. I'm sorry, Uncle Wilbur."

"Talk to us, Michael," Helena begged, getting scared now.

"Don't worry about the cows now, jest keep talkin', Michael. We'll follow your voice. Is the water deep where you are, boy? Are you OK?"

"It's nearly two feet deep here, Uncle Wilbur. And...I think I'm hurt."

"He's in the middle of the swamp, Helena, probably fifty feet away from us in the worst part of the swamp. I'll go git him, Helena. You stay right here near the edge of the swamp. I hope he's not hurt bad."

"Be careful, Uncle Wilbur."

Wilbur, eager to help Michael, turned and kicked his horse, moving quickly toward where he thought Michael was, while yelling, "I'm coming! Keep talkin' to me!"

Wilbur's horse splashed through the thick cluster of trees in the swamp water, leaping across fallen trees. Just as Wilbur moved toward Michael's voice, he saw the bright flash of light of a large lightning bolt in the darkening sky, followed by the crack of a very loud thunderclap. Instinctively he tightened his grip on the reins, but the loud and threatening noise scared his horse, which reared instantly, throwing Wilbur off to the ground. He landed on a cluster of underwater cypress knees, hitting his head and back.

"Oooh," he groaned, knocked out of breath, yet somehow still holding onto his horse's reins, unable to move.

"Uncle Wilbur, are you coming? I heard a large splash!" Michael yelled. "Where are you? I need you!"

"Uncle Wilbur!" called out Helena, remaining near the edge of the trees and swamp as she had been told to do. "There's a lot of wind blowing across the pasture! It's getting stronger." At that moment, she saw another large flash of lightning, and heard a second, louder thunderclap, scaring her pony. But she held him in place, tightly gripping her reins, and tightening her thighs against the horse. "Whoa, baby…whoa. It's OK," she said softly, patting the pony's neck, trying to calm him. "Where are you, Uncle Wilbur?" she called out frantically.

But Wilbur could only groan, laying flat out with his head above the fairly shallow water, slowly regaining consciousness, but not yet able to move, helpless to find Michael. Becoming more aware of the growing winds and rainfall, he grew frustrated, and frightened for his charges. With great pain, he could only whisper, "Helena…oooh…"

Scared and worried, Helena directed her pony toward where she last saw Wilbur going to find Michael. She walked slowly, hoping to avoid any cypress knees as Uncle Wilbur cautioned her. Another flash of lightning. Another very loud thunderclap. Growing more frightened as she felt the drenching rains, Helena pulled on her rain hat and slicker.

"Uncle Wilbur! Please answer me!" she cried out as she directed her pony through the swamp toward where she last saw Uncle Wilbur, "I'm getting scared!"

Finally, she reached where Wilbur fell, and whispered, frightened, "Oh, there you are! What happened to you? Are you hurt?"

She looked down at her mentor, her expert horseman lying flat on his back, partially submerged in the dank swamp water.

"Oh, no," she said as she looked at Wilbur's motionless body, now more scared than ever as she heard torrential rains begin to fall, more aware than ever of their desperate situation. Although his eyes flickered open occasionally, he didn't speak, and his breath appeared labored.

"What should I do, Uncle Wilbur? What can I do to help you?" she started to cry, her voice becoming frantic, terrified at her situation, the rains and winds growing in intensity and the lightning and thunder more frequent.

As Wilbur slowly regained consciousness, he delicately rolled off the painful cypress knees, and carefully sat up in the shallow water. "Help me, Helena, onto that mount over there, he whispered. "I gotta git out of this water because it's gonna git deeper and we don't know how soon. This thunderstorm sounds bad!"

"I know!" she exclaimed positively. "What should I do?"

"Take that rope there and I'll tie it around my middle, then you take it and tie it to your saddle horn. Your pony can pull me."

After what seemed forever, Helena succeeded. With her pony's help, she pulled Wilbur's entire body about thirty feet up onto the earthen mound out of the water.

After resting for a few minutes, Wilbur instructed, "Helena, it's now up to you to find Michael and bring him here to dryer ground…not dry, mind ya, just higher. We may be stuck here for hours."

"Hours? But Mommy and Daddy will be really mad at us…and worried!"

"Yes, they will be. Mad at all of us, Helena, especially me. I should have gotten you back home before now. It's gittin' dark and there's no way we can build a fire. Not in this storm!

"I was following Michael's voice that way. But you'd better walk slowly with your pony so you won't bump into any more cypress knees. There are plenty here." He gestured over his shoulder toward where he last heard Michael's voice. "Go that way, Helena."

Suddenly, another large flash of lightening, followed quickly by a loud thunderclap, scared Helena even more. Slowly, carefully, she pulled the reins as she led her pony toward, she hoped, her brother, Michael. The rains were getting heavier and heavier, the winds blowing so hard she could hardly see.

Helene arrived home from the church, followed shortly by Alexander, who drove back from St. Cloud around four o'clock.

"Helene! I'm home!" he called out urgently as he entered the house. "Where are you?"

"I'm in the kitchen starting dinner."

"Where are the children," he asked, looking around as he stepped into the kitchen, soaking wet, his hair disheveled from the wind.

Helene reached for her husband. "I don't know, Alexander. They're not in the house. I looked everywhere, in their rooms, everywhere. I'm getting concerned. It looks like a bad storm outside, and they're always home by this time."

"They're with Wilbur, aren't they?"

"Yes, at least I think so."

"I'll check the stables and see if their horses are there. Maybe they're keeping the hoses calm during this thunderstorm. The horses could be really nervous." Walking to the kitchen door, turning back, he said, "I'll be right back. I'll bet that's where I'll find them, all three."

"Oh, I hope so. I'm getting worried. It's really bad out there."

"Have you heard, Helene?"

"Heard what?"

"It's all over the radio. Everybody is talking about it."

"About what?" she asked impatiently.

"We got a call from a customer in Miami an hour ago that a really intense hurricane came out of nowhere from east of the Bahamas and headed toward South Florida and upper Florida Keys last night with a storm surge of eighteen to twenty feet. Can you believe it? It just about destroyed every building in Islamorada! There was no warning! My customer told me the storm's moving west very fast around South Florida, heading for Ft. Myers and Tampa. They say winds reached over 155 miles per hour, a category five. It's a meaner hurricane than in 1926 and 1928 when thousands were killed south of Lake Okeechobee. Much worse. More intensive."

"Then the winds we're getting must be from the hurricane approaching us!"

"Yes, Helene. They say the winds could be as bad here in Central Florida."

"Oh, my God, Alexander. Can our house stand up with winds that high? Are we safe here? It's blowing really hard already, and the rains are fierce, almost horizontal. I'm worried these winds and severe rains may blow out our windows!"

"Yes, this house can stand those winds," he assured her quickly. "I'll be right back. I'm going to check out the stables where I'd better find Wilbur and the children and their horses."

"Alexander stepped back toward the door, now even more anxious to get to the stables.

"Wear your boots, slicker, and hood. And please, be careful. I don't want anything to happen to you. There's debris flying everywhere, and the wet ground is slippery. It's very dangerous. Please, please find our children!" She was almost begging now.

He nodded to her confidently, though uncertain in his mind, and, pulled the door against the wind, watching the screen door pull off its hinges and fly away. Bowing into the gale-like winds, his face struck by the rain biting into his face, he slowly made his way to the stables, step after uncertain step, watching for flying objects blown by the now seventy mile per hour winds. He witnessed again the fierce lightning bolts, then silently counted, convinced each second before the coming thunderclap measured a mile. Each second would tell him how far away the lightning struck. Just five seconds passed before the loudest thunderclap he could remember blast the air. Head bowed, very determined, he remembered for just a few seconds walking in the freak snowstorm on the mountain top in Lebanon. "Oh Lord," he prayed, "keep Michael and Helena safe." *My God*, he thought, *Michael's only ten, and Helena is even younger. Ten years old, exactly my age when I did that crazy, childish thing.*

Finally, he reached the stable door, struggled against the driving rain and winds, to open it, and fell inside. After searching the stables, he realized neither Wilbur nor the children or their horses were there. "My God! They're out there in this hurricane! I've got to somehow find them before it gets too dark!"

After a long twenty minutes, he returned to Helene, trudging in the raging winds and horizontal rains as fast as he could, now more worried than ever.

"They're not out there! And their horses are gone too, Helene! Even Wilbur's horse is not in the barn!"

"Oh, my God, Alexander," she exclaimed, looking out the kitchen window, "that means our children are out in this hurricane with Wilbur!"

"We can be grateful, Helene, that Wilbur is with them. He's an expert at surviving out there and knows better than anyone how to survive in these conditions."

"But, my husband, I am so worried. They could be killed! What are you going to do?"

"It's getting dark now, too dark to go out and search for them, Helene. The winds will blow our truck over, and I can't take a horse out there in these winds and rains! It cuts into you like knives. And there's debris flying all over the place."

"But they're out there all alone, even though Wilbur's with them. I know they're scared and in great danger. I can't stand this, Alexander! We could lose our babies!" she cried out, tears welling in her eyes.

"It's terrible out there, Helene, but they'll be alright…I hope."

"Let's pray together now, Alexander," she said quietly, shaking in fear for her young children, tears flowing onto her cheeks.

"Of course," he replied, as he embraced his wife, the mother of his endangered children. He gently rubbed her back as he held her, hoping to soothe her nerves. They prayed together, asking for Providence to protect their young children from this catastrophe.

"It's late, Helene, and there's nothing we can do, and that is hard for us," he said, as they listened to the harsh winds and rain beat against the house. "It breaks my heart knowing they need me and I can do nothing."

"Then, we must stay here and wait, Alexander. There's no way for me to sleep. I cannot. My babies need me." Helene broke down and sobbed, feeling she somehow let them down. They both sat at the kitchen table, consumed with worry.

"They're so young, Alexander, so fragile."

"I know, Helene. Now I know how my mother and Milhelm must have worried when I was gone for two days in that freak snowstorm when I was Michael's age." He stared out the window, sad and worried, desperate to the core.

Suddenly, their electric power went off.

"Oh, my God, Alexander! It's totally dark!"

Throughout the night, Alexander and Helene sat in a pitch dark vigil, hoping, praying, and fantasizing that any moment their children would step through the door, soaking wet, but happy and excited. The rains kept beating against their windows, rattling the house, incessant thunder rumbling in the distance, and enormous lightning bolts making the outdoors appear like daytime, keeping their nerves on edge all night.

Alexander woke first, still at the breakfast table, his head on the table only inches from Helene's, where they both fell asleep late at night, emotionally drained. He saw through the kitchen window that it was, indeed, morning. The winds and rains were even more severe than before. He quietly went to the counter and began making a pot of coffee on their gas stove that Alexander bought when he built the house, for just this situation. In just a few minutes, the reassuring fragrance of the brewing coffee aroused Helene. "Is it morning, Alexander?"

"Yes, my dear, it is. But the winds and rains are even stronger than yesterday. We were told yesterday by our friend in Miami that for us, the prediction was that today the winds hitting Tampa could reach over one hundred miles per hour. I don't know how high they are here, but if yesterday they were at least seventy, now they are much stronger. And the rains! I hate to say this, but the Kissimmee River must have overflowed by now, and the pastures in the flood plain must be flooded by now."

"What about Helena and Michael? And Wilbur?"

"We can only pray that they are hunkered down somewhere safe."

"Michael!" Helena called out urgently, yelling over the loud noises of the relentless wind in the trees, thunder, and heavy rains. "Where are you, Michael?"

"Helena! Over here! You're getting closer. Be careful. There are lots of fallen trees and Cyprus knees. But keep coming. You're not far."

"I'm coming, Michael, but I have to walk slow."

After what seemed like an hour, Helena finally saw Michael to the side, laying in the water, a fallen small tree across his legs.

"Are you hurt, Michael?"

"I think so. My legs hurt. Help me get up, Helena."

As she pulled her pony toward Michael, she handed him her reins and began to pull the tree off his legs. "Ugh, this is heavy. I know! I'll tie my rope around the tree and have my pony pull it off you," she said, still having to shout over the rumbling thunder, the rains hitting the trees, and, now, hurricane level winds.

"I'll pull you out too, Michael, like I had to pull out Uncle Wilbur."

"Is he hurt too? Is that why he's not with you?"

"Yes, Michael. It's up to us."

After she had her pony pull the small tree off his legs, she reached to him. "Can you stand up?"

"I…I…don't know. Bring your pony closer. Maybe I can lean on you and pull on her saddle horn."

It took longer than either wished, but Helena kept pulling and pushing. Michael, suffering through his pain, finally fell over the saddle and held on.

"OK, Michael, don't move. Here we go. I'm taking you to Uncle Wilbur."

"Watch out for the cypress knees, Helena. We can't let the pony stumble now!"

She guided the pony through the clusters of trees along a crooked path, avoiding the fallen trees. She finally saw Wilbur on the mound.

"Oh, thank the Lord!!" Wilbur yelled when he saw them. "Come here!"

"Uncle Wilbur! We need you!"

"We gotta hunker down together, kids. Here's what we gotta do." Gesturing, he ordered, "Lay my slicker on the mound. We'll lay on it and cover ourselves with your two slickers. But first, Helena, it's up to you. Take my knife and start chopping those small trees. We can make a small lean-to with 'em."

By nightfall, Helena placed several small trees over them. She then put cut branches above the lean-to as thick as she could. The effort did cut down much of the harsh rains falling on them. They huddled together under the two slickers, one on either side of Wilbur. "I'm so tired, Uncle Wilbur," Helena murmured as she cuddled against him.

"I'm hungry," Michael added quickly.

"Mmmm, so am I," Helena echoed.

"By gosh!" Wilbur exclaimed, "I plain fergot! I got some beef jerky in my coat. Want some?"

"Yeah!" they cried out as they eagerly reached for their share.

"It ain't like your mother cooks, but it'll taste good now, I bet," he said as he smiled at them.

"It's gonna be a rough night, kids, but we'll be fine. These trees will protect us a lot, and the cypress are strong. Now, after you eat your beef jerky, best try to sleep. We're all tired."

"I hope Mommy and Daddy aren't too worried," Helena whispered as drowsiness overcame her.

They all slept, although the sharp thunderclaps disturbed them throughout the night and the winds and rains, though not totally constant, raged on and on.

Wilbur woke first, and let the children sleep as long as they could. Daybreak finally came, yet the winds were even stronger than the night before. "We're gonna stay right here, kids, until this storm passes. We could be here all day. I believe this is no ordinary summer thunderstorm. It feels more like a hurricane. But we got no warning. This one sure beats what we had in 1926. I don't understand why nobody warned us. But we're here and we're gonna wait it out."

"But I'm hungry again, Uncle Wilbur. Do you have any more beef jerky?"

"Yeah, me too," Helena added.

"I do, but we'll have to be careful not to eat it too fast. Helena, take my knife and go cut some of them big leaves over there near the water. We can eat the stems; they're full of good water, safe and good for us, and they'll fill us up."

"But I bet they don't taste much good, Uncle Wilbur."

"I know, Michael, but you won't be as hungry if you eat some of those leaves."

"Awww," Michael groaned, "OK, if I have to."

"Boy, Michael, we'll have some stories to tell at school, won't we?" Helena laughed as she thought how impressed her girlfriends would be when they heard she'd rode out the hurricane in a cypress swamp.

"This will pass by. How soon I don't rightly know, kids. The winds are still too strong for anybody to get out here and look for us. We may as well do the best we can all day."

For Helene and Alexander, it was the longest day of their lives. All they could do was worry and pray for the safety of their two young children.

"Where can they be, Alexander?"

"It's hard to say. Maybe they found a safe place to hunker down. I hope they're not near the Kissimmee. I know it must be flooding into the flood plain. And the winds and rains are so bad there's no way I can find them. Wilbur can't bring them home! You can't even see fifty feet!"

By nightfall the second day, there was still no word. Debris was everywhere, and while there were distinctive breaks in the winds and rains, the hurricane continued to rage outside the safety of their home.

"Dammit, I feel so helpless, Helene. I can do nothing! Everything that can't drain must be flooding. We're lucky we're on this ridge and we still have our windows and roof!"

"Huh? I'm sorry, Alexander," she responded, distressed. As she turned her head to him, he saw her swollen eyes, her cheeks still moist from nearly two days of crying. "Uh, I didn't hear what you said."

He stepped to his heartbroken wife, embraced here, trying to comfort her. "Helene, everything is going to be alright. You'll see. Wilbur is a wise and good man who will find a way to shelter them."

"Oh, Alexander," she replied, looking out the window, "I must hope for the best, but it's been two days and it will be dark soon. What am I going to do without my babies? How could they survive this hurricane?"

"Michael! Helena! Look!" Wilbur yelled, pointing, "We're gonna have to climb higher up this here mound. The water's arisin' and if this keeps up much longer we're gonna be in the water. Dang it all!"

"I can't move, Uncle Wilbur, my right leg hurts so bad."

"I ain't so hot either, Michael. I can't move my body, Helena. We need your help again."

"I'm so tired and hungry, Uncle Wilbur. I don't know how I can pull you two up."

"You'll have to use your pony again, Helena, like you did yesterday when you pulled me up the first time. Remember?"

"Yes. I'll get the pony."

"It is deeper, Uncle Wilbur," she exclaimed loudly, over the noise of the continuing winds howling through the trees. Helena struggled through the water, now nearly two feet deep, bringing her pony in place, and, wrapping her rope under the arms of first Wilbur and then Michael. She struggled to lead the pony to pull them further up the earthen mound clear of the water. Then, she moved the lean-to and branches, spread out their slickers and, exhausted, joined them, laying down under the remaining slickers. She started crying.

"Do you have any more beef jerky? I'm hungry again," she sobbed.

"There's not a lot left. We gotta hope this hurricane passes soon so yer Daddy can come lookin' for us. Best we try to sleep some more. It's gittin' dark."

"Tomorrow has got to be a better day, Uncle Wilbur. It's just got to be," cried out Michael, tears flowing from fear, pain, and frustration. "It's just gotta!"

By morning on the second day, the hurricane did pass through the area.

"The rains have stopped! And the winds have calmed down too," yelled Helena happily, as she looked through the trees out onto the pastures.

Seeing the same signs, Alexander shook Helene, still at the kitchen table, exhausted and depressed, having spent the last forty-eight hours keeping vigil, hoping, praying, nearly without hope, for the safe return of their children.

"I can go out now, Helene. I'm going to go into town and get some help. We've got a lot of searching to do to rescue Michael, Helena, and Wilbur, wherever they are."

Within an hour, Alexander returned to the house with six friends. Two took their small truck and four rode their horses as they headed south and began their desperate search, not knowing where to look first, not knowing what they would find. Would they be alive? Or injured and unable to move? Would they be in the open? Huddled in the pines? Or would they be under palmetto clumps? Or, God forbid, in one of the many cypress hammocks and swamps?

"I'm riding hard, fellows. I'm sure they're not nearby. Let's go to the first hammock as fast as we can," directed Alexander to the men.

For two hours the group rode as hard as they could, sometimes through a foot of water, in the river's flood plain, careful not to overheat their horses or the truck.

Helena," Wilbur announced, "it's up to you to go fer help. Better git on yer pony and ride toward the house. Best you keep the Kissimmee River on yer right and in sight the whole way."

"Maybe Daddy will be out there looking for us!"

"I'll fire a couple rounds into the air after you leave, and I'll do it agin every hour so you'll know where we are. Now git along, Helena. You can do it. I know you can. You're our heroine now. Go git yer Daddy and bring him here jest as soon as you can so we can git to the doctor. And be very careful."

It took Helena a good two hours of riding north toward the house before she tired. Sitting still on her pony, she spotted the truck, and her Daddy with some other men on horseback. Excited, bursting with joy, she kicked her pony's sides and took off toward them, anxious to reach them, waving her arm and yelling as loud as she could, "Daddy! Daddy!" Her eyed filled with tears of joy, just as did his when he saw her racing toward him

"Helena!" he yelled, kicking his horse's sides, galloping eagerly to his little girl, a good two hundred yards away. "Come on, fellas!" Alexander shouted, motioning them with his arm, "Bring that truck up here! Let's go get them!"

You work that you may keep with the earth
and the soul of the earth
Kahlil Gibran

CHAPTER 25

Years of the Great Depression

Alexander, always concerned about his family in Lebanon and Madeleine in France, knew that Hitler's growing power and armed forces were beginning to threaten the entire continent. Communism spread across Eastern Europe from Russia into the Ukraine and the Baltics, and was even becoming a growing influence in America. To those in America and on the continent who were out of work, Socialism was a very attractive solution. The cattlemen of Central Florida were concerned about how to cope with the terribly low prices and low demands for beef and citrus. Alexander and Abraham also worried about how to keep their stores open for business.

"Alexander," Big John asked, "what's your opinion on Europe? You know more about Europe than the rest of us. Do you think France, England, and Poland can survive this German threat?"

"Well," Alexander replied, "certainly the political conditions and threat of war in Europe are getting more and more serious. The harsh reality is that Germany invaded Poland and then marched into France, took over the government, and occupied most of the country. This does not bode well for the French or my friends and family there. I'm very concerned about my Uncle Hanna and his close friends Danielle and her daughter Madeleine in Marseille. They were all very kind to me during my stay there while on my way to America. I've been through an occupation when the Turks invaded Lebanon, so I know how frightening it can be."

"We're feeling the effect of what's happening over there, Alexander. Economic conditions are so bad here that the state of Florida and its counties are nearing a revenue crisis. Tax receipts are dangerously low. As in 1884, when Hamilton Disston saved the state of Florida from bankruptcy with his first $200,000 purchase, a new state law is required to save Florida from bankruptcy in 1938. This new law allows the private purchase of land from the government for only the taxes owed on the land."

Alexander later discussed his conversation with Abraham. When the new law came into effect, they began to carefully invest from their "bank in the field" in the new "buy for taxes" program. They sat at the same spare table in Abraham's apartment for hours, scouring page after page of tax sales announcements in the newspapers.

Along with a few others, Alexander, the Stewarts, Big John and the Perkins bought tens of thousands of acres during those months near the end of the Great Depression for virtually pennies per acre. Many fine properties, including buildings constructed during the Land Boom, were bought for hardly anything. Sometimes, hundreds of acres were bought for as little as 50 cents per acre.

As economic conditions began to improve in the late 1930s, Alexander bought more land at very depressed prices when the opportunity arose. He purchased acres of citrus land with fruit bearing trees and pastureland for as little as seventy-five cents per acre. Some available land, with better access and less wet land, cost no more than $2.00 per acre. The market for citrus and beef had almost disappeared, but he found his cattle loved the chopped citrus fruit, so he began to feed his herd with the fallen or harvested unsold oranges during the winter season. When the grasses were dry, the citrus was ready for harvest. That year Alexander bought two used trucks for $100 on credit to haul the fruit to the herds.

Trusting the future, and seeing their beef sales slowly but steadily improve due to the needs of Europe, Alexander and Abraham accumulated numerous improved rental properties in towns throughout the area, as well as thousands of acres of productive pasture and citrus land. By 1941, they were poised for good times, even though the Depression era was not completely over.

Alexander's children were growing up, and he felt great pride in their dedication to schoolwork, church duties, and good behavior. Michael was now a tall and rugged 14-year-old, and Helena, at 12, was a beautiful dark-haired young, tomboy who loved her horse Sheikh, and could ride him as well as her brother rode his horse. Most of the time she wore her long wavy, dark hair in a ponytail like a lot of her girlfriends. "It's cooler this way, Dad," she would explain when her father asked her to wear it down. "Your hair is so pretty when you let it be natural, Helena," was always Alexander's response.

Michael, looking much like his father and nearly as tall, rode his horse expertly. He worked the cattle as Wilbur taught him, and was doing well in school.

Alexander and Helene were very proud of their children and watched over them, hoping to keep them from getting into trouble that could threaten their safety, especially since their scare during the 1935 hurricane when they thought they might lose their children. At every opportunity, he brought Michael with him as he inspected his herds, citrus groves and juicing plants. For pleasure, they fished and hunted for hours of camaraderie. He loved his son more than life itself.

The children worked the herds with Wilbur and their father, and played at the lake with their friends. Like most first generation Lebanese, they stayed close to home, church, and their parents.

Alexander took Michael in his 1937 Ford pickup truck, ready with his .12 and .410 gauge shotguns, .22 Winchester rifle for hunting, and fresh water fishing gear. He found Sunday afternoons with Michael to be a wonderful respite. He loved to sit at the kitchen table and watch Helene teach Helena how to roll grape leaves, stuff *koosa*, and make *tabouleh*.

Alexander taught his children from a young age how to drive the truck, and to fish and hunt small game like quail and rabbit, and, in the fall, turkey and deer. All were plentiful in the area, especially deer who were overpopulated. Michael proved to be an excellent hunter and impressed his father with his accuracy. Most of what they brought back went to the church for the poor townsfolk. He taught his children to give of themselves, and to help the church. "Help the poor," he would admonish, "and always share your blessings."

"We are so lucky," Helena often commented to her brother. "We get to ride, hunt, and fish almost every day."

"Yes, Helena, and we have mom, dad, and *Jiddy*, our grandfather, in our lives."

Times during the Great Depression were very difficult, but, since the Thomas' always had food, they were better off than many. They grew into a close-knit family, and well-known to be very generous to those less fortunate.

"I will take care of your needs, children, but there are times when your mother and I can't take care of your wants. You must learn the difference."

Alexander could only afford a single cowman, Wilbur, on his payroll throughout the entire 1930s. Because he survived and Wilbur was still employed, Alexander's reputation was strong, especially among the cowmen who were searching for any kind of work they could find.

Alexander, now in his twenty-first year in Kissimmee, was considered a good family man and a shrewd, honest businessman in the region. By 1941, he was asked to serve on several boards of directors: a bank board, a hospital board, and the corporations that owned those juicing plants in which he now held substantial and growing ownership. They found his counsel and advice to be sound, seasoned, and wise. And he enjoyed responsibilities outside his own holdings.

By early 1941, Alexander, through cattle crossbreeding with the Brahman and purchasing dirt cheap pasture lands with cattle, had accumulated a total of 30,000 acres of pasture, 5,000 head of cattle, and two thousand acres of productive citrus groves. He was now among the more successful farmers and ranchers in Central

Florida, and was well-respected for his integrity and his commitment to his family and his holdings.

"Life is good, Helene. We have been tested. And we have survived."

"I always believed in you, Iskandar. Always."

During 1941, conditions continued to get somewhat better. Federal government initiatives under President Franklin Roosevelt during the early 1930s lowered the growth of unemployment, changing the conditions of the country. But times were still not very good. The creation of the Federal Reserve System guarantee on deposits restored faith in the banking system. Federal Work Programs were creating jobs and making more money available for spending.

Still, times were difficult for most of the world, especially in Europe. In America, prices and profits were still too low to empower companies to hire more help or expand. In 1940, new automobiles could be bought for just $400, only slightly more than during the early 1930s. Bare necessities were very cheap, but many people had to do without. Many even bartered their talents for food. Too many Americans were still too poor even to feed themselves despite efforts by the government. Many people in Kissimmee were willing to work for pennies a day.

But Alexander's world in Florida was still innocent and mostly insulated from the battles taking place overseas. He had his family, and his businesses. His son, now fifteen, was becoming an adept cattleman. His popular cowgirl daughter, Helena, was beautiful, tall, slender, and dark-haired, with large brown eyes, who shared a ready smile with everyone. Her mother carefully watched over her...as did all the boys in school. Helena, though confident in herself, was also, in a disarming way, modest and feminine. The boys loved being around Helena. So did the girls. She was everyone's friend. And Alexander was proud of both.

"Why don't you have a boyfriend, sis?" Michael asked her.

"I do, Michael. I have lots of friends...most are boys, so I have lots of boyfriends," she would giggle, then smile over her shoulder as she stepped away, teasing her brother.

Helena could run as fast as her brother, and could ride her horse now as well as Michael and his friends. She won many impromptu races.

"Last one to the lake is a spoiled brat," she yelled to her brother as she kicked her heels into Sheikh's sides. With her long dark hair trailing behind her, she crouched in the stirrups, laughing and bending forward into the wind, racing to the shoreline. Michael sometimes matched her, and sometimes beat her, laughing if she won their race. When Alexander watched Helena beat Michael, he would smile, remembering his friend Abigail racing ahead of him so many years ago.

Sometimes, on Sundays, Alexander and Helene rode their horses along with their children.

"Helene, you have made me very, very happy," he commented as they rode side by side. "I am forever grateful to you for all you have added to my life."

"Thank you, my husband. I have loved you since that day in Boston at Salim and Julia's house. I knew then that you would take good care of me and our children. I am still very much in love with you."

He admired Helene. She was a good and devoted wife, his companion, partner, and mother. And, as his father had advised him, he indeed had come to love Helene very much. He shared all his life with her, good times and bad, appreciated her, confided in her, kept her informed of his work, and even suggested she keep some of the books.

Sometimes, when he watched Helena, he saw Madeleine, remembering his first and lost love running up the hill overlooking the Mediterranean Sea, laughing and calling for him, just like young Helena was doing now. He could not extricate himself from his secret story, and, while torn emotionally with his past, he made sure he devoted his present to Helene.

Even before the Japanese attacked Pearl Harbor, the demand for beef was increasing as the government that year was buying huge amounts of beef products for shipment to its European Allies. Though America was doing its best not to go to war, President Roosevelt was acquiring large quantities of food, materiel, and armaments for the allies in Europe under the Lend-Lease Program.

Alexander, along with his fellow ranchers, including Big John Sommerland, the Parkins family, and the Stewarts were called on to increase their production of beef, milk, citrus and citrus products. While his pastures required ten acres of raw pastureland (including large clumps of palmetto and pine trees) per head of cattle in the 1920s, by the 1940s, on his cleared pastures could raise nearly ten times more cattle on the same grass lands.

Looking out over the rolling open pastures one afternoon, Wilbur said to his friend and employer, "Y'know, Alexander, we've had a lot of tough times, but look at all those rich open pastures…the hills…the clear lakes…we did some good things out here…"

"We survived, didn't we, Wilbur?"

Because, finally, there was a good and growing market, Alexander called on Wilbur to hire more men, increase breeding, move the stock to better pastures, and teach Michael all he could.

"Hey, boss," Wilbur said, "T.J. came by lookin' for work. He's been outta work for quite a time."

"You think he'll be okay?"

"He's a good cowman who had stupid ideas about immigrants, but I figure it's been more than twenty years since you and him disagreed. He told me awhile back he sure made a bad mistake 'cause you did good since you came to Kissimmee and he'd like another chance. Yeah, boss, I think he's learned the hard way like a lotta people did these past ten years. All of us have. I'd give him a chance. He'll work with me."

Rubbing his chin, thinking on it, Alexander finally responded, "Well, OK, Wilbur. Sure, I think everyone deserves a second chance. Go ahead and hire him and a few others. I'll count on you to watch over them."

...you can only be free when even the desire of seeking freedom becomes a harness on you...
Kahlil Gibran

CHAPTER 26

December 7, 1941

Times began getting better for the food and munitions businesses, even though the overall economy was still languishing. And then came "The Day of Infamy," December 7, 1941. That day, life for all Americans changed dramatically and forever.

On that memorable date, Helena was fourteen, and Michael sixteen, when America was reluctantly drawn into war. As usual, the family had attended church that morning, and visited with friends during coffee hour after the service.

By one o'clock, they were home, sitting together around the dining room table, sharing their customary Sunday dinner while listening to the background music of Sammy Kaye and his orchestra emanating from their radio, the favorite Sunday afternoon sound for millions of Americans.

Sunday afternoon meals always included *Jiddy* who was there to enjoy his grandchildren, unless on occasion he was in Orlando with his daughter, Leila, and her family. Honoring the Sabbath, the entire community of Kissimmee, as well as most of Central Florida's conservative southern traditional towns, was quiet. All stores were closed.

It was about 3 p.m. that day when the music was interrupted by a deep male voice who spoke with a surprisingly serious tone:

"We interrupt your afternoon of listening pleasure to announce that the United States Naval Base at Pearl Harbor on Oahu in the Hawaiian Islands was attacked this morning by the Imperial Japanese Armed Forces. It was a sneak attack that began early in the morning. Casualties are high. Many battleships have been sunk in just a few hours."

Everyone around the table looked at each other, stunned by the news. All day the radio brought announcements by the government with words like "needing all men over the age of 18." President Roosevelt's speeches and "mobilization" announcements filled the airwaves that day, and the country went into shock, anger, and fear. The next day, President Roosevelt, before a joint Congressional session, called for a "Declaration of War," and gave his famous "Day of Infamy" speech.

The impact on the lives of the people of Kissimmee and the Thomas family was as sudden and as severe as it was across the country. Alexander's mind flashed back to the days of his youth when the Turks occupied his homeland. Would the Japanese be his next oppressor?"

Suddenly, the prospect of Michael going to war engulfed the family.

"*Biyee*, will they come and get Michael?" Helena asked her father fearfully, looking for guidance and reassurance. Her peaceful, happy childhood was suddenly changed, jarred by the reality of war. America was at war.

"Michael is sixteen," Alexander replied. "I think he will be exempted while he is in school. And maybe, God willing, the war will be over before he becomes eighteen," he said hopefully, but not too convincingly. He, too, was deeply concerned for his beloved only son. Then, turning to his wife, he said "We must look into this and see if it changes his plans for college, Helene."

As Michael's eighteenth birthday and high school graduation drew closer, the more the Thomas family realized their personal world was facing a major crisis.

In late June, 1943, at Sunday dinner, Michael, barely a high school graduate, hesitatingly cleared his throat, and proudly announced to his family at the dinner table that night while looking at his father, "Dad, I want to join the Air Force."

Alexander was stunned. Initially, his emotions rolled between anger at Japan and the U.S. government, and pride in Michael's decision. After a few moments of thought, pride won out.

Michael sat nervously, darting his eyes around the table at his family, waiting for reactions, expecting a negative response. "I want to help. It's the right thing to do."

He paused, hoping for a response. But none came quickly. "Sure, I could get a deferment by going to college, but would that be right? You always taught us to do the right thing. I hope you'll support my decision, Dad."

Helena and Michael turned their heads to their father, grandfather, and mother waiting for their guidance, their quiet wisdom. There was a long moment of stunned silence.

Letting his son's profound words sink in, Alexander, at the head of the table with his beloved son, Michael, next to him, slowly looked around, in serious thought, hands folded on the table before him. Memories of his son swept through his mind. As a newborn baby he had held him in his arms and kissed him. He remembered the young boy sitting on his lap, the first time he caught a fish, rode his pony. Tears of joy filled his heart; a lump grew in the back of his throat. Clearing his throat, he stared at each of them, circling the table with his eyes, acknowledging his own father's focused stare, waiting, not interrupting. Then he reached for Michael's hand and squeezed it, conveying the pain of fear for all his family.

He spoke softly, "Michael, you are my firstborn, my son, and while I love you and Helena equally, you were the first. Your life is the fulfillment of my destiny. You are to carry on the family name. You and Helena will receive all that your mother and I have worked so hard to hold onto. I cannot bear the thought of anything happening to you. Neither can your mother." He took a deep breath, gathering his thoughts. "I was eighteen, your very age, when I left all that I knew and came here to a place I knew nothing about. I was driven from my homeland, as was Jiddy, by an oppressive, brutal foreign army. Your grandmother and many of our friends in Lebanon died at the hands of the foreign occupiers."

He stopped for a moment, tears flowing down his cheeks from his deep concern for his son. Michael focused on his father's face, feeling the emotional struggle his father was going through. He knew this wouldn't be easy for his father, and listened lovingly to every word, wanting to know his wishes.

"All we ever wanted was freedom, the right to come and go, simply the opportunity to work, to have a family…to have a life. That freedom we found in America. This is the greatest country in history. It provides freedom and opportunity to everyone, even immigrants like us." He paused again, thinking with great deliberation as he recalled the terrible agony of his youth, blended with a growing sense of anger at having his son forced to become part of war.

Misreading his father's thoughts, Michael interrupted, "But, Dad…"

Alexander held up his hand, quieting Michael. "And so, my son, as much as we want you to be safe here with us, there is no safe place if angry animals are on the loose. And I believe Germany and Japan are those animals. They must be stopped. As much as it pains me to acknowledge this fact, only America and its people can stop them. You make me very proud that you want to be part of that. *Allah ma'ak*, Michael, may God be with you. Trust all that your mother and I, who love you so much, have taught you. Follow your trust and faith in God, pray for guidance, help those who need help, and when your job is done, come back safely to us." He turned to his wife. "God help us, Helene, and God be with Michael. I am deeply saddened but I am very proud of my American son. This will not be easy for us, Helene." He said, turning to her.

Helene extended her hands to touch him, tears in her eyes. "Michael, my son, like your father, I want this to be your decision, just as any major decision of your life must ultimately be made only by you. And I too am proud of you and will pray daily for your safe return. We will worry every minute until you return safely to us."

Then Alexander smiled as he turned to his daughter. "And, of course, Helena, we are very proud of you. But we want you to stay here with us, so don't you be thinking about following in Michael's footsteps just yet!"

Helena laughed, "I'm only sixteen, Papa. I'm not nearly ready."

As he completed all he wanted to say, which seemed to be more than his family had ever heard from him at one sitting, Alexander, saddened, turned his head slightly, stood up, and with tears in his eyes, pulled Michael to him, embraced his son with both his strong arms, kissed him twice on his cheeks, and pursed his lips into a reluctant proud smile as he wiped the tears from his cheeks with his handkerchief. Without hesitation, Helena stood, embraced her brother, kissed him, and, honoring her parents, hugged and kissed them both. Then they all stepped to embrace Abraham, patriarch of the family, still seated at the table, quiet, teary-eyed, representing the link to their culture, their roots, their traditions, and their way of life.

By late summer of 1943, Michael joined hundreds of thousands of other teenage American boys, enlisted in the U.S. Army Air Corps, and was immediately sent to training camp to become a pilot. After basic training, he was sent to Tampa for flight training and shipped to England by the summer of 1944 to join the 8th Air Force where he would pilot bombers over France and Germany.

The British, under siege for five years, were exhausted. Their Air Force, weakened by the German attacks, buzz bombs and aggressive bombers and fighters, were assigned the task of nighttime bombing of German cities.

In contrast, the American heavy bombers, mostly B-17s and B-24s, were assigned the much more risky daylight strategic bombing missions to destroy Germany's war-making machinery, including fighter factories, rail yards, manufacturing plants, and submarine bases. Their missions were extremely vulnerable and dangerous, drawing incessant plane-shattering flak and attacks from hundreds of German fighters defending their homeland, and by ground-based cannon fire. By the time Michael arrived, nearly fifty percent of all U.S. Army Air Corps bombers of the 8th Air Force planes had been lost. Thousands of airmen were killed. Hundreds of the huge bombers, each with ten crew members, were shot down. Until D-Day, when the rules changed, a pilot had to fly twenty-five missions before he could be returned to America. After that date, the missions required was increased to thirty-five missions.

At home, Alexander and Helene kept a daily vigil, praying for their son to beat the odds and somehow return safely to them.

But it was not to be.

When love speaks to you, believe in him.
Though his voice may shatter your dreams
as the north wind lays waste the garden.
For even as love crowns you so shall he crucify you..."
Kahlil Gibran

CHAPTER 27

Marseille, 1920

"Goodbye, my love. Until we meet again. I will always love you." Madeleine said aloud as she waved for the last time to Iskandar, her departing lover. She still saw him standing at the rail of the stern waving to her and she watched him grow smaller and smaller as the ship sailed out to sea into the bright orange setting sun. As she finally turned to leave the pier, a long painful hour after the ship was out of sight, Madeleine felt slightly light-headed and weak.

During the next several weeks, nausea and discomfort kept her from her work some mornings. For weeks, she said nothing to her mother, thinking it was nothing. Finally, she decided she must confide in her mother. They scheduled an appointment with the doctor at the hospital.

"You are going to have a baby," the kindly doctor smiled.

"Oh my goodness, *Maman*, what shall I do?" she asked when they were alone.

"You will have the baby, Madeleine. It is God's will. But we must prepare."

That night, with enormous emotions, Madeleine prayed to God that the baby be healthy, that the baby look like his father, and that soon, Iskandar would come back and take care of her. She missed him so much. The next day and many days thereafter, as she did every morning, she caressed her...his...cross in her fingers, sometimes all day. Now, a bit frightened, she thought of Iskandar even more. *What am I to do?* she asked herself.

Often she went to the hill overlooking the sea, and prayed, "One day, dear Lord, bring Iskandar back to me. I will wait forever. Please, Lord, but please have him hurry," she pleaded.

After a few days, she and her mother spoke about her dilemma.

"Shall I tell Iskandar or not, *Maman*? I have received many letters from him, but they were all from New York. I don't even know where he is. I think I should not tell him yet. He must come for me. I don't want him to come back to me because of an obligation, because I am bearing his child. That would not be good. But I cannot lie to him. It would require a month for my letter to get to him even if I knew where he was, another month for him to find passage, and another month for his ship to arrive in Marseille."

"You...no...we must be realistic," Daniella replied firmly, holding up her hands.

"But..."

"Hush. We must go to Paris to be with our family, to stay for awhile. You are with child, we have no man in our home, and we will have another mouth to feed. We do not have much money. But you are young, very pretty, and you must attract a man to marry."

But, *Maman*, I love only Iskandar..."

Late November, 1920 Madeleine bore a six-pound, eight-ounce baby, a handsome son who looked exactly like Iskandar. "I am so happy, *Maman*. He has his father's nose, his eyes. He is beautiful. Look at his beautiful hair. I will call him François, after papa. Would that please you, *Maman*?" Daniella replied, gently touching the baby's head, smiling proudly, "Yes, my love, and I know it pleases your father who I am sure is watching over us today."

That same month, Iskandar, now known as Alexander Thomas, opened his small store, and was now on his own, on Broadway in Kissimmee, hoping every day for a letter from Madeleine. But none came. "None today?" he asked the postman as he did each day, receiving a shaken, lowered head in return. Still, he longed to be with his love, Madeleine.

Because of the need to conceal a child with no apparent father, Daniella initially told Hanna she and Madeleine were going to visit family in Paris for awhile as Madeleine was not well. But as the weeks progressed, she felt she should be totally honest with Hanna and told him what was happening. But she made him promise not to tell anyone, especially his family members in Lebanon and America.

After two years in Paris with their family, Daniella, Madeleine, and François returned to Marseille. Madeleine's life was almost fulfilled with her love child, "Little François," and yet, there was something missing. She longed to be held by Iskandar, to listen to his voice, to gaze into his eyes. She imagined how proud and happy Iskandar would be to hold his son. Because Iskandar's letters were never forwarded to Paris, she never again saw his letters. And did not write him.

Madeleine took François with her to her shop, keeping him nearby all the time. Most days found her busy in the shop making clothes for those few wealthy ladies of Marseille who still had funds for their custom-made clothes. In the early days, she kept François in a basket by her feet. Evenings alone with François were actually easier for her than before he was born when she was so lonely. Now she had her growing son, a beautiful, dark-haired, handsome child a constant, living personification of her love, Iskandar.

"Run to me, François," Madeleine would laugh, clapping her hands. "Come to *Maman*, my darling."

On Sundays, she would place him in the carriage and walk to the park, the *Jardin du Pharo*, where she and Iskandar enjoyed their too few days. As François began to walk, they walked hand-in-hand, skipping, laughing, enjoying the days together. She was a young mother, still less than nineteen years old.

In the spring of 1924, when he was nearly three and a half years old, Madeleine began taking François to the hill overlooking the sea. There, she would spread her blanket and place her picnic basket on the very spot of grass where François was conceived in love. When François first asked of his father, Madeleine explained as best she could, with emotion, from her heart, not from knowledge. She would serve them lunch on a blanket as she told François of her undying love for his father, Iskandar, and of his love for her. Her explanation to his inquiries of his father's absence in their lives always included, "Your father loves you, but he cannot be with us here. He is in America looking for a better life for us." She also told him all she knew of his father's heritage, of Lebanon, Douma, and the mountains.

THE IMMIGRANT

PART TWO

OF A

TRILOGY

Your Friend Is Your Needs Answered
Kahlil Gibran

CHAPTER 1

Paris; Spring, 1924
Philippe

"I know they are up to something that will change Europe forever," Philippe Moreau told his superiors in secretive French Intelligence meetings in Paris. "There are hundreds of German undercover agents operating all over Belgium, Austria, and Denmark. This man Adolph Hitler is crazy! He's taken over the German Workers' Party and renamed it the National Socialist German Workers' Party… the Nazi party. He hates France and blames Germany's economic depression and the plight of the German workers on France's Versailles Treaty demands. The Nazis have co-opted many Frenchmen as well. These are difficult times, and I am convinced they are going to get much worse, and very soon." But Philippe's was a lonely voice seeking to alert the indecisive politicians who were too consumed with disputes to respond. His was a lonely, futile effort. If they would just listen. But they didn't. The French government drifted during most of the 1920s, still believing they had defeated Germany forever.

Later, on a visit to his offices in Marseille in the summer of 1924, Philippe called on his good friend, Hanna Chalhoub, in the Lebanese section. The Lebanese were skilled at operating under occupation and during political turmoil with ubiquitous spies and compromises. They would know, especially Hanna, of subversive activities in Marseille as they related to the local media and to shipments in and out of the busy port and the rail station. Because the Panier district, with its large Lebanese immigrant community, was strategically positioned between the docks and the rail yards, he knew Hanna was his key man in Marseille.

It was during one of these visits that Philippe met Daniella and Madeleine at a dinner engagement with Hanna. Philippe was immediately struck by Madeleine's vibrancy and beauty.

Later he inquired, "Tell me, dear friend, what is the story about Daniella's daughter, Madeleine. She is the most beautiful creature I've ever met."

"Aah, Madeleine," Hanna replied, "she is a magnificent woman. You are correct, *mon ami*. Madeleine is the finest. She is just twenty years old, and yet, she is an exciting, insouciant woman, Philippe. She also has a beautiful son, François, who is nearly four years old."

Hanna felt a strange sense of conflict of loyalty and betrayal while introducing his good friend to the lover of his nephew. While Daniella and Madeleine had finally informed Hanna, they had obtained his promise not to tell Iskandar of his love child. Madeleine was insistent that the child not be the reason for Iskandar to return. She was absolutely convinced he would return to find her when he could, that he loved her as completely as she did him, and that he had had to go to America or he might always regret it and ultimately blame her. Certainly, if this was true, she felt, she did not want him ever to blame her or his own child for ruining his life. "This way is better," she told Hanna. "He will come. I know it. But it must be for the right reasons. Telling him he has a son in France is not the right reason for his return. Trust me, *Maman*. Trust me, Hanna," she pleaded that day before they left for Paris "for family reasons."

"Well, I would like to see Madeleine, my friend. Can you help me? I realize that I am much older than Madeleine, but I am entranced by her, and cannot get her out of my mind. Perhaps in time I can become important to her as well."

Hanna put his arm on his friend's shoulder and spoke candidly to his friend, "Philippe, these are difficult times, and Madeleine is doing her best. She is raising her son by herself as the boy's father left France to go to America in 1920. I'm certain he does not know he has a son. She has worked hard with her mother, and yes, she needs a good man. But I think her heart belongs to, and will always belong to, the father of François. You must know this from the outset, *mon ami*."

Philippe looked directly at his friend and replied, "You say she has not seen him since 1920? If that is the case, perhaps there is a possibility for me then, Hanna."

"Perhaps, Philippe, perhaps."

Madeleine found herself frequently being visited by Hanna's friend, Philippe. He was always kind and charming, and took her to dinners at the finest dining establishments and to cultural events in the city. Over time, she became more willing to accept Philippe in her life.

"I love the bouillabaisse of Marseille, especially at Henri's by the *Vieux Port*," smiled Philippe as they taxied to his favorite seafood restaurant. "His fish are freshly caught each day. Remarkable! Paris doesn't have bouillabaisse like this."

While he spent much of his time in Paris, he returned every available weekend to Marseille. His excuse was to see his family and to meet with his colleagues, including Hanna, in the Marseille offices. His real but unspoken desire for being in Marseille was to see this enchanting twenty-year-old beauty named Madeleine. Within weeks, he knew he was falling in love although he was twenty-five years older than she. But she was a mature, delightful, feminine young woman with a child, making her way with her mother, an excellent and popular *couturière*, graceful, cultured, and fully aware of the fashions of the day. Madeleine, like her mother, made her own dresses that reflected the *au courant*, creating a stir wherever they went together. They emulated the latest designs of Paris so to inspire the ladies of Marseille to visit them and order their wardrobe from these two esteemed fashion models and designers. Strikingly attractive, tall, slender, and finely attired, Daniella and Madeleine personally maintained their shop's reputation.

Philippe felt very proud to have this stunning beauty on his arm even though he knew some looked askance at the "May-December couple." Some were perhaps envious, some judgmental, respectfully holding back, with a stifled smile, the query, "Oh, Philippe, is this your niece?"

He could only smile without comment. But he didn't care. He was quite self-assured. His hope and concern was to somehow gain her affection, and in time, her love, by overcoming with his physical presence and charm what her son's father couldn't provide in his absence. This, indeed, was becoming the principal emotional focus of his life. *I will win her over*, he kept telling himself.

www.ingramcontent.com/pod-product-compliance
Lightning Source LLC
Chambersburg PA
CBHW050632160426
43194CB00010B/1635